# ARE GIRLS NECESSARY?

# ARE GIRLS NECESSARY?
## Lesbian Writing and Modern Histories

Julie Abraham

University of Minnesota Press
*Minneapolis*
*London*

Copyright 1996 by Routledge

First University of Minnesota Press edition, 2008

Published by the University of Minnesota Press
111 Third Avenue South, Suite 290
Minneapolis, MN 55401-2520
http://www.upress.umn.edu

Library of Congress Cataloging-in-Publication Data

Abraham, Julie.
    Are girls necessary? : lesbian writing and modern histories / Julie Abraham. – 1st University of
Minnesota Press ed.
        p. cm.
    Includes bibliographical references (p.   ) and index.
    ISBN 978-0-8166-5676-9 (pbk. : acid-free paper)
    1. Lesbians' writings, American–History and criticism. 2. Lesbians' writings, English–History
and criticism. 3. Lesbians–English-speaking countries–Intellectual life. 4. Lesbians in literature.
5. Homosexuality and literature–English-speaking countries. 6. Women and literature–English-speaking countries–History–20th century. 7. American fiction–Women authors–History
and criticism. 8. English fiction–Women authors–History and criticism. 9. American fiction–
20th century–History and criticism. 10. English fiction–20th century–History and criticism.
I. Title.
    PS153.L46A27 2008
    810.9'9206643–dc22                                                          2008005619


Printed in the United States of America on acid-free paper

The University of Minnesota is an equal-opportunity educator and employer.


15  14  13  12  11  10  09  08                          10  9  8  7  6  5  4  3  2  1

*For Amy Schrager Lang*

# Contents

A very great many have very many prejudices concerning loving. . . .
This is very common. Not very many are very well pleased with other
people's ways of having loving in them. Some are very much pleased
with some ways of having loving and not with other ways of having
loving. Some are wanting people to be very nice in having loving
being in them. Some are pretty well ready to let most people do the
kind of loving they have naturally in them but are not ready to let all
people do the loving the way loving naturally comes to be in them.

———Gertrude Stein, *The Making of Americans* (1906–1908)


Don't you understand
if you today in a crude speech
in a dark landscape hope to say,
to speak one word of the joy we had
(to people who anyway don't want to understand)
. . . . . . . . . . . . . . . . . . . . . . . . . . . . . . . . . .
O don't you know, don't you understand
you must count yourself now, *now* among the dead?

———H. D., "I Said" (1919)


Form in fiction . . . is emotion put into the right relations.

———Virginia Woolf to Roger Fry (September 22, 1924)

# Preface

# "Are Girls Necessary?"

In the nineteenth-century chapters of *Orlando* (1929), her fantastic biography of Vita Sackville-West, Virginia Woolf offers a parable of "the transaction between a writer and the spirit of the age." This transaction, she observes with conscious irony, "is one of infinite delicacy, and upon a nice arrangement between the two the whole fortune of [the writer's] works depends."[1] While all writers engage in such transactions, it is hardly coincidental that Woolf was thinking of these matters while writing about a woman she loved. Lesbian writing remains unintelligible as "lesbian writing" if these transactions, their complexity, and their influence over what was written and how it was read are not acknowledged.

In *Orlando*, Woolf illustrates one aspect of the history of lesbian writing: cultural policing of the representation of women's relationships. Orlando is, of course, a writer, but until she succumbs to the spirit of the Victorian age and marries, her pen produces nothing but the conventional pieties of the period. Ironically, marriage frees her from the worst of the nineteenth century's literary tyranny. The newly wed Orlando begins immediately to write freely:

> "And then I came to a field where the springing grass
> Was dulled by the hanging cups of fritillaries,
> Sullen and foreign-looking, the snaky flower,
> Scarfed in dull purple, like Egyptian girls—"

But Orlando is not exempted from scrutiny by her social conformity to (hetero)sexual imperatives. The spirit of the age now scans her verses for signs of transgression. And any pairing of female figures—even "Egyptian girls" from "a lady's pen"—gives the spirit pause:

As she wrote she felt some power . . . reading over her shoulder, and
when she had written "Egyptian girls," the power told her to stop.
Grass, the power seemed to say, going back with a ruler such as gov-
ernesses use to the beginning, is all right; the hanging cups of fritil-
laries—admirable; the snaky flower—a thought, strong from a lady's
pen, perhaps, but Wordsworth, no doubt, sanctions it; but—girls?
Are girls necessary? You have a husband at the Cape, you say? Ah,
well, that'll do.
    And so the spirit passed on. (187)

While propriety of both life and work are demanded by the spirit of the age,
Orlando is allowed to proceed. But her literary options are inseparable from
her social status, which is a matter of class and race as well as sexual distinctions. "Girls" are acceptable in the work of a woman if the woman is a "lady"
and the "lady" is safely married. The marriage need only be a form. That the
husband is engaged in imperial adventures "at the Cape" makes life simpler all
around. So does the fact that the girls are not Shropshire lasses: "Egyptian" girls
are less real, if more easily eroticized, from the perspective of a British spirit of
the Victorian age.

    At the same time that Woolf identifies literary options with social status,
she presents interpretation as key to the relation between a lesbian writer and
her age. "The spirit of the age" polices suggestions of women's interest in other
women partly by determining what constitutes such a suggestion. Orlando,
due to accidents of birth and decisions about marriage, has "so ordered it that
she was in an extremely happy position; she need neither fight her age, nor
submit to it; she was of it, yet remained herself" (188). But the "spirit of the
age" is, if anything, happier. It has one less lesbian reference to deal with, not
because Orlando has stopped writing or because a particular sentence has been
censored, but because, if the "girls" can be neutralized by their author's class,
her position within imperial structures, and her marriage, Orlando's poem
need not be interpreted as lesbian.

    The history of *Orlando* itself demonstrates the politics of interpretation.
Woolf dedicated the book to Sackville-West and incorporated photographs of
her lover and even her writing into the text; it is Vita Sackville-West's poetry
that "Orlando" is producing.[2] But *Orlando* was not "officially" read as a lesbian
text until fifty years after its publication when, in 1988, it became the subject
of *PMLA*'s first foray into lesbian criticism.[3] Such "failures" of interpretation
are a more common and effective form of social control than publicly brand-
ing and casting out offending sentences and writers. The refusal to interpret
elides the possibility of lesbianism. At the same time, "the age" can continue to
set the terms under which lesbianism is understood, through setting the terms
on which a text—and by extension a gesture, a relationship, a person—is understood as lesbian.[4]

Are girls necessary? In one sense, this is a purely rhetorical question: Woolf can expect her readers to understand that there has yet to be an age that finds desire between women, much less its literary representation, necessary. But in another sense this question, asked in this fashion within Woolf's text, opens a crucial area of inquiry. Given policing by the spirits of various ages, and given the centrality of interpretation—especially interpretation as not-lesbian—to the process of policing, how might we now, in the last decade of the twentieth century, at a moment of unprecedented possibility for lesbian cultural production, criticism, and theory, identify a lesbian text or a lesbian literature? Given the particular social pressures surrounding the writing and reading of lesbianism over the past century, can we assume anything about what a text "about" desire between women might look like? Does a text have to be "about" desire between women in order to be "lesbian"?

These questions, produced by historical circumstances and ideological formations, can only be answered in historical and ideological terms. The circumstances that produced the questions have produced, out of the possible relations between lesbianism and the literary, two types of work. There are those texts written, presented, and read as representations of lesbianism by lesbian, gay, and heterosexual writers and readers. This is a field so dominated by as to be synonymous with the female couples of the "lesbian novel." In Anglo-American culture, fiction has been a primary arena for the representation of sexuality and gender and the construction of identities. First cousin to the case study, and more accessible than scientific texts, novels remained over the first half of the twentieth century easier to produce and harder to censor than theater or film. So, for a combination of formal, cultural, and material reasons, the novel has been *the* genre in which representations of lesbianism have been recognized.

There is also, however, a much larger body of lesbian-authored fiction—as well as poetry, drama, essays, journals, and so on—that is not "about" female couples. All of what I will call "lesbian writing" is shaped by the historical circumstances of lesbian writers as Woolf began to represent them in *Orlando*. But lesbian writing has no fixed subject or form. And given modern Anglo-American culture's investment in not interpreting texts as lesbian, this work has not, for the most part, been read as "lesbian."

Needless to say, there is some intermingling among "lesbian novels" and "lesbian writing." Lesbian novels produced by lesbian writers, of course, function under both rubrics. However, most of the novels written by lesbians have not been "lesbian novels," and many "lesbian novels" were not written by lesbians. Nonetheless it is surprising—given how little lesbian writing is interpreted as "lesbian"—how much lesbian writing contains aspects of the subjects and formula of the lesbian novel.

This is a study of lesbian writing. Given the hegemony of the lesbian novel, however, it is not possible to discuss lesbian writing without first considering the lesbian novel and the relations between the lesbian novel and lesbian writing. The formula and authority of the lesbian novel have contributed to patterns of interpretation which continue to limit the readings of much lesbian writing. When I move beyond my discussion of the lesbian novel, narrative and the novel remain the focus of my account of lesbian writing, for some of the same reasons that the lesbian novel exerts so much influence in the world: not only because of the cultural role of fiction/narrative as an arena for the representation of sexuality and gender and the construction of identities, but also because of the authority of narrative convention as simultaneously a repository and a source of cultural ideology about sexuality, gender, and women's identities.

Any discussion of lesbian writing must take into account not only cultural prohibition and policing through interpretation, but also literary questions. "A more committed analysis of homosexuality," Thomas Yingling argued in 1990, "is not content to stop with having established the homosexual content of this or that text or writer but sees homosexuality as the beginning and not the end of a certain literary question."[5] I hope to carry this argument a step further. I will propose that no distinction can be drawn between "establish[ing] the homosexual content of . . . [a] text or writer" and "literary question[s]." Literary conventions are one method through which "the age" determines where we look and what we see as "homosexual content," while assumptions about "the literary" as a realm of aesthetic abstraction obscure the role of the literary in producing both "homosexual content" and reader expectations.

This study is focused on British and American fiction of the first six decades of the twentieth century, post-Wilde and pre-Stonewall. While there were earlier literary representations of lesbianism (often in poetry), and earlier examples of the lesbian novel (often in French), modern lesbian writing became possible, as recognizably modern lesbian identities became available, in Britain and the United States by the beginning of the twentieth century. The cultural as well as material possibilities of lesbian writing were fundamentally changed by the end of the 1960s. The gay and women's liberation movements produced new publications and new publishers committed to lesbian and gay material, offering new means of access to a new audience committed to challenging dominant social hostility and claiming authority and even power.

This study depends on two terms—"lesbian" and "lesbian writer"—the former highly contested and the latter, as a result of this contest, barely recognized as a cultural possibility. Post-Stonewall discussions of lesbian subjects routinely begin with an attempt to define "the lesbian." This practice can be traced back over the past century to the decades when "the lesbian" was first proposed as a social/sexual type. Despite their best efforts from the late 1960s to the early 1990s, neither lesbian-feminists nor queer theorists have managed to resolve the problem of definition.

Some contemporary critics, such as Terry Castle, argue that the ongoing problem of definition represents a failure of common sense on the part of lesbian and gay scholars, a refusal to recognize the self-evident significance of desire between women.[6] But women have engaged in a range of homosexual, homosocial, and gender-transgressive behaviors (including a commitment to feminism) to which, over the past century, the term "lesbian" and its variants (Sapphist, invert, female homosexual, gay girl, butch, femme, bulldagger, dyke, and so on) have been applied. Moreover these terms, and the relationships among behaviors and terms, have not only varied according to the nationality, class, race, sexuality, religion, and political convictions of the speaker, but have varied as well over time. Desire between women has not always been sufficient to identify lesbianism.[7] Nor has desire between women been consistently interpreted *as* desire between women: just as frequently it has been labelled a form of man-hating, or a retreat from or distortion of heterosexuality.

At the opposite extreme from those urging common sense, critics such as Biddy Martin have interpreted the fact that "the lesbian" remains undefined as a sign of the peculiar indeterminacy of lesbianism, or of sexual categories more broadly, in implicit contrast to categories of gender, race, class, nationality, and so on.[8] But each of these categories—gender, race, class, nationality, as well as sexual preference—has been thought at some moment to be inscribed on the body, represented simultaneously as self-evident and inexplicable, and considered in need of border patrol.

Given the history of the category, neither stabilizing a "commonsense" definition of lesbianism based on an ahistorical common sense, nor celebrating lesbianism as uniquely unstable (and therefore peculiarly subversive) seems an adequate response to the problem of definition. It seems to me to be necessary, in fact, to resist both these moves, one limiting and the other romanticizing, and to resist as well any attempt to represent sexuality as the source of unique social categories, or lesbianism as simply a sexual phenomenon.

Lesbian and gay studies in the 1990s has been further complicated by two interrelated developments: the rejection of social categories as mechanisms above all of social control ("regulatory fictions"), and the subsequent invocation of sexuality or "desire" as an alternative subject—as if sexuality/desire was significantly exterior to the social.

The observation that, as Judith Butler proposes, "identity categories tend to be instruments of regulatory regimes, whether as the normalizing categories of oppressive structures or as the rallying points for a liberatory contestation of that very oppression," has produced her defensive insistence that:

> It is always finally unclear what is meant by invoking the lesbian-signifier, since its signification is always to some degree out of one's control, but also because its *specificity* can only be demarcated by exclusions that return to disrupt its claim to coherence. What, if anything, can lesbians be said to share? And who will decide this question, and in the name of whom?"[9]

Insofar as the "signification" of the "lesbian-signifier" "is always to some degree out of one's control," the same could be said of any social designation. The members of any stigmatized group are likely to be anxious about who will decide on the meaning of the label that they bear.[10] The relative weight of the "regulatory fiction" of identity categories has to be considered in relation to the weight of the other modes of regulation to which "lesbians" are subject. The losses represented by the social and psychic exclusions that identity categories produce have to be considered in relation to the enabling potential of the terms. Even Michel Foucault, often credited as the source of category anxieties within lesbian and gay studies, posited the possibility of "a 'reverse' discourse," and precisely in relation to homosexuality as a source of identification: "homosexuality began to speak in its own behalf, to demand that its legitimacy or 'naturality' be acknowledged, often in the same vocabulary, using the same categories by which it was medically disqualified."[11]

"Sexuality" is the term with which everyone hedges their bets.[12] Henry Abelove, Michèle Barale, and David Halperin argue, in the introduction to their Lesbian and Gay Studies Reader, that "lesbian/gay studies . . . intends to establish the analytical centrality of sex and sexuality within many different fields of enquiry," while nevertheless "advance[ing] the interests of lesbians, bisexuals and gay men" (xvi). Halperin and Carol Dinshaw announce, in their introduction to the first issue of GLQ, the first academic "Journal of Lesbian and Gay Studies," that they "seek to publish work that will bring a queer perspective to bear on any and all topics touching on sex and sexuality."[13] But "sexuality" hardly presents fewer problems of definition than "lesbian." Halperin and Dinshaw go on to explain that GLQ will consider "the complex interplay among sexual and social meanings, individual and collective practices, private fantasies and public institutions, erotics and politics" (iii), aligning the "sexual," the "individual," the "private," and "erotics," over against the "social," the "collective," the "public," and "politics." Would you buy a definition of sexuality from these people?[14] Particularly when "lesbian and gay" is unproblematically identified as "the sexual"—"We have used the terms lesbian and gay" in the journal's subtitle, they explain, "in order to foreground what is specifically *sexual* about the subject matter of GLQ."

My goal in this book is to elaborate interpretations, rather than to fix—either in the sense of correcting or stabilizing—definitions. I assume Teresa de Lauretis's and others' arguments for the premise of "queer theory," "that homosexuality is no longer to be seen simply as marginal with regard to a dominant, stable form of sexuality (heterosexuality) against which it would be defined either by opposition or by homology."[15] But obviously my work is not in line with those "queer" projects committed, in Diana Fuss's words, to "bring[ing] the hetero/homo opposition to the point of collapse."[16] I am more interested in the task de Lauretis outlines, whereby:

male and female homosexualities . . . may be reconceptualized as social
and cultural forms in their own right, albeit emergent ones and thus still
fuzzily defined, undercoded, or discursively dependent on more established forms. . . . both interactive and yet resistant, both participatory
and yet distinct, claiming at once equality and difference, demanding
political representation while insisting on . . . material and historical
specificity." (iii)

And this is in particular a book about social and cultural forms.

The "lesbian" has always been and remains controversial. As for "lesbian
writers," Eve Sedgwick has noted the dismissive response of last resort to discussions of writers as lesbian or gay: "The author or the author's important attachments may very well have been homosexual—but it would be provincial
to let so insignificant a fact make any difference at all to our understanding of
any serious portrait of life, writing, or thought."[17] There has been important
work on lesbian writers as lesbian writers, such as Catharine Stimpson's essays
on Gertrude Stein and Sharon O'Brien's studies of Willa Cather's fiction. But
still, too often when the possibility of a writer's lesbianism is raised, its implications are strictly contained, or figures such as Stein and Woolf are romanticized,
particularly as biographical spectacles.[18] Nancy Miller, justifying feminist discussions of "women writers,"

> locates the problem of identity and difference . . . on the level of the text
> in all its complexities: a culturally bound, and . . . culturally overdeter-
> mined production. . . . There are no infallible signs, no failsafe tech-
> niques by which to determine the gender of an author. But that is not
> the point of the *post*-compensatory gesture that follows what I call the
> new literary history. At stake instead is a reading that *consciously* recreates
> the object it describes, attentive always to a difference . . . not depen-
> dent on the discovery of an exclusive alterity.[19]

While unwilling to abandon biography, I have, like Miller, focused on "the
level of the text." I am interested in the "*post*-compensatory gesture . . . not
dependent on the discovery of an exclusive alterity" or an exclusively biographical alterity.

Teresa de Lauretis, following Sue-Ellen Case, has observed that "it takes two
women, not one, to make a lesbian."[20] I am arguing that all it takes, in the period under consideration in this book, is one woman and a novel. Most simply, I mean by this that as a reader a woman could interpret herself as lesbian
and find her interpretation of lesbianism through a novel. (This form of discovery was likely when, before Stonewall, novels were the primary [textual]
source of popular understandings of lesbianism.) More importantly, I mean
that, for the lesbian writers of the first half of the twentieth century, lesbianism

was produced not only out of the emotional and/or sexual details of their lives, and/or out of the social consequences of their lesbian desires, but also through literary activity itself. Given the highly problematic relation between lesbianism and narrative, the lesbianism of the lesbian writer could be constituted, in part, through/in the very process of writing.

This study is not intended as a history of the lesbian writing of the first half of the twentieth century: it is not organized chronologically, nor is it sufficiently broad or detailed to make such a claim. If nothing else, it is skewed by its attention to the novel and narrative. None of the lesbian poets, essayists, short story writers, playwrights, or journal writers of the period are addressed, nor for the most part are the poems, essays, stories, plays, and journals of the writers I do consider. I am not offering a canon of lesbian literary production, nor the basis of a tradition.

The writers I focus on were white, middle- or upper-class women whose capacity to negotiate their worlds depended in part on their privileges of race and class, as Woolf acknowledges in *Orlando*. The women I am writing about would not have produced the amount of work they did, would not have received whatever popular and critical attention they achieved—and we would not know enough about their lives to identify them as lesbian—if not for the material and cultural privileges conferred by their white and middle-class or upper-middle-class status. Their privileges gave them more cultural space than was available during the first half of the twentieth century to their black and white, working-class, lesbian peers, and their middle- and upper-middle-class, black, lesbian counterparts. (Gloria Hull's account of Angelina Weld Grimké suggests, paradoxically, the particular constraints imposed on an upper-middle-class, African-American, lesbian writer by her genteel status.)[21] Their work provides a basis for examining the formal literary constraints that come to the fore in the absence of material obstacles, the constraints experienced even by lesbian writers with money, time, and cultural capital.

In my introduction I discuss a range of lesbian novels produced between 1900 and 1969, although I concentrate on a superficially unlikely pair, H. D.'s modernist *HERmione*, from the 1920s, and Patricia Highsmith's realist *The Price of Salt*, from the early 1950s, to demonstrate the consistency of the structural patterns of the lesbian novel, and the modes of resistance to the limits that structure produced. I go on to focus on five writers: Willa Cather, Mary Renault, Gertrude Stein, Djuna Barnes, and Virginia Woolf. But this is neither a biographical study, nor a study of identity. All of these women lived in a period in which few women identified themselves as lesbians. There are now more and less responsible biographies of each of them. The journals and letters of many of them are now available. They expressed very different understandings of themselves, their sexuality, their writing, and their relations to the world. These women did not in any obvious sense form a group: Stein and Barnes were friends; Woolf and Stein had certainly met. Yet they were all born in the last decades of the nineteenth or the first decades of the twentieth century, and all began writing either before World War I or during the interwar period. Even Renault, who continued to publish into the early 1970s, produced the bulk of her work before Stonewall. More to the point, all of these writers were shaped by the decades from the 1880s to the 1950s. These women were all expatriate, in some sense or for some significant period of their lives, whether the journey made was Gertrude Stein's transition from the United States to Paris, France, in 1903, or the symbolic break marked by Virginia Woolf's move across London from Hyde Park Gate to Bloomsbury after her father's death in 1904. Their writings spanned two national cultures (British and North American), modernist and realist literary forms, and mainstream and genre fictions. Each of these women produced a significant body of work and shared a measure of success, insofar as that was available to women writing at the time. Their work can be found in early twentieth-century high cultural canons and on late twentieth-century best-seller lists.

Dr. O'Connor asks rhetorically, in Djuna Barnes's *Nightwood*, "What am I?" and answers himself, "I'm damned, and carefully public!" If these women were "damned" by their lesbianism, they were also "public," however "carefully." They were public in that they produced culturally significant and/or widely read literary work. But they were also public insofar as they allied themselves with public life, claiming most of Western and all of twentieth-century history as their subjects, and rewriting the accounts of past and present that would erase them.

\* \* \*

My introduction, "I Have a Narrative," begins with a discussion of narrative and of the plot of heterosexual romance that was, at the beginning of the twentieth century, still *the* convention on which literary representations of women and expectations of women's writing were based. Consequently, twentieth-century lesbian writers faced a particular narrative disenfranchisement. "Lesbian novels," I argue, rather than a solution to this problem of narrative, are formula fictions based on the heterosexual plot. I demonstrate the ways in which lesbian novels are constructed out of heterosexual plots, and consider the ideological limitations of this situation, as well as various modes of resistance lesbian writers employed. I consider the effects of the explicit and implicit focus on the lesbian novel for the development of lesbian criticism. I propose, as the basis for an alternative—nonrepresentative—analysis of the possible relations between lesbianism and the literary, to focus on the problem of narrative disenfranchisement, and read lesbian writing via the responses of lesbian writers to heterosexual narrative hegemony, including responses other than lesbian novels. For example, many early twentieth-century lesbian writers, faced with the limitations of the heterosexual plot, turned to history as an alternative source of narrative convention.

In Part I, "Tell the Lacadaemonians," I discuss Willa Cather and Mary Renault as historical novelists. Their writings span the period under discussion in this book: Cather published fiction from the 1900s until 1940, and Renault from 1939 until the early 1970s. That period encompasses the careers of two other lesbian writers who were major contributors to the genre of historical fiction in the twentieth century—Marguerite Yourcenar and Bryher—and others who, like Sylvia Townsend Warner, produced historical novels in the course of their careers. Of this group, however, Cather, with her interest in formal innovation and in the possibilities of North American New World histories, is the most unconventional as a historical novelist. By contrast Renault, who relied on literary realism and the cultural authority of ancient Greece, was the most conservative.

Cather's early fiction, written at the beginning of the century, reflects her conflicted response to the heterosexual plot. Renault, on the contrary, in her early work, explores the limits of the lesbian novel that was, by mid-century, being produced out of that plot. In patterns also traceable in the work of Bryher and Yourcenar, both Cather and Renault found in history, even if in very different forms, possibilities for narrative and for the representation of same-sex relationships.

In my discussion of Cather I focus on one of her first novels, *O Pioneers!* (1913), and two novels from the middle of her career, *One of Ours* (1922) and especially *The Professor's House* (1925), and end with a consideration of her two late attempts at representing female pairings in history, "The Old Beauty" (1936), and *Sapphira and the Slave Girl* (1940). My discussion of Renault begins with her early lesbian and gay novels, *The Friendly Young Ladies* (1944) and *The Charioteer* (1953). I then move on to survey the patterns in the development of her historical novels. As I demonstrate, Cather's writing reflects the conflict between her interest in formal innovations and her desire for the authority history might offer, a conflict often played out in her representation of same-sex pairs. Renault's fiction, more formally and historically conventional, extended the possibilities for popular representations of homosexuality by offering a country in which gay men could be citizens.

In Part II, "Love is Writing," I discuss the ways in which such key modern literary innovators as Gertrude Stein, Djuna Barnes, and Virginia Woolf redefined "history" in their pursuit of narrative and of complex representations of lesbianism. History became both a subject in their writings and, like writing itself, a medium of representation. The literary self-consciousness that can be traced in the work of Cather and Renault is central to the writing of Stein, Barnes, and Woolf. This section begins with a consideration of Stein, whose account of history is the most abstract and elaborately self-conscious of these authors.

Stein adopted the term "history" at the beginning of her career as a way of signifying her rejection of conventional narrative. I focus on her use of reference to history (history as a source of narrative, the history of "daily living" and the history of "events"), in the 1920s and 1930s as a basis for her explanations of her own writing in "Composition as Explanation" (1926) and *Narration* (1935), and her return to her own version of narrative in the 1930s and 1940s, in *The Autobiography of Alice B. Toklas* (1932), *Everybody's Autobiography* (1937), and *Wars I Have Seen* (1945), as well as *Four in America* (1933) and *The Geographical History of America* (1936). Her use of history in this process depended on understandings of narrative and history derived from her relationship with Alice Toklas, and enabled her to produce a public "history" of that relationship reaching far beyond the bounds of the lesbian novel.

Djuna Barnes invoked what Stein called the history of events, the official historical record, to gain access to history and consequently to representation for those who lack a place in that record—circus performers, gay men, lesbians. In *Nightwood* (1936), but also in her stories, in *Ladies Almanack* (1928), and in *The Antiphon* (1958), Barnes records a lesbian desire for and fear of other women that is inextricable from desire for and fear of representation.

Virginia Woolf's narrative experiments, her accounts of history, and her representations of lesbianism have all been analysed, but never in such a way as to bring these terms together, and never for the purpose of a broad reading of Woolf as a lesbian writer. Instead, critical responses to Woolf's fiction have offered particularly clear examples of the ways in which the literary effects of lesbianism are still contained. I am interested in the interdependence of her accounts of history, her uses of history as a source of narrative, and her representations of lesbians and gay men. In a pattern that can be traced back to and through the work of Cather and Renault, Woolf's recourse to "history" at once enables and limits possibilities both for the representation of homosexuality and for the lesbian as writer. My discussion focuses especially on *Mrs. Dalloway* (1925), a novel which represents lesbianism without being a lesbian novel; it concludes with a reading of Woolf's last novel, *Between the Acts* (1941). The account of a lesbian writer, in history, dealing with the consequences of the heterosexual plot in literature and in history, *Between the Acts* brings together all of the elements of my study.

\* \* \*

While I focus on specific writers and on a particular historical period, on the pre-Stonewall decades of the twentieth century, the problem of narrative disenfranchisement I identify and its consequences can be traced in the work of other lesbian writers of the time, and in more recent developments in lesbian writing. It might help to explain the choice by some early twentieth-century lesbian writers—Amy Lowell, Alice Dunbar-Nelson, Janet Flanner—of poetry, journals, journalism, and so on, rather than fiction, as genres in which to work. Even for those who chose to write novels, "history" was not the only alternative source of narrative structure, and turning to history was not the only way for lesbian writers to solve the problem posed by the heterosexual plot; other forms of genre fiction were chosen by mid-century writers such as Patricia Highsmith and M. E. Kerr. But "history" was a highly productive choice, crossing and even blurring conventional literary boundaries, producing historical novels, high-modernist experiments, and a whole range of texts between. As I have just noted, this was a choice made earlier in the century by more lesbian writers than those I have chosen to focus on here. "History" is still a choice being made in the post-Stonewall period; Jeannette Winterson's historical fantasies are a notable example of this pattern. The problem of narrative disenfranchisement, and lesbian writers' consequent dependence on the heterosexual plot, might explain as well the difficulties of those lesbian writers who, in the post-Stonewall decades, have written novels about lesbians but have been hampered by the limits of the lesbian novel formula, limits compounded by a general lack of recognition of the lesbian novel's formulaic nature. These difficulties are reflected in the centrality of genre fiction—detective stories, science fiction—in contemporary lesbian work, although writers such as Joanna Russ continue to demonstrate the potential of genre fiction in the post-Stonewall period, as Renault does earlier in the century.

In the quarter-century since Stonewall, other literary forms besides the novel have flourished, and other forms of cultural production have proliferated: poetry, the essay, autobiography; video, performance arts, 'zines. But literature continues to be a significant source of representations of lesbianism, and anxieties about the parameters of "lesbian writing" have not been resolved, rendered academic, or ceased to undermine the possibility of our interpreting a range of writers and texts as lesbian. The novel continues to be the focus of these anxieties. When Dorothy Allison's *Bastard Out of Carolina*, nominated for a National Book Award in 1993, was not considered for the 1993 Lambda Literary Awards (for the best "lesbian and gay" books in a range of categories), the resulting debate was reported in lesbian and gay community and mainstream media. Allison's novel was excluded from consideration because the judges decided to "focus on lesbian and gay content," which meant that "lesbian fictions" were "books whose main characters were lesbians consciously concerned with exploring their identity."[22] Allison has a history of commitment to post-Stonewall lesbian and feminist politics and community, and her poetry, stories, and essays are well known among lesbian and gay readers. *Trash*, a collection of her stories, won a Lambda Award in 1989. Moreover, *Bastard Out of Carolina* is one of a series of novels by lesbian writers about intense mother-daughter relationships, from Radclyffe Hall's *The Unlit Lamp* (1924), to Maureen Duffy's *That's How It Was* (1962). But the story of Bone, the protagonist of *Bastard Out of Carolina*, ends as she reaches adolescence, before she is able to interpret her own story as lesbian or otherwise.

Allison's comments on the controversy illustrate the ongoing interpretive dilemma it reflects. In an interview in *The Nation* she recalls her own earlier battles with Bertha Harris, whose novels *Catching Saradove* (1969), *Confessions of Cherubino* (1972), and *Lover* (1976) were major contributions to the first wave of post-Stonewall lesbian writing. According to Allison, Harris "used to say there was no such thing as a lesbian novel because no little female books ever ran off with other little female books. I got into a furious argument with her in 1975 because I needed there to be a category called lesbian fiction. I realize now that what I really needed was to know that my life was a proper subject for fiction, that my life was as valid as heterosexuals' lives."[23] The Lambda Awards decision suggests this desire for validation and the belief in fiction as a source of validation still flourish, as well as the assumption that stories of "female[s who] . . . ran off with other . . . female[s]" are the only source of such validation. Even while Allison says, "I don't think I'm capable of writing a non-lesbian novel," she still talks about a given text as more or less lesbian, declaring that her "next book . . . is going to be much more lesbian in content, in the traditional definition" (20).[24]

These assumptions about the subjects of "lesbian" texts still limit our interpretations of what it might mean to consider any given writer as a lesbian writer, and consequently our identification of writers as lesbian writers. Allison acknowledges the distinction between lesbian writers and lesbian novels: "Awards for lesbian writers," she concludes, "would in many ways be more valuable" than awards for lesbian fiction (20). And she defines herself in post-Stonewall terms, in relation to a self-conscious lesbian community rather than either her emotional/sexual life or her fiction: "I always have felt like a lesbian writer. I have felt like there was not any other community in which I could have developed my craft or published" (20). But Allison was being interviewed here by Blanche McCrary Boyd, whose own most recent novel, *The Revolution of Little Girls*, won a Lambda Award in 1991, but who insists, "I don't feel like a lesbian writer, I feel like a lesbian and a writer." Her distinction is still based on the test of "content": "I'm trying to give voice to what it feels like to try to be an authentic person in the world, and my lesbianism is a key to that, but it's not exactly my subject." For Boyd (as for the Lambda judges) lesbianism remains a subject, and the only subject of the implicitly limited "lesbian writer."

The premise of this study is that there are more complex connections between sexuality and the literary than can be traced through literal or metaphoric representations of relationship, romance, sex, or body parts, and that, since lesbianism is as much a social as a sexual phenomenon, there are other axes of connection between lesbianism and the literary than can be encompassed by any connections to be drawn between sexuality and literature. As Gertrude Stein observed, "Literature—creative literature—unconnected with sex is inconceivable. But not literary sex, because sex is a part of something of which the other parts are not sex at all."[25]

The "other parts" of this story are gender and history, feminist criticism and the study of literary modernism. My analyses depend on the archival, critical,

ARE GIRLS NECESSARY?

and theoretical work, as well as the activism, of a generation of feminist scholars. My consideration of a range of twentieth-century women writers reflects
and, I hope, contributes to recent debates about the interpretation of modernism and of twentieth-century literature more generally.

When I began this study, I relied upon the efforts of those lesbian and gay
scholars and activists who began considering these issues before Stonewall. Now
this work is part of a field of lesbian and gay studies in literature, history, anthropology, queer theory, cultural studies, and so on that has only recently taken
shape. This new work often divorces the study of sexuality from the study of
gender, while proposing to consider gay male and lesbian subjects in conjunction. I am skeptical about both of these efforts. In practice, most of the work
to date in the field of lesbian and gay studies has been gender-specific, and has
produced analyses that cannot easily be transferred across gender lines. While I
share the goals of the gay literary criticism that draws on feminist models and
offers an expansive reading of lesbian and gay subjects, what follows is a study
of lesbian subjects. It could not be otherwise, given all that feminist criticism
has indicated about the particular conditions of the representation of women
and of women writing.

* * *

I am grateful to the Emory University Research Committee for lending its
support to this study.

For their intellectual, institutional, and practical help and for their generous encouragement at various stages over the course of this long project, I
would like to thank Elizabeth Blackmar, Elsa Dixler, Ann Douglas, Martin
Duberman, Ralph Freedman, Amanda Gable, Nancy K. Miller, Elizabeth
Pochoda, Ann Snitow, Catharine Stimpson, and Carole Vance. My thanks to
Miranda Pollard for the time she spent with this study; to Grace Goodman
and to Ellen Marakowitz for years of friendship; and to Esther Newton for her
companionship in the task of thinking and writing about lesbian and gay cultures. Meryl Altman's contributions to my history have been invaluable. Despite the distances between our lives, my parents, Joseph and Janet Abraham,
have always given their love. Amy Schrager Lang brought to this project all her
intellectual clarity and the possibility of an ending.

# Introduction

# "I Have a Narrative"

## I. "I Have a Narrative, but You Will Be Put to It to Find It": The Heterosexual Plot

Insofar as there yet exists a critical commonplace about the relationship between lesbianism and literature, it is that literary lesbianism is to be found in "lesbian novels"—tortuous romances of fragile female couples. Embedded in this commonplace is the assumption that lesbian novels offer the sum of lesbian existence, even though, with their conflicted heroines poised at the border of a twilight world, they tend to represent lesbianism as an excess of sex, sin, and torment. However contested the accuracy of any particular novel, the formula on which lesbian novels depend has been treated by readers and critics alike not as a literary artifact, but as authentic and representative. Not surprisingly then, lesbian novels have dominated twentieth-century British and American popular and critical analysis of literary lesbianism, as well as shaping public understanding of lesbians. Even when the lesbian novel has not itself been the subject of literary analysis, it nonetheless has set the terms of critical discussion. Moreover, even when the literary is not the subject of analysis, the lesbian novel sets the terms for discussions of lesbianism. In order to talk about the larger field of lesbian writing, it is, then, first necessary to talk about the lesbian novel. And in order to talk about the lesbian novel, it is necessary to talk about narrative.

This discussion assumes that the cultural significance of narrative is, as Peter Brooks proposed, as "a form of understanding and explanation," a central "way of speaking our understanding of the world."[2] But narrative is not simply a means of expressing "understandings of the world." Our understandings are in

part produced by our interactions with preexisting narrative conventions. As
Teresa de Lauretis has argued, "the very work of narrativity is an engagement
of the subject in certain positionalities of meaning and desire." Moreover, this
subject is being simultaneously "engendered . . . by the process of its engagement in the narrative genres," because "subjectivity is . . . constituted in the
relation of narrative, meaning, and desire."[1] The aspect of this work of narrative that is crucial to the following discussion is the engendering of "sexual difference," where sexual difference is a matter of both masculine/feminine and
homosexual/heterosexual distinctions. "The work of narrative," de Lauretis argues, "is a mapping of differences, and . . . first and foremost, of sexual difference into each text; and hence . . . into the universe of meaning, fiction,
and history, represented by the literary-artistic tradition and all the texts of culture" (121). If narrative is the overarching structure, "plot," in Brook's words,
serves as "the logic and dynamic," "the syntax" of this system (10).

As feminist critics have demonstrated over the past two decades, representations of female characters and expectations of the work of women writers
have both been dominated by a romance plot. Twenty years ago novelist and
critic Joanna Russ commented pointedly on the "one occupation of a female
protagonist in literature . . . [the] one thing she can do, and by God she does
it and does it and does it, over and over and over again. She is the protagonist
of a Love Story." Russ points to the way in which the love story subsumes all
possible narrative destinations: "For female protagonists the Love Story includes not only personal relations as such, but *Bildungsroman*, worldly success
or worldly failure, career, the exposition of character, crucial learning experiences, the transition to adulthood, rebellion (usually adultery) and everything
else."[3] More recently, Nancy Miller has demonstrated the inseparability of "fictions of desire" from "the desiderata of fiction," of ideology and form.[4] Ideology made form ensures, in Miller's words, that "in so much women's fiction a
world outside love proves to be out of the world altogether" (45). Rachel Blau
DuPlessis has elaborated the ideological consequences of this merger of literary convention and love story. "As a narrative pattern," she argues,

> the romance plot muffles the main female character, represses quest, val-
> orises heterosexual as opposed to homosexual ties, incorporates individ-
> uals within couples as a sign of their personal and narrative success. The
> romance plot separates love and quest, values sexual asymmetry, includ-
> ing the division of labor by gender, is based on extremes of sexual differ-
> ence, and evokes an aura around the couple itself. In short, the romance
> plot, broadly speaking, is a trope for the sex-gender system as a whole.[5]

If we recognize that plot conventions do more than impose expectations on
the work of women writers and preemptive "explanations" on women as literary subjects, that they construct sexual as well as gender systems, it becomes

clear that narrative conventions do more than "valorise heterosexual as opposed to homosexual ties." The "desiderata of fiction" rely not on any "fiction of desire" but on the fiction of heterosexual desire. DuPlessis's "romance plot"—which I will call more accurately the heterosexual plot—constructs the heterosexuality it represents.

The heterosexual plot constructs heterosexuality—which is to say it constructs heterosexuality as the norm—not only by supplying the structure and the focus for representations of women but, regardless of whether love or sexuality are the subjects of the text, by providing a basis for narratives into which the heterosexuality of the subjects can disappear. When it is not the focus, heterosexuality remains the precondition for whatever is being addressed, whether that is the intricacies of particular relationships, adolescent angst, or adult ambition.

There is no corresponding "lesbian plot." There could be no "lesbian plot" equivalent to the heterosexual plot, because the construction of heterosexuality is in modern culture the construction of heterosexuality as the norm, and because the function of literary conventions, like all conventions, is to normalize. When Doctor Matthew O'Connor declares, in Djuna Barnes's *Nightwood*, "I have a narrative, but you will be put to it to find it," he is voicing a contradiction in terms—it is in the nature of narrative to be easy to find.[6] But lesbian writers have no narrative for the representation of lesbianism that is easy to find, because a narrative about a woman that is easy to find must finally be about finding a man.[7] Consequently, if lesbianism is to be represented in the way that heterosexuality is represented within the novel—through narrative, as a matter of emotional, sexual, and social relations—it has to be represented through the heterosexual plot.

Lesbian novels, then, are inevitably based on the heterosexual plot. But if lesbianism is represented through the heterosexual plot, it can only be represented as deviant.[8] Whatever the author's goal, lesbian novels cannot "normalize" lesbianism. In fact lesbianism, which is to say lesbianism as problem, is always the subject of the lesbian novel, because, in terms of the heterosexual plot's structuring of fiction about women, lesbianism is a problem. Lesbianism cannot be represented simply as a variation on heterosexuality, which might be presented in more or less hostile or sympathetic terms, because the heterosexual plot produces gender difference and heterosexuality partly through correlating gender and sexuality. Within the heterosexual plot, femininity and masculinity are ensured by heterosexuality, and ensure heterosexuality. That is, the heterosexual plot is a key element in what Judith Butler calls the "heterosexual matrix," "a hegemonic discursive/epistemic model of gender intelligibility that assumes that for bodies to cohere and make sense there must be a stable sex expressed through a stable gender (masculine expresses male, feminine expresses female) that is oppositionally and hierarchically defined through the compulsory practice of heterosexuality."[9] Lesbianism disrupts this system.

In those lesbian novels that replicate the heterosexual plot's sexual prescriptions—masculine desires feminine—with a masculine and a feminine woman, the masculine woman remains a problem. In those lesbian novels that model the heterosexual plot's gender prescriptions—women are feminine—with two feminine women, the problem of accounting for a relationship between two women remains.

There are two broad consequences. Because "lesbianism" is a problem, it is extremely difficult to submerge "lesbianism" as a question of gender and/or sexuality into either a narrative that elaborates particular lesbian relationships, or narratives about lesbians whose lesbianism-as-problem is not the focus of their story. That is, it is hard to produce a novel about lesbians/lesbianism that is not a "lesbian novel." At the same time, insofar as lesbian novels are always *about* lesbianism, they are about the problem of "woman" and "heterosexual" not being identical terms. The subject of the lesbian novel is always, in a sense, the problem of not-heterosexuality, which is to say, finally, that the subject of the lesbian novel remains, like the subject of all other novels about women, heterosexuality.

The immediate consequences of this narrative disenfranchisement can be traced through the structure and ideological implications of the lesbian novel. The ramifications of this narrative disenfranchisement can be traced through all forms of lesbian writing. The distinction between the "lesbian novel" and lesbian writing, as I discuss in my preface, was reinforced by social prohibitions against the representation of girls and a cultural refusal to interpret much else as lesbian. But the distinction was founded on this narrative disenfranchisement, which left the novel itself as a limited option for lesbian writers.

## II. "Carol, in a Thousand Cities": Writing the Lesbian Novel

Lesbian novels have been formula fictions constructed out of the heterosexual plot and according to the same patterns whether they were written by heterosexual women, by straight or gay men, or by lesbians; whether they were produced by reputable writers and published by respectable presses, or written anonymously and published as pulp paperbacks; whether they were intentionally derogatory, intended to titillate, or self-conscious pleas for understanding. The history of the lesbian novel is a history of refinements, extensions, and challenges to a formula.

Versions of what would become the lesbian novel began to appear in English in Britain and the United States in the late nineteenth century, for example Henry James's *The Bostonians* (1886). Gertrude Stein's *Q.E.D.* (1903) signals the beginning of the production of lesbian novels by lesbians; Stein's lesbian self-consciousness was reflected in her making no effort to publish the manuscript. This first phase of the history of the lesbian novel ended with the publication and prosecution of Radclyffe Hall's *The Well of Loneliness* in 1928. Hall's sympathetic portrait of a gifted writer and congenital invert with the class background and conservative instincts of a country gentleman, who gives up the love of her life so that her lover might have a chance of heterosexual respectability, was charged with obscenity in Britain and the United States within weeks of its initial publication, and banned in Britain for decades.[10]

For the next two decades, the 1930s and 1940s, which included the upheavals in lesbian and gay history produced by the social displacements of World War II, the second phase in the history of the lesbian novel was dominated by responses to *The Well*. Hall's novel became the touchstone, invoked in the reviews and on the covers of later works: G. Sheila Donisthorpe's *Loveliest of Friends!* (1931) was "More revealing than *The Well of Loneliness*"; Elisabeth Craigin's *Either is Love* (1937) was "like . . . *The Well of Loneliness*"; and as for Vin Packer's *Spring Fire* (1952), "Not since *The Well of Loneliness* has there been such an honest, provocative novel on a theme too important to keep from the light." The lesson of such references was always that these less immediately identifiable works were "lesbian novels," "like" Hall's work in subject and form.[11]

The inception of the postwar pulp paperback industry in the United States in the early 1950s marked the beginning of a third phase in the history of the lesbian novel: writers were solicited to produce romantic melodramas for what was increasingly available and understood as a lucrative market; lesbian novels from the 1920s through the 1940s were republished at an increased pace; and these old and new lesbian novels were all more widely distributed. These increases in production and circulation increased the volume of repetitions of the basic stigmatizing formula, but also provided more space for the development of variations. Moreover, in the postwar decades the increasing permeation of popular fiction by modernist literary techniques, and the initiation of postmodern literary experiments, all contributed to undermining the dependence of representations of lesbianism on the heterosexual plot.

Nevertheless, from the late nineteenth century through the 1960s, the lesbian novel's narratives of relationships between women were consistently constructed out of—through, around, against—heterosexual plots. The chief method of creating lesbian narratives out of heterosexual plots was triangulation. The persistence of this pattern can be traced across the decades, from James's *The Bostonians*, to Sylvia Townsend Warner's historical drama *Summer Will Show* (1936), to Dorothy Baker's appropriately named *Trio* (1949). So *The Bostonians* is organized around the struggle between a woman, Olive Chancellor, and a man, Basil Ransom, for the allegiance and affections of another woman, Verena Tarrant. In Townsend Warner's *Summer Will Show*, Sophia Willoughby is drawn to Minna Lemuel, once her husband's mistress.[12] In *Trio*, the trio are a female French professor, a female graduate student, and a young man who rejects the hypocrisies of academic life and tries to save the young woman from the clutches of both the older woman and the university. But the male-female relationship from which the lesbian couple is developed need not be that of lovers. In Gale Wilhelm's *Torchlight to Valhalla* (1938), the protagonist is introduced as a daughter extraordinarily devoted to her extraordinarily compelling father: only his death makes possible her love for another young woman. Or the heterosexual plot may be the basis for the presentation of the narrative rather than narrative events, as again in *Torchlight to Valhalla*, where the women's relationship is represented entirely from the perspective of an aggrieved male suitor.[13]

Lesbian stories could also be superimposed over the heterosexual plot, with one of the women in the central couple represented as "really" male. This pattern can be traced through the narratives of the various masculine heroines of lesbian novels, from Radclyffe Hall's Stephen Gordon in *The Well of Loneliness*, to Ann Bannon's pulp novel series of the late 1950s and early 1960s, invariably identified with her butch heroine Beebo Brinker. Discussions of gender difference within such lesbian novels do not usually take into account the ways in which their emphases on masculine/feminine distinctions within the lesbian couple dovetail with heterosexual narrative conventions. But the masculinity of Radclyffe Hall's Stephen Gordon or Ann Bannon's Beebo Brinker places them in the male role in narrative as much as social terms in relation to their more feminine lovers.

After the connection between two women is established, the formula of the lesbian novel is completed by some punishment, because heterosexual plots produce heterosexual endings, with lesbianism as problem. In *The Bostonians*, *Summer Will Show*, and *Trio*, neither Olive Chancellor, nor Sophia Willoughby, nor the evil French professor get to keep their girls: two of the girls marry and one is killed. But the punishment that completes the representation of lesbianism could take forms other than the disruption of the female couple by marriage or death. In *The Well of Loneliness*, Stephen Gordon is disowned by her mother, exiled from her beloved family home, and shut out of respectable society long before she surrenders the love of her life to a man.[14]

Both the construction of the narrative through the heterosexual plot and the subsequent punishment of the female couple signify that the central relationship should be read as sexual, that is, that the relationship is lesbian. Constructing a lesbian narrative out of the heterosexual plot—for example, juxtaposing heterosexual and lesbian couples through the story of a woman who rejects a male suitor for the sake of her love for another woman—establishes that the relationship between the women is lesbian by analogy to the heterosexual relationship it has challenged. The implication of the punishment of the female couple is less direct but equally significant. If lesbianism is considered not only a form of sexual behavior, but transgressive behavior to be rejected and punished, these fictional punishments "prove" the transgression. This evidence that the relationship was transgressive then "proves" that the behavior being described was sexual.[15]

\* \* \*

Both the consistency and the detail of the lesbian novel's dependence on the heterosexual plot can be traced through the similarities between such ostensibly different lesbian novels as H. D.'s *HERmione* (1926/27) and Patricia Highsmith's *The Price of Salt* (1952). *HERmione*, written just before the publication of Hall's *The Well*, is the work of a high-modernist poet as well as novelist. H. D. preserved the manuscript, but the novel did not appear until the 1980s, after her death. Highsmith, who was subsequently successful as a writer of sophisticated psychological thrillers, published *The Price of Salt* under a pseudonym. Appearing at the beginning of the fifties' heightened production and reproduction of lesbian novels, *Price* was frequently reprinted and widely distributed. The realist writer of the 1950s made use of the same formula as the modernist writer of the 1920s, even though the earlier text was invisible to the next generation of lesbian writers.

At the beginning of the novel that bears her name, H. D.'s Hermione is in the position of many of the heroines of her own and preceding literary generations: from the Emmas, Elizabeths and Janes of Austen and the Brontës, Eliot's Maggie Tulliver and Dorothea Brooke, to Virginia Woolf's Rachel Vinrace and Katharine Hilbery. The question of what Hermione might do with her life is both entirely open and completely closed. She is living with her respectable upper-middle-class family, expected to hand small sandwiches and tea to gossiping "university ladies," the wives of her father's colleagues who attend her mother's "afternoons." This is Pennsylvania, just outside Philadelphia, at the beginning of the twentieth century: George Bernard Shaw is the quintessence of modernism. Unlike the heroines of the English novels of this generation, H. D.'s American girl has had access to a college education. She has just returned from Bryn Mawr, after failing her examinations, which means "fresh barriers, fresh chains, a mesh here. The degree almost gained would have been redemption, ... would have brought her in a 'salary'."[16] That teaching is the only possible work mentioned serves to emphasize the continuity between Hermione's situation and those of the heroines of previous generations.[17] Having failed to order her life through education, she lacks any sense of what she might be and do: "She said, 'I am Hermione Gart,' but Her Gart was not that. She was nebulous" (3). However nebulous she feels, one option always remains, marriage: "She must have an image no matter how fluid, how inchoate. . . . She dragged things down to the banality. 'People don't want to marry me. People want to marry me. I don't want to marry people.' She concluded, 'One has to do something' " (5).

The role of narrative conventions in the shaping of Hermione's situation is confirmed when she is offered a way out of her stasis by a suitor, George Lowndes, who provides a heterosexual plot for Hermione's life and H. D.'s narrative. His presence erases her academic disgrace and resolves her lack of purpose: "Was it possible that she wasn't quite a failure?" (44). He proffers adulthood: "She wanted George as a little girl wants to put her hair up or to wear long skirts" (63). He offers a way out of her family and her country.

What distinguishes *HERmione* from the stories of Elizabeth Bennett, Dorothea Brooke, Rachel Vinrace, and Katherine Hilberry, is that H. D. places this heterosexual plot—the pattern of George's courtship, their engagement, her mother's resistance and then reconciliation to the marriage, the announcement and preparations for a wedding—in counterpoint to the story of Hermione's developing love for another woman, Fayne Rabb.[18] Through the stories of Hermione's relationships with George and Fayne, which, as Susan Stanford Friedman and Rachel Blau DuPlessis observe, "intersect . . . with great complexity," H. D. uses the heterosexual plot as a means of gaining access to representation for an experience for which there is no literary as well as no social form.[19] The expectations of a romantic narrative created by Hermione's conventional situation, and advanced by George's arrival, are challenged and fulfilled by Fayne. H. D. turns the literary advantages of the heterosexual plot (the access to a very specific social and textual mobility) back on itself. "George got [her] loose, lifted, as it were, a tangle," of family relations, H. D. emphasizes, "but she had been too tired to run and shout. She hadn't cared to, simply. [Yet] She had run and shouted at the sight of Fayne . . . had run to far hills, and found foothold on odd continents" (166).

H. D. indicates the comparable status of Hermione's relationships with both Fayne and George by constantly bringing "Fayne" and "George" into contact. Hermione receives the letter announcing George's arrival in the same post as the letter inviting her to meet Fayne. Her first meeting with Fayne is followed by her first meeting with George, and so on. But the pattern is even more elaborate: Hermione's first conversation with Fayne begins with Fayne's enquiry, "Who is George?" (61). When Hermione subsequently meets George, she tries to explain to him her response to Fayne. Hermione, kissing George, recalls her world-shattering vision of Fayne, "As she looked up into [his] eyes that were grey, that were green, she recalled the dynamic splendour of [her eyes,] two gambler's gems, star sapphires" (75). Hermione talks about George to Fayne before she kisses her; "But you haven't told me yet if you like George?" Hermione protests, to which Fayne responds, "I don't like George. I don't *care* for him," before "Her bent forward, face bent toward Her" (162–164). The presence of "Fayne" during Hermione's encounters with George suggests the sexual possibility in her response to the woman, which is confirmed by the invocation of "George," of the heterosexual plot, before she kisses Fayne. If marriage to George represents social and geographical mobility, the proof of Hermione's love for Fayne is a rejection of that mobility: George " 'Said that London was soporific and so restful.' 'And you?' 'Would rather stay on here with you, Fayne Rabb' " (217). At the same time, paradoxically, the movement (to London/Europe) that marriage to George implies is contradicted by the web of constraining social obligations Hermione's engagement brings, along with George's rapidly developing sense of her obligation to him. Her relationship with Fayne is, in contrast, repeatedly associated with physical movement and freedom. The importance of the relation between the two women is confirmed when it disrupts a heterosexual relationship, when Hermione decides, because of Fayne, that she will not marry George.

H. D. can record the diverging social implications of the two relationships by contrasting other characters' responses to Fayne and to Hermione's love for Fayne with their responses to George and the heterosexual plot he represents. As her daughter becomes closer to Fayne, Hermione's mother becomes increasingly willing to overlook what she had previously considered an insurmountable obstacle to Hermione's marriage, George's social and sexual disrepute. After a scene in which George almost rapes Hermione, a moment H. D. presents as entirely within the range of the heterosexual plot ("Now more than ever she knew they were out of some bad novel. Sound of chiffon ripping" [173]), her mother declares, "I don't think [Fayne] is good for you. Don't let her come here any more, Hermione. . . . I think the whole thing is wrong, a strain on us all. You ought to marry George Lowndes" (176).

H. D. employs two of the central tropes of the heterosexual plot in order to contradict them. Hermione expects that her male lover will define her: "she wanted George to correlate for her, life here, there. She wanted George to define" (63). And he does offer social and sexual definition, herself as his decorative wife: "He wanted Her, but he wanted a Her that he called decorative." This is a definition she rejects. "There was something stripped of decoration," she insists, "something of somewhat-painful angles that he would not recognize" (172). Fayne is the source of the definition she accepts: in Fayne's presence, "she felt somehow something in her taking shape" (136). The defining act in the heterosexual plot is the sexual act, too frequently represented as a kiss that literally and metaphorically "awakens" the heroine. But George's kisses "smudge" and "blur" Hermione: "George like a sponge had smudged her smooth face with kisses, had somehow . . . smudged out something. . . . had done away with something" (118). Hermione's awakening takes place, instead, during her first meeting with Fayne, when she "came to as from an anesthetic" (61).

Inevitably, though, the heterosexual plot creates a crisis in the lesbian narrative it enables. After Fayne, Hermione cannot marry George. But for literary as well as social reasons, the text cannot be concluded by her "marriage" to Fayne. The heterosexual plot H. D. has invoked must end with some form of marriage, some heterosexual relation (or death): Fayne betrays Hermione with George. George's promise to Fayne is identical to his promise to Hermione, the promise of normality—the security of the plot—as Fayne admits, "George said that I was merely human, that I wanted love. . . . that I wasn't so odd really" (185–186). This form of closure ensures the hegemony of the heterosexual plot. All of Fayne's responses to Hermione are put in doubt—overshadowed by a retrospectively "conventional" explanation, a desire for George that led her to cultivate George's affianced. The challenge that Fayne and Hermione's love for her represented has been reincorporated into the heterosexual plot, and the formula of the lesbian novel completed with the punishment of Hermione's deviant desire.

\* \* \*

Thirty years after H. D. completed *HERmione*, Patricia Highsmith based *The Price of Salt* on a similar triangulation of the heterosexual plot, though the triangles have been multiplied and even inverted. Highsmith's protagonist, Therese, is, like Hermione, a young woman at the point of establishing her adult life. Her evolution as a lesbian follows the pattern of Hermione's, out of a specific heterosexual relationship. Each move Therese makes towards Carol, the woman she discovers she loves, moves her away from her boyfriend Richard. When he is finally convinced that she will not marry him, and disappears cursing from the picture, she has to reject still another heterosexual proposal, from the more appealing Dannie. Highsmith is explicit about the connections between these choices: Therese's "consciousness . . . stopped in a tangle where a dozen threads crossed and knotted. One was Dannie. One was Carol. . . . One went on and on out of it, but her mind was caught at the intersection. . . . she clutched at Dannie. But the strong black thread did not lead anywhere" (275).[20] Only when heterosexuality has been rejected twice can the lesbian couple be confirmed.

In *The Price of Salt*, as in *HERmione*, the progress of the lesbian relationship is shaped in detail by its relation to the heterosexual plot, although the structure of Highsmith's novel is developed out of the dissolution of an already established heterosexual relationship, Carol's marriage. So Carol spends her first evening with Therese after her first meetings with the divorce lawyers result in her husband's initial victory, his winning custody of their daughter for the next three months. This loss of access to the child provides the rationale for the cross-country trip Carol asks Therese to take with her. They are pursued by a detective sent by Carol's husband to collect evidence he can use in the divorce. As the women move closer to each other, he moves closer to them, appearing first on the morning after they have become lovers. The novel's crisis and the lovers' punishment—their confrontation with the detective on a country back road, and their subsequent separation as Carol returns to New York to fight for her child—are produced by his spying. This spying will determine the outcome of the divorce proceedings which will, in turn, determine the future of the women's relationship. Even the "happy ending" the lovers achieve in *The Price of Salt* is represented in terms of the heterosexual plot, down to the details of the novel's concluding paragraph. Therese stands:

> in the doorway, looking over the people at the tables in the room where a piano played. The lights were not bright, and she did not see her at first, half hidden in the shadow against the far wall, facing her. Nor did Carol see her. A man sat opposite her, Therese did not know who. Carol

raised her hand slowly and brushed her hair back, once on either side, and Therese smiled because the gesture was Carol, and it was Carol she loved and would always love. . . . It would be Carol, in a thousand cities, a thousand houses, in foreign lands where they would go together, in heaven and in hell. Therese waited. Then as she was about to go to her, Carol saw her, seemed to stare at her incredulously a moment while Therese watched the slow smile growing, before her arm lifted suddenly, her hand waved a quick, eager greeting that Therese had never seen before. Therese walked toward her. (276)

The anonymous man sitting with Carol when Therese enters the room represents all of the men in the novel who have tried to separate the women. Therese, arriving, challenges the heterosexual pair he and Carol represent. Carol, greeting Therese across his body, confirms the disruption of that pairing. But he must be there. The women's union must be represented, even in this schematic fashion, as the rejection of heterosexuality, if it is to have either social meaning or literary form.

* * *

The effects of the lesbian novel's dependence on the heterosexual plot are ideological as well as formal. This dependence is not just a matter of "the 'presence' of so-called heterosexual conventions within homosexual contexts," which Judith Butler warns should not "be understood as the pernicious insistence of heterosexual constructs within gay sexuality and identity."[21] Butler argues that "The repetition of heterosexual constructs within sexual cultures both gay and straight may well be the inevitable site of the denaturalization and mobilization of gender categories," because "The replication of heterosexual constructs in non-heterosexual frames brings into relief the utterly constructed status of the so-called heterosexual original."[22] But the lesbian novel is not a "homosexual context," if there is such a thing. Moreover, the kinds of "replication of heterosexual constructs" Butler is anxious to justify—wearing drag, butch-femme lesbian couples—are quite different from most of the effects of the lesbian novel's dependence on the heterosexual plot. The repetition of masculine/feminine pairings in the lesbian novel is only one possibility of the range of effects of the lesbian novel's dependence on the heterosexual plot.

As already noted, the lesbian novel represents lesbianism as a problem, as deviant and to be punished. Moreover, as the narratives of *HERmione* and *The Price of Salt* demonstrate, because the heterosexual plot provided the basis for representations of lesbianism, "the outcast world of twilight love," as the jacket of an early 1960s paperback describes its subject, is above all a world of love. The construction of lesbian novels out of the heterosexual plot focuses their representations of lesbianism on sex/romance. Highsmith's novel is often referred to as a breakthrough text because of its "happy ending."[23] No one finds

a man, no one is felled by a falling tree or a psychiatric breakdown, no one
jumps or is pushed to her death. Carol declares: "the rapport between two men
or two women can be absolute and perfect, as it can never be between man and
woman, and perhaps some people want just this, as others want that more
shifting and uncertain thing that happens between men and women" (246).
The punishment is deflected, finally, from the couple to Carol, who loses her
daughter. But the novel's "happy ending" only reinscribes the romance as the
focus of representations of lesbianism.[24]

Unfortunately, to inhabit "the outcast world of twilight love" was hardly to
be cast out at all. If lesbians are only identifiable as lesbian through their appearance in a love story, they are simultaneously contained within the fe-
male/feminine role within the novel, by the novel, which limits female subjects
to the plot of romance. These romantic narratives processed lesbians into the
culture as "women," that is, as partners in sexual or love stories, and confined
to the private realm of the sexual and the emotional. This occurs whether the
lesbian is represented as feminine or masculine, femme or butch, within the
narrative.

The lesbian novel based on the heterosexual plot also reinscribes the "scientific" identifications of "lesbianism" with sexual life that began in the work
of late nineteenth- and early twentieth-century sexologists such as Krafft-
Ebing and Havelock Ellis, and continued with the pronouncements of the
medical authorities of the twentieth century. In the lesbian novel, lesbianism
produces only desire and female couples. No one lives a life not dominated by
romance.

Even though "the novel" implicitly generalizes women's experience, and
lesbian novels explicitly generalize about lesbianism—each lesbian novel is
presented as offering the whole truth about its subject—the novel also indi-
vidualizes the stories it offers. Given the heterosexual plot's construction of
lesbianism as private and sexual, lesbian experience cannot be represented as
an effect of political, social, or cultural forces. The "twilight woman" occupies
the "twilight" because she "love[s] . . . other women," not because women
who love other women are stigmatized and marginalized in modern Anglo-
American culture.[25]

Lesbian novels' dependence on the heterosexual plot means that their protagonists are invariably engaged in becoming or not becoming lesbians. In
order to produce an extended narrative, like Hall's *The Well,* the number of potential lesbians has to be multiplied so that the processes can be repeated: first
we have the story of Stephen's "coming to terms" with her lesbianism, and then
the story of Mary's waverings between two worlds. In a novel series like Ann
Bannon's, in which the same characters reappear, some go through the process
of "becoming a lesbian" over and over: in college, then in Greenwich Village,
then again after trying to go straight, and so on. Moreover, insofar as lesbians
are represented through narratives of relationship, and these narratives of rela-

tionship are of necessity constructed from heterosexual plots, to become or not become a lesbian is to be coming from or going to a heterosexual relationship. Consequently, in the lesbian novel the lesbians are always in circulation in a system that remains heterosexual. And the lesson of this circulation is that "lesbian" is not a stable identity. The lesbian remains always recoverable for heterosexuality. So, in *The Well of Loneliness*, Mary Llewellyn loves and lives with Stephen Gordon, but a single turn of the narrative sends her into Martin Hallam's arms.

This fluidity is sometimes checked by the representation of lesbians as gender-transgressive: the masculine Stephen Gordon is physically repulsed by the only heterosexual proposition she receives. But this is implicitly horror at a homosexual proposition, the gesture of one masculine character towards another. Moreover, there are lesbian novels—such as Vin Packer's pulp *Spring Fire*—in which the butch goes straight while the femme stays gay.

Finally, if through the lesbian novel the lesbian is defined by her position in a relationship, the lesbian novel ties the lesbian to the novel as a genre, insofar as the novel is, after all, the genre which places a premium on the representation of personal relationship. The cultural and critical consensus about the lesbian novel as *the* arena for literary lesbianism is in part a function of this factor, the lesbian novel's self-perpetuating representations of lesbianism.

## III. "Dozens of Ways of Being Queer"?: Rewriting the Lesbian Novel

The heterosexual plot and its ideological effects could be challenged from within the formula of the lesbian novel. The protagonist does not have to be the one who comes to a heterosexual end: *The Well of Loneliness* concludes with a wedding, but it is the marriage of Stephen's lover Mary, which disrupts the novel's central lesbian relationship but leaves one lesbian committed to her deviance. The heterosexual ending in marriage could be parodied, as in the strange concluding scene of Djuna Barnes's *Nightwood*—Robin Vote, Norah Flood, and Norah's dog "bowing down" grotesquely before the altar of a candlelit chapel. The heterosexual plot could be queered from within, by the use of a gay man in the male role. The generically labelled Jack Mann—a kind but alcoholic, intelligent but unambitious fellow, exploited and abandoned by a string of handsome boys—is on hand throughout Bannon's pulp series to provide half of a sequence of male-female couples that keep the narratives moving forward, while mixing up heterosexual expectations of male-female relationships. In *I Am a Woman* (1959) it is Jack who introduces protagonist Laura Landon to the gay life. He proposes to her at the beginning and they marry at the conclusion of *Women in the Shadows* (1959). By the time her old lover Beth arrives in New York City to seek her out again, in *Journey to a*

*Woman* (1960), Laura and Jack have a daughter, and gay lovers on the side. In *Beebo Brinker* (1962) the reader is first introduced to Beebo, Laura's great love, through Jack's eyes, that is, through a frame simultaneously heterosexual and gay.[26]

The lesson that women are always in circulation in a heterosexual system can be challenged even in those novels in which the lesbian relationship is patterned over the heterosexual plot, with the central couple divided into masculine and feminine women. When the couple is divided in gendered terms, the masculine woman is routinely cast as the "real" lesbian, while her more feminine partner is represented as not really lesbian. Not only is the femme not a lesbian, but the couple's status as lesbian is compromised because they look like a heterosexual pair. One woman is sacrificed to lesbianism—the one who, insofar as she can be masculinized, can perhaps be moved out of the category of woman altogether—but there is still always a woman to be recuperated. Moreover, lesbianism is bounded, restricted to the figure of the visibly unwomanly woman. But, as already noted, there are occasions when the narratives push the butches toward heterosexuality. On the one hand, such refusals to identify the masculine woman as the "real" lesbian keep both partners in heterosexual circulation. But on the other hand, if ascriptions of "real" lesbian status are undercut, so are ascriptions of "not real lesbian" status. If neither woman in a given couple is "really" lesbian, then any woman might find her way into a lesbian couple.

The circulation of women within a system of heterosexual plots is also interrupted by the representation of romantic triangles among women. In *The Price of Salt*, Therese's second male suitor responds liberally to her account of her relationship with Carol, when that is presented as an isolated event. "Are you going to see her again?" he asks, and she responds negatively: " 'But somebody else?' 'Another woman?' Therese shook her head. 'No.' Dannie looked at her and smiled, slowly. 'That's what matters. Or rather, that's what makes it not matter' " (258). As long as Therese is convinced that she can love only Carol, their relationship can "not matter." But Therese returns to Carol at the novel's conclusion, after she discovers that she can be attracted to another woman. If Therese is choosing between female lovers rather than between lesbianism and heterosexuality, then she is a "real lesbian," not just a woman accidentally or incidentally attracted to a "real lesbian." She will not return to heterosexuality with the next turn of the narrative. Moreover, the female triangle allows Highsmith to present the relationship between Therese and Carol as specific rather than generic. The happy ending affirms the possibilities of this relationship, as much as of lesbianism *per se*.[27]

The heterosexual plot's production of the lesbian as an exclusively sexual being can be undermined by the subject of work, which takes characters out of romance and into the world. In *HERmione*, Hermione's failure at work is a precondition for her dependence on the heterosexual plot. In *The Price of Salt*, the possibility of paid work enables lesbianism: Therese and Carol meet over a temporary department store job Therese has taken, outside the confines of domestic life.[28] Carol's desire to work had already been interpreted as a threat to proper order when it was opposed by her husband, and her first job led to her first lesbian experience. Although she is wealthy, Carol must find a job again before she asks Therese to live with her at the novel's conclusion. After Therese initially refuses, she relents not only because of the self-knowledge produced by her flirtation with another woman, but also because she has completed the first step of her career. The Therese who is able to return to Carol is confirmed as both a lesbian and a working woman, which are identified as interrelated conditions by her return to the couple.

\* \* \*

In Maureen Duffy's *The Microcosm* (1964), Matt concludes defiantly: "There are dozens of ways of being queer and you have to find out what your kind is and make something of it even if the answer leaves you a kind of little half-chick, a natural eunuch, the stock figure of fiction. You have a choice."[29] Nevertheless, despite any individual writer's efforts to escape the effects of the lesbian novel's dependence on the heterosexual plot—by disrupting its heterosexual ending, by challenging its gendering, through representing female triangles and/or working women—there were not "dozens of ways of being queer." In lesbian novels before Stonewall there were only two queer lives—as a lover, and as a writer: writers are the most frequently represented workers in these texts. Lesbianism and writing are persistently joined through lesbian-writer protagonists. H. D.'s eponymous Hermione, Virginia Woolf's Miss La Trobe (*Between the Acts* [1941]), Bryher's Nancy (*Development* [1920] and *Two Selves* [1923]), Mary Renault's Leo Lane (*The Friendly Young Ladies* [1945]), and, if we include the critic as a writer, Jane Rule's Evelyn Hall (*Desert of the Heart* [1964]), as well as the paradigmatic literary lesbian, Radclyffe Hall's Stephen Gordon, and Gertrude Stein as a character of her own creation (*The Autobiography of Alice B. Toklas* [1933] and elsewhere)—all of these women write as well as love.[30]

The writer-protagonist takes the lesbian out of the heterosexual plot as a sexual story and as a female story. Because she writes as well as loves, she contravenes the lesbian novel's exclusive identification of lesbianism with love/sexuality. The lesbian-as-writer's challenge to the lesbian-as-lover is reflected in the fact that writing is invariably the practice of the single lesbians in these texts—or the lesbian who has lost her lover, which is how you get a single lesbian in an economy in which sexual identity is constructed relationally. The conclusion of *The Well*, where Stephen is represented as turning from her loss of Mary to writing a novel that will plead for social justice, is paradigmatic in this regard. Of course the history of the female *Künstlerroman* suggests that writing is something "women" do in addition to loving, but not without conflict.

Moreover, as Sandra Gilbert and Susan Gubar and other feminist critics have shown, over the course of the twentieth century there has been a continuing struggle over the gender identification of the writer.[31] The unstable gender of "the (modern) writer" makes him/her available as a figure through which lesbians can exit the female role, and enter representation as more complex selves. After all, Stephen Gordon's turning from her lost relationship to the task of writing about it, which will, by implication, produce *The Well of Loneliness* itself, and be the fulfillment of her career as a writer, is predicated on her final admission that she is not a man—she cannot give Mary the life that her male suitor Martin Hallam might—as well as not a woman. The gender ambiguity of the writer, then, offers a way to elude the constraints of gender as well as the exclusive identification of the lesbian with sexuality.

Moreover, the lesbian as writer directs attention to the world beyond the novel, and to the possibility of a literature beyond the lesbian novel. She demonstrates that lesbians can produce novels as well as serve as their subjects, that is, that they might exist outside the confines of the lesbian novel, and moreover that they can produce something other than lesbian novels. In an acknowledgment of the possibilities of lesbian writing, most lesbian writers in novels conspicuously do not write lesbian novels. Nevertheless, lesbian novels about lesbian writers insist that a lesbian writer's work is shaped by her life, whatever her work is "about." So, in *The Well*, Stephen Gordon's first novel—drawing on her childhood—is a success, but her second and third novels are "sterile." This is not the sterility ascribed to lesbian and gay lives. This sterility is produced by the social hostility that restrains her from writing about her adult life.

* * *

The writers within lesbian novels also reflect literary self-consciousness, and literary self-consciousness is inimical to both the dependence of the lesbian novel on the heterosexual plot, and the authority of the lesbian novel. Literary self-consciousness that takes the form of linguistic experimentation threatens narrative itself. In *HERmione*, H. D. replaces the naturalizing surface of realism with a modernist style that directs attention to the subject of writing. *HERmione* suggests that if the subject of writing (even writing about lesbianism) becomes the subject of a lesbian novel, this allows a representation of lesbianism not bounded by the heterosexual plot. "Writing about lesbianism" becomes an alternative subject for this lesbian novel, which produces a nonnarrative model of the relation of lesbianism to the literary ("love is writing") that undercuts the heterosexual plot by shifting the focus from narrative. If love might be writing, or writing love, the heterosexual plot, and so the lesbian novel, are confounded, because plot is no longer the repository of value.

Like lesbianism, "writing" is introduced into *HERmione* via the heterosexual plot. Hermione's sense of herself as a writer is represented through discussions about art with her male suitor, George Lowndes. He praises Hermione's poems, but criticizes her mother's painting, objecting that "Love doesn't make good art." But Hermione disagrees, silently, "Writing. Love is writing" (149).[32] Hermione's relationships with George and with Fayne Rabb, and the choice she is faced with between the two, are subsequently played out within the novel as an aspect of the question of writing. George is correct in the sense that love for him will not help Hermione to "good art." He has been her teacher, given her books to read and praised her first poems, but she is aware that: "George . . . was flattering her, tribute such as some courtier might pay to a queen who played at classicism; he did not proffer her the bare branch" (172–173). George, when he is courting her, kisses her to stop her from speaking. In contrast H. D. represents Hermione's recognition of the possibility of desire between women as an awakening to language:

> Just what had she been saying? She seemed to have answered this odd girl, word for word, click, snap and click, the exact requisite counter, the same game but involving something very different from the casual af-terdinner sort of auction-whist her words meant with these others. Her words now were a gambler's heritage, heady things, they would win for her, they would lose for her. . . . She could use the same counter, the same sort of password that she used with all these people, but she had passed out in a twinkling of an eye into another forest. This forest was re-ality. . . . A whole world was open. She looked in through a wide door-way. (61–62)

But H. D. does not propose a symmetry in which Fayne offers Hermione the support for her writing that George cannot. The relation between lesbianism and writing that H. D. constructs is instead analogous to Hermione's under-standing of her relation to Fayne: "She is Her. I am Her. Her is Fayne. Fayne is Her" (181). Loving is writing.[33]

Love is writing in the sense that Hermione experiences desire as a revelation of the value and complexity of language.[34] In two key sequences in the novel—at the transition between the first half, dominated by George, and the second half, dominated by Fayne; and during the breakdown Hermione suffers as a re-sult of Fayne's turning to George—the focus is not on a contest between the heterosexual and lesbian couples, but on the literary implications of lesbian-ism. The first half of the novel ends with Hermione's and George's attendance at a play in which Fayne is to perform the leading role, of Pygmalion.[35] A brief but crucial conversation between the two women takes place in the corridor before the play begins, which concludes with Hermione's declaration, "I al-ways knew you" (139). They are interrupted by George. "Who are these wretched dramatists, these highbrow art sort of college girls?" he asks, using gender as a means of concluding the attack he had begun earlier on the artis-tic value of everything connected with this play (139). As they are entering the

theater and being seated, she responds to his question, obscuring the fact that
they are there because she wants to see Fayne, and Fayne, wanting to see her,
has sent tickets:

> "I don't know who they are. I mean I only know who one is. I mean that
> girl I spoke to is Pygmalion. I met her at a party. A sort of hot day when
> the dust was so hot . . . it's so much, isn't it, cooler . . . it's quite isn't it
> cool?" And she knew [. . .] that she would always say to George now and
> to all the Georges "The dust was so hot . . . it's so much isn't it cooler . . .
> it's quite isn't it cool?" hearing an overture on a violin and seeing a form
> step forward . . . (139)

The passage ends here, with Hermione's decision, a decision with literary as
well as sexual and social consequences. Hermione's exchange with Fayne has
completed their "courtship." Hermione's exchange with George completes her
education as a writer. The implication is that the "form step[ping] forward,"
the figure Hermione will be watching as she placates "all the Georges" with
conversational conventions, is Fayne (or another woman). But that is not
spelled out: there is, instead, ellipsis. Hermione's decision is already the basis
of the text, which suggests that Hermione the writer should be understood as
the writer of this text.

The possibilities of writing are also the focus of H. D.'s account of Hermione's breakdown, after the hegemony of the heterosexual plot has been re-
asserted through Fayne's turning to George. Hermione's emotional and sexual
dilemmas are brought to a symbolic resolution through the subject of writing,
in a dreamlike passage in which she identifies herself as a Greek messenger:

> run on and on Hermione. You are doomed Hermione for the message
> you carry is in forgotten metres . . . run, stripped across snowbanks, fly
> downward with pulse beating and pummelling veins at either side of a
> burning forehead. [. . .] Pheidippides run, run. You have a message but
> you are doomed Hermione. [. . .] You know running and running and
> running that the messenger will take (lampadephoros) your message in
> its fervour and you will sink down exhausted . . . run, run Hermione.
> For the message-bearer next in line has turned against you . . . dead,
> dead or forgotten. [. . .] you have a double burden . . . run, run
> Hermione, run for yourself and Fayne Rabb.

This sequence concludes with a version of Simonides' "For the Spartan Dead
at Thermopylae": "Tell the Lacadaemonians . . . that . . . we . . . lie . . . here
. . . tell the Lacadaemonians that we lie here . . . tell the Lacadaemonians that
we lie here . . . Obeying their orders" (220–221). The resolution achieved
through this passage depends on the figure of Hermione as a message-bearer—

Hermione as a writer. Simonides' epigram is a message of obedience and a message of defeat. The cost of obedience is death, but the message-bearer has escaped death, excused from obedience in order to report obedience. There is the verbal message of compliance destined for the Lacadaemonians, those who command obedience. Then there is the message the runner inscribes with her body on the landscape she traverses, the message "in forgotten metres." That Fayne was the runner next in line, who would have carried on had she not turned against Hermione, indicates the lesbian content of these messages. H. D. elaborates on the contradiction between these two messages: "Obeying their orders? Whose orders? I have been almost faithful. In order to be faithful I will forego faith, I will creep back into the shell in order to emerge full fledged, a bird, a phoenix. I will creep back now in order to creep out later … tell the Lacadaemonians that we lie here obeying their orders" (221). If the authority that the orders of the Lacadaemonians represent is the authority of convention, lesbian faith can be kept only behind the appearance of obedience to the rule of the heterosexual plot. But questions—"Whose orders?" and who "the Lacadaemonians" might be—remain.

Through the character of Hermione, who is both heroine and writer, H. D. perpetrates an elaborate sleight of hand. Love is writing. Hermione's love for Fayne is shown, in the course of the novel, to be the source of the understanding that leads Hermione to become a writer, and ultimately the writer of this text, but is also the source of the novel's structure and its subject. The book would not have been written if Hermione had not desired Fayne. If love is writing, writing is also love. If the choice between Fayne and George is a choice between writing and silence, Hermione's constant questioning of herself— "One I love, two I love. I am in love with . . ." (219)—is answered by the fact that she can ask. The book could not have been written unless Hermione chose Fayne. H. D. seems to be declaring the necessity of a doubled exchange, one part of which will be constructed of the most obvious conventions for negotiating a hostile social and literary landscape. But by staging her own understanding of the necessity of duality within the narrative, H. D. also undoes the practice of double communication: the message of obedience that *HERmione's* plot conveys for all the Georges is belied by the fact of the book itself, whatever the conclusion of its narrative. In such a literarily self-conscious version of the lesbian novel, narrative is no longer where meaning lies.

But even self-consciousness about genre can undermine the heterosexual plot and the lesbian novel simultaneously. Even within *The Price of Salt's* realist love story, Highsmith pushes at the boundaries of the romance, flirting with the picaresque and, most significantly, with the crime novel. The trappings of detection do not produce a "detective story." There is a gun that is never fired, a case that does not make it to trial. And while the effect of the heterosexual plot is to privatize, Highsmith's melodramatic parable of surveillance—the detective bugs their hotel rooms, producing an alternative representation that mirrors the novel, tapes that allow the voyeuristic presence of Carol's husband and the legal system he deploys against her, at the scenes of the women's love-making that the novel has also already described—displays the "lesbian novel" as a public document. As they are being stalked, the couple is overtly presented as necessarily hidden:

> Carol teased [Therese], leaning on her shoulder as they stood in front of a cigarette machine, touching her foot under tables. . . . [Therese] thought of people she had seen holding hands in movies, and why shouldn't she and Carol? Yet when she simply took Carol's arm as they stood choosing a box of candy in a shop, Carol murmured, "Don't." (184)

Later Carol says to Therese:

> "Is it anything to talk about? Is it anything to be proud of?"
>     "Is it anything to be ashamed of?"
>     "Yes. You know that, don't you?" Carol asked in her even, distinct voice. "In the eyes of the world it's an abomination. . . . And you have to live in the world." (189)

Such emphasis that what is happening must not be revealed to "the world" implies that the space of the novel is private. But there are no private spaces in the novel: Therese and Carol meet in a department store, and are reunited in a restaurant; neither of them has a personal space over which they have control, hence the trip across country and the hotel rooms. The hotel rooms themselves, provisional spaces that are never really private, are a model of their situation. As the detective demonstrates, the lesbian novel, like the hotel room, offers only an illusion of privacy.

## IV. "Clear Explanations Are Not Clear": Readers and Critics

The lesbian novel has dominated popular and academic understandings of the possible relations between lesbianism and the literary from at least the 1920s through the post-Stonewall decades. The lesbian novel was the basis of the lesbian criticism that began outside the university in the 1950s and sixties, with Jeannette Foster's *Sex Variant Women in Literature* (1956) and reviews in the lesbian periodical *The Ladder*.[36] They became the basis of *The Lesbian in Literature* bibliographies produced from the mid-sixties to the early eighties (1967, 1975, 1981) under the aegis of *The Ladder*'s original reviewer, Barbara Grier, and J.R. Roberts' 1981 *Black Lesbians*. Foster's vision was expansive: "Not all women," she pointed out, "recognize a sexual factor in their subjective emotional relations, particularly in the intrasexual field so heavily shadowed by social disapproval."[37] Nonetheless, her emphasis remained on the representation of relationships between women. Grier's assumptions—reflected in an elaborate system of identification for the hundreds of texts she listed—were similar. As, Bs, and Cs indicated the amount of "lesbian" material in a given book while asterisks (* to ***) signified the quality of its treatment. (T identified trash.)[38] "Lesbian" material consisted of representations of relationship. Moreover, if there could be more or less "lesbian" material in a given text, lesbianism was implicitly represented as a discrete element within texts, and certainly then independent of literary form. Nevertheless the lists return consistently to the novel.

Throughout the preceding half-century, literary journalists and publishers had emphasized the similarities and the limits of the novels they identified as lesbian. So a reviewer of Djuna Barnes's *Nightwood* began with the image of a "solid, well-tailored figure pacing distractedly up and down, rearranging a bow tie, angrily shooting her stripped cuffs, furiously glancing at a masculine wrist-watch, as she expects in vain the absent and faithless beloved." This image has everything to do with *The Well of Loneliness* but nothing to do with Barnes's novel.[39] The only question to be asked of a lesbian text was, as another reviewer wondered of Mary Renault's *The Friendly Young Ladies* (1944), "precisely *how* friendly the young ladies have been to each other."[40] Publishers continuously reprinted a few British and American texts that fit the lesbian novel pattern, such as Elisabeth Craigin's *Either Is Love* (1937), Gale Wilhelm's *We Too Are Drifting* (1935) and *Torchlight to Valhalla* (1938), Diana Frederics's *Diana* (1939), and *The Well*.[41] By the time these were being reissued for the North American pulp paperback market of the 1950s and 1960s, alongside a raft of written-to-order girl-girl melodramas, the publishers ensured that it was not even necessary to open the book to get the message. The pulps were adorned with lurid covers featuring pairs of agonized-looking young women, one blonde and one brunette, invariably in carefully posed proximity (but not embracing), and often in carefully posed states of undress, beneath breathless invocations of love, the forbidden, and shadow, twilight, or outcast worlds.[42]

Through the 1970s and 1980s and into the 1990s, the lesbian novel has prevailed in a range of guises in academic writing. Critics and theorists continue to foreground the lesbian novel: so, for example, Teresa de Lauretis moves between *The Well of Loneliness* and contemporary film in her essay, "Sexual Indifference and Lesbian Representation" (1988). The "lesbian novel" is still casually treated as a self-evident category: Judith Roof offers without clarification Jane Rule's *This is Not for You* (1970) and Rita Mae Brown's *Rubyfruit Jungle* (1973) as "two more or less typical contemporary lesbian novels" (1991)[43]; Cassandra Laity notes without elaboration references to *Paint it Today* as "H.D.'s most 'lesbian' novel" (1992). [44] Or earlier assumptions about the form of the lesbian novel are articulated: Bonnie Zimmerman suggests, in *The Safe Sea of Women: Lesbian*

*Fiction, 1969–1989* (1990), that identifying factors "vary according to historical era," but still insists: "A lesbian novel . . . places love between women, including sexual passion, at the center of its story."[45]

The authority of the lesbian novel has continuously been bolstered by the
assumption that lesbian novels could offer accurate representations. This assumption can be traced through post-Stonewall criticism. Barbara Smith's
varying judgments of Gloria Naylor's *The Women of Brewster Place* (1983),
Alice Walker's *The Color Purple* (1982), and Audre Lorde's *Zami* (1982) are
based on what she describes as these texts' "varying degrees of verisimilitude
and authenticity."[46] The demand for authenticity is implicit in Terry Castle's
assertion that including "pornographic or semi-pornographic texts of male
voyeurism" such as Diderot's *La Religieuse* (1760) under the rubric of "lesbian
fiction" "does not feel exactly right," although it is unclear whether the problem is pornographic or masculine perspectives.[47] Bonnie Zimmerman accedes
to this pattern when she declares that "Fiction is a particularly useful medium"
for the representation of lesbianism, because "of all literary forms, [it] makes
the most complex and detailed use of historical events and social discourse. . . .
novelists give the appearance of reality. . . . Novels can show us as we were, as
we are, and as we would like to be" (2).

But the desire to see the lesbian novel as authentic pre-dates this critical literature. The lesbian novel's dependence on a formula, and the limits of that
formula, have been obscured and the problematic effects of those limits exac-
erbated by the truth claims routinely made on behalf of lesbian novels. These
appear within the fiction itself. In *The Well of Loneliness*, for example, the
novel's novelist heroine is explicitly charged with the task of explaining homosexuality to "the so-called just and righteous. . . . [who] persecute those who,
through no known fault of their own, have been set apart from the day of their
birth." Books are presented as the remedy for this persecution, which is ascribed to ignorance. But scientific studies will not help: "they will not read
medical books. . . . And what doctor can know the entire truth? Many times
they meet only the neurasthenics, those of us for whom life has proved too bitter." The doctors, all presumably heterosexual, lack the skills of novelists as well
as the knowledge of a "normal invert": "The doctors . . . cannot hope to bring
home the sufferings of millions; only one of ourselves can some day do that"
(389–390). This kind of claim to truth within the lesbian novel was, however,
supported by medical prefaces. After Havelock Ellis's commendation of *The
Well* for "present[ing] in a completely faithful and uncompromising form, one
particular aspect of sexual life"—a commendation Hall herself solicited to val-
idate her work—introductory testimonials to the scientific value of the tragic
story the reader was about to encounter became commonplace. Typically, "Dr.
Arthur Guy Mathews" declares of Sheila Donisthorpe's *Loveliest of Friends!*: "If
I had taken a typical case of lesbianism out of my files . . . I could not have im-
proved on the subject as presented by the author in this story."[48] The language

of authenticity, if not science, appeared likewise in reviews: the *New York Times* commended *The Price of Salt* for "sincerity" as well as "good taste." Jacket copy routinely declared the truth of the lesbian pulps: Vin Packer's *Spring Fire* was touted as "frankly, honestly written." By the early 1960s, a pulp writer like Ann Aldrich could announce that "literature is a mirror to life," "However [the lesbian] may have been presented by the writer, and whether or not the writer had any personal experience with lesbianism."[49]

These truth claims depend on the broadest cultural assumptions about fiction: Aldrich's "mirror to life" is, after all, a resounding cliché. Even as that consummate realist Arnold Bennett argued with Virginia Woolf over the formal innovations of modern fiction, the two were equally committed to the representational possibilities of the novel. "The first thing is that the novel should seem to be true," Bennett insisted.[50] But Woolf defended her own work as well as that of her contemporaries with the claim that "they attempt to come closer to life" than the novelists of previous generations.[51] Truth claims are made most vociferously whenever a novel's subjects are sensational or sensationalized; truth justifies the shock and titillation the reader is promised. At the same time, as my discussion of narrative convention presupposes, the "lesbian novel" was overidentified with literary realism.[52] Modernist texts such as Barnes's *Nightwood* were read as "lesbian" only to the extent that they could be read in terms of the realist romantic narrative exemplified by *The Well*. The realist novel's particular identification with verisimilitude further naturalized the lesbian novel's representations of lesbianism. And the success of this naturalization helped to further naturalize the lesbian novel as the primary site of representations of lesbianism.

When lesbian critics have tried to expand on the model offered by the lesbian novel, they have too often simply relocated its romantic couple. So modernist texts around which female couples can be established have been brought into the discussion, but as versions of lesbian novels: *Orlando* becomes the story of the relationship between Virginia Woolf and Vita Sackville-West; Stein's experimental writing becomes the dialogue of her decades with Alice B. Toklas. Alternatively, lesbian critics have set themselves up in couples around the texts they want to discuss: in *(Sem)erotics* (1992), Elizabeth Meese's account of Brossard, Barnes, Woolf, and Stein is embedded in a dialogue with her own lover; in *The Apparitional Lesbian* (1993), Terry Castle presents herself as flirting with "the lesbian" who is her subject, while she frames her text with autobiographical essays about her own attractions to specific women.

\* \* \*

Even when the discussion is not explicitly focused on the lesbian novel, or its subsidiary, the female couple, lesbian criticism in the 1970s and 1980s relied on patterns of reference to "silencing" and "coding" that presuppose the lesbian novel as the only authentic lesbian text. The emphasis on the silencing of the lesbian has been extraordinarily consistent. In twenty years, the critical discussion has moved only from protests to a valorization of the "disappearing trick" as a newly claimed "unwriting." In 1976 Adrienne Rich argued powerfully of "relationships between women," that: "Whatever is unnamed . . . whatever is misnamed as something else . . . whatever is buried in the memory by the collapse of meaning under an inadequate or lying language—this will become, not merely unspoken, but *unspeakable*."[53] Barbara Smith, in "Towards a Definition of Black Feminist Criticism" (1977), writes about the "invisibility" of black lesbians, "which goes beyond anything that either Black men or white women experience and tell about in their writing."[54] Catharine Stimpson, in "Zero Degree Deviancy: The Lesbian Novel in English" (1981), argues that "the lesbian writer . . . learned that being quiet, in literature and life, would enable her to 'pass'."[55] The very title of Bonnie Zimmerman's often-reprinted 1981 overview of lesbian-feminist criticism, "What Has Never Been," signals her understanding of the lesbian as silenced, while Teresa de Lauretis insists, in "Sexual Indifference and Lesbian Representation" (1988), that the space to speak remains "hard-won and daily threatened by social disapprobation, censure, and denial."[56] More recently, in a 1992 discussion of what she calls "lesbian : writing," Elizabeth Meese elevates the question of silence into a metaphysical principle: " 'Lesbian' is a word written in invisible ink. . . . an unwriting as carefully prepared and enacted as the act of lesbian: composition itself."[57]

The discussion of silencing began as the feminist recovery of women's writing was in its first phase; it could continue, however, in the face of new information about lesbian lives and literary contributions, only because of the continuing acceptance of the lesbian novel as the standard. Prolific writers such as Virginia Woolf, Gertrude Stein, Willa Cather, Amy Lowell, Janet Flanner, H. D., Vita Sackville-West, and so on, who nevertheless did not produce lesbian novels, can be seen as having been silenced only if the lesbian novel is understood as *the* lesbian text. The gap between the multitude of lesbian writers and the comparative paucity of lesbian novels, especially of lesbian novels produced by respected or even identifiable writers, then only reinforces a reading of lesbians as silenced. This insistence on the silencing of lesbians either renders invisible most of what I have called lesbian writing, or at best relegates this work to secondary status as inauthentic or opaque—coded.

These writers had to be acknowledged in some fashion, hence the concept of coding. "Silenced by a homophobic and misogynist society," critics have argued, lesbian writers "have been forced to adopt coded and obscure language and internal censorship."[58] Lesbian writers, these critics presume, encoded lesbian references in texts that to straight readers appear neutral—asexual, heterosexual, or exclusively concerned with the fall of the Roman Empire. To a privileged group of readers, however—those having knowledge of the writer's sexuality or sharing it—these texts reveal their "real" lesbian subject. Critics could then speak of covert and overt lesbian texts, the former privately coded, the latter presumably both public and transparent. The repression hypothesis from which coding derives implies that there were other, more direct ways for saying what was being said, of writing "about lesbianism," that the writer avoided because of social pressure. It implies, moreover, that we know the forms lesbian writing would take were it not for social hostility—that within each Clarissa Dalloway there is a Stephen Gordon waiting to come out.

"Coding" implies that heterosexual and lesbian writers occupied different literary worlds, and that public and private speech can be clearly differentiated. It does not take into account the "codes," the references to mannish women or to the Greeks, used by both heterosexual and lesbian writers as signs of the lesbian.[59] It obscures, moreover, both the extent to which certain forms of writing "about lesbians" are not only constructed but at times promoted in the mainstream, and the role of lesbian writers in developing and/or employing these forms. Lesbian meanings, if not persons, are consigned to the "private." If the connections between publicly recognized lesbian references and mainstream forces are erased, so too are the gaps between those same lesbian images and what lesbians were writing. This masks the fact that lesbian writers could work unchallenged "in public" simply by avoiding those tropes already publicly identified as lesbian—the broad shoulders and narrow hips—or those genres, such as the novel, in which the tropes would signify. Similarly, the concept of "coding" distracts attention from the question of acculturation by implying a group of natural readers of "lesbian" texts. There may be readers with greater and lesser stakes in understanding such work, but lesbians are hardly born to read Gertrude Stein.

The concept of coding, applied most often to experimental or nonrealist texts, provided the basis for an unproductive critical opposition between realist and modernist writing. This opposition furthered the naturalization of the formula lesbian novel—by obscuring the extent to which Stephen Gordon's broad shoulders, narrow hips, and literary pretensions are as much a "code" as Gertrude Stein's cows and tender buttons. What was posed as a distinction between realist and modernist texts by lesbian writers was usually a distinction between lesbian novels and the work of the lesbian modernists. Those lesbian novelists who did not produce lesbian novels were erased, as was the possibility that "lesbian novels" could be produced by anyone other than lesbians. Equally significantly, the extent to which realist and modernist lesbian texts share in the use of the narrative paradigms foregrounded in "lesbian novels" was also obscured.

Literary modernism should be seen as offering new possibilities for lesbian representation. But the critical emphasis on coding turns formal innovation into a defensive choice, a deliberately obscurantist gesture whose only function is to conceal taboo meanings. "Coding" implies neater correspondences and simpler meanings lurking behind modernist texts than these texts can bear: it initiates searches for kinds of meanings different from those the texts were created to convey. It also deflects attention away from texts by modernist authors that are less experimental, or those that defy the terms of both the discussion of coding and conventional discussions of modernism: Woolf's *Orlando* and *Between the Acts*, or Stein's narratives, such as *The Autobiography of Alice B. Toklas* and *Wars I Have Seen*, hover on borders other than those between "obscurity" and "clarity," coded and open.

## V. "Narrative as It Has Been and Narrative as It Is Now": Writers and Conventions

The persistent emphasis on the lesbian novel as a form, and as a frame for the explanation of the relations between lesbianism and the literary, suggests that it fulfills many, even contradictory, needs. The lesbian novel serves the dominant culture's interest in controlling lesbianism. The dire consequences of lesbianism could be demonstrated within the narratives of individual novels, through threats of censorship, and through the processes of censoring individual texts. Moreover, if lesbian novels were the only kind of text to be interpreted as lesbian, the meaning of lesbianism could be limited to whatever could be represented in a lesbian novel. At the same time, despite its basis as a formula fiction, the lesbian novel supplies the kind of explanation and understanding of the world that narrative offers. And it provides explanations of lesbianism to lesbian readers as well as to the dominant heterosexual culture, explanations that are accessible insofar as fiction is widely available, and insofar as narrative is a generally familiar literary mode.

Lesbian writers' relations to the "lesbian novel" are equally contradictory. Most twentieth century lesbian writers of the pre-Stonewall period did not produce lesbian novels. As already discussed, because of its dependence on the heterosexual plot, the lesbian novel was a limited literary vehicle for the representation of lesbianism and/or for dissent from dominant heterosexist ideology. In addition to literary and ideological problems, there were obviously external pressures shaping lesbian writers' relations to the lesbian novel: the threat of censorship; and the stigma surrounding lesbianism, which might be drawn to a writer by her production of a lesbian novel. *The Well of Loneliness*, read since its initial appearance as its author's autobiography, demonstrated not just that identifiably lesbian texts might be banned, but that female writers of lesbian novels faced being publicly identified by their texts.[60] Lesbian novels that were either not presented for publication during their author's lives, such as H. D.'s *HERmione*, or published under a pseudonym, like Highsmith's *The Price of Salt*, testify in particular to the power of this threat of identification.[61] But paradoxically, lesbian writers also benefited from the existence of the "lesbian novel." The public identification of stigma with lesbian novels drew hostile attention to texts that could be made to fit the lesbian novel formula, but meant that it was not difficult for a writer to avoid identification. In particular, if there was not only a specific kind of work that might be identified as "lesbian," but that kind was extremely narrow, this left a great deal of space for the development of a wide range of other lesbian writings. As Gertrude Stein observed, "explanations are clear but since no one to whom a thing is explained can connect the explanations with what is really clear, therefore clear explanations are not clear."[62] If "no one . . . can connect the explanations with what is really clear"—in this case because they are expecting another kind of explanation, a lesbian novel—then no other form of writing will be read as lesbian.

In a system of interpretation dominated by the lesbian novel not only is most lesbian writing either erased or dealt with as secondary, but lesbian writers disappear from view except as potential authors of lesbian novels, or as the inhabitants of lives that might have been the stuff of a lesbian novel. But all lesbian writers share with the lesbian novel (or all lesbian writers share with writers of lesbian novels) in the narrative predicament posed by the heterosexual plot—the narrative disenfranchisement produced by the heterosexual plot. While the lesbian novel is based on the heterosexual plot, the distinctive qualities of lesbian writing can be more broadly traced out of lesbian writers' reactions to the heterosexual plot, insofar as they did not produce lesbian novels.

Not only because of stigma, but also because of their narrative predicament, lesbian writers' formal position within literary history is broadly but fundamentally different from that of heterosexual women writers. Obviously not all lesbian writers had the same reaction to the problem of the heterosexual plot, and to the absence of other than stigmatizing conventions the heterosexual plot represents. Nor have all heterosexual women writers accepted the constraints of the heterosexual plot. In *Writing Beyond the Ending*, DuPlessis traces a history of "twentieth century women writers'" rejection of the heterosexual plot's limitations. In *The Mother/Daughter Plot*, Marianne Hirsch argues specifically that "the mother-daughter narrative tries to displace the narrative of heterosexual romance."[63] But although lesbian writers were key figures in the reaction against the heterosexual plot they describe, both DuPlessis and Hirsch mention lesbianism only as a mode of reaction to the heterosexual plot or as a minor variation on the mother-daughter theme.[64] If we reexamine the history of resistance to the heterosexual plot that DuPlessis and Hirsch propose, with the question of lesbian subjectivity in mind, the patterns shift significantly, complicating any account of why and how modern women writers rejected this plot, and broadening the scope of feminist discussion of narrative and of lesbian criticism more generally.[65]

Lesbian writers were not necessarily alienated from the appeal of narrative as an explanatory system because they stood in such a problematic relation to narrative conventions. The attraction of narrative remains, as Teresa de Lauretis suggests, "in the possibility, glimpsed if not assured, to make up one's story, the possibility to speak as subject of discourse, which also means to be listened to, to be granted authorship and authority over the story."[66] Lesbian writers' alienation from dominant representations was hardly likely to produce less of a need for alternative stories and authority. Moreover, literary conventions could not be easily abandoned, even if those conventions replicated oppressive social prescriptions. Despite her commitment to new subjects and formal experiments, even Virginia Woolf insisted on the necessity of literary conventions. "A convention in writing is not much different from a convention in manners," she wrote, identifying literary and social convention in "Mr. Bennett and Mrs. Brown" (1924):

> Both in life and in literature it is necessary to have some means of bridging the gulf between the hostess and her unknown guest on the one hand, the writer and his unknown reader on the other. The hostess bethinks her of the weather. . . . She begins by saying that we are having a wretched May, and, having thus got into touch with her unknown guest, proceeds to matters of greater interest. So it is in literature. The writer must get in touch with his reader by putting before him something which he recognizes. . . . And it is of the highest importance that this common meeting-place should be reached easily, almost instinctively, in the dark, with one's eyes shut.[67]

Moreover, that Woolf imagines the connection between writer and reader as "reached easily . . . instinctively, in the dark, with one's eyes shut," suggests perhaps a particular conjunction between her concern with literary convention and the sexual.

Critics' difficulties in conceptualizing alternatives to the lesbian novel echo lesbian writers' difficulties in conceptualizing alternatives to the heterosexual plot. These difficulties are reflected in the terms through which Virginia Woolf states her narrative predicament. In her 1928 essay, "The Narrow Bridge of Art," she observes, "we long sometimes to escape from the incessant, the remorseless analysis of falling into love and falling out of love, of what Tom feels for Judith and Judith does or does not altogether feel for Tom. We long for some more impersonal relationship. We long for ideas, for dreams, for imaginations, for poetry."[67] The personal here is the realm of the heterosexual couple; the only alternative is the impersonal, the abstract. Similarly, in *A Room of One's Own*, Woolf insists on the importance for women writers of confronting an impersonal reality, rejecting the male figure who would stand between them and the universe. Even Chloe's liking for Olivia, which is the alternative personal subject Woolf suggests in *A Room*, must be identified with the impersonal, with the laboratory they share and the liver they dice. The problem for the lesbian writer is how to reject the heterosexual but retain the personal, when the heterosexual and the personal are identified, especially in narratives about women. At the same time, Woolf's placing of Chloe and Olivia in their laboratory suggests the difficulty of containing lesbianism within the private/public, personal/impersonal divisions the heterosexual plot imposes on the representation of sexuality and relationship, the difficulty of articulating lesbianism as only personal.

Given heterosexual conventions for the narrative representation of women, lesbian writers faced at least four different options: to represent women through the heterosexual plot; to give up on writing about women, at least as protagonists; to give up on plot/narrative; or to reconstruct narrative. In practice, different writers pursued different combinations of these paths at different points in their careers. Some lesbian writers were so committed to the possibilities of narrative that they were willing to reconfigure narrative; Gertrude Stein, for example, insisted on a "difference between narrative as it has been and narrative as it is now."[69] Others were so committed to the possibilities of love that they were willing to reconfigure conventional understandings of the relations between love and representation. Many of the lesbian writers of the first half of the twentieth century turned from an understanding of the personal that both distorted and failed to contain their experience, to the discourse of "history," to merge the personal and the public as a way of constructing narratives beyond the heterosexual limits of literary "reality."

## VI.  Clio Liked Olivia: The Promise of History

Modern lesbian writers were acutely aware of the freedom from social accountability historical settings offer. "Where Scott will go back a hundred years to get the effect of distance, Mrs. Radcliffe will go back three hundred," Woolf observed: "With one stroke, she frees herself from a host of disagreeables and enjoys her freedom lavishly."[70] Mary Renault was blunter: "Even to the most serious and sophisticated artists, the past gave invaluable safeguards."[71] The license supplied by a historical setting is illustrated by the differences in content and publishing history between two of H. D.'s autobiographical fictions: "Hipparchia," the first part of her story trilogy *Palimpsest* (1926), and *Bid Me to Live* (1960). In "Hipparchia," H. D. set the end of her marriage to Richard Aldington against the decline of Classical Greece; she becomes the title figure, and he appears as a Roman army officer. This "historical" version of events also includes H. D.'s lover, Bryher, as "Julia." Although Hipparchia and Julia are not shown as lovers, H. D. presents Julia as Hipparchia's savior in a fictional version of the critical moment in the development of her relationship with Bryher: Bryher's visit to H. D. in London in early 1919 when, finding the older woman gravely ill from the Spanish flu, she summoned doctors and friends and—according to their own mythology—saved her life and the life of the child she was carrying.[72] In "Hipparchia," Julia arrives when Hipparchia is dying of fever, and calls her back to life. As Bryher took H. D. to Greece when she had recovered, in 1920, Julia provides a conclusion to the "fictional" historical narrative with her promise to keep alive the "spirit of Greece." But Bryher did not appear when H. D. retold the ending of her marriage in a contemporary setting in *Bid Me to Live*. H. D. could only write Bryher into the earlier historical work, and publish such a potentially lesbian autobiographical narrative under historical guise: "Hipparchia" appeared in 1926, but *Bid Me to Live* was not written until the 1930s, and not published until after H. D.'s death.

But lesbian writers in particular turned to "history" as a source of narrative alternative to the heterosexual plot. This was possible because, as Hayden White argues, in the Western tradition, history *is* narrative: "the very distinction between real and imaginary events, basic to modern discussions of both history and fiction, presupposes a notion of reality in which 'the true' is identified with 'the real' only insofar as it can be shown to possess the character of narrativity."[73] To choose history as a framework for fiction was to gain access to an already established narrative. But more broadly, to locate one's text in relation to the dominant cultural understanding of "history" was to gain access to the assumptions of narrativity embodied by that history. Either way, history offered a structural refuge from the heterosexual imperative. The historical novelist could excuse herself from the heterosexual plot by claiming prior allegiance to a particular historical subject, such as Renault's Alexander (in *Fire From Heaven* [1969] and *The Persian Boy* [1972]). Even local/social histories provided an alternative frame of meaning: the North American pioneering story of the conquering of the Divide gives an impersonal coherence to Willa Cather's *O Pioneers!* (1913), *My Ántonia* (1918), and even *A Lost Lady* (1923). History as a subject frees an author from the necessity of establishing personal relationships among her characters or of focusing on a single protagonist. At the same time, individual life stories can be given shape by their relations to history: so Stein's *Autobiography of Alice B. Toklas* and *Wars I Have Seen* are organized around World War I and World War II respectively.

Moreover, "history" has been a source for defenses of homosexuality since at least the Renaissance. In 1592, Christopher Marlowe was explaining the king of his own historical drama, *Edward II*, in historical terms:

> The mightiest kings have had their minions;
> Great Alexander lov'd Hephaestion,
> The conquering Hercules for Hylas wept,
> And for Patroclus stern Achilles droop'd.
> And not kings only but the wisest men;
> The Roman Tully lov'd Octavius,
> Grave Socrates wild Alcibiades.
>
> I,iv, 390–396

Such lists of "gay" historical figures are typical of modern gay fiction. In Mary Renault's *The Charioteer* (1953), Ralph Lanyon numbers "Plato, Michelangelo, Sappho, Marlowe; Shakespeare, Leonardo, and Socrates if you count the bisexuals—we can all quote the upper crust."[74] Although there is only one woman on Lanyon's list, lesbians could also make use of this kind of historical reference. In *The Well of Loneliness*, the fey gay playwright Jonathan Brockett takes Stephen Gordon to Versailles, and, while they are touring Marie Antionette's apartments, points to:

> the simple garniture on the mantelpiece of the little salon . . . "Madame de Lamballe gave those to the queen," he murmured softly. . . . "Those two would often come here at sunset. Sometimes they were rowed along the canal in the sunset—can't you imagine it, Stephen? They must often have felt pretty miserable, poor souls; sick to death of the subterfuge and pretences. Don't you ever get tired of that sort of thing? My God, I do!" (239).

Brockett comes out, invites Stephen to speak to him, claims a queen and her lady, and offers an embryonic protest against "subterfuge and pretences," via this historical reference. But women were always at a disadvantage when the "history" that provided these identifications was a record of political or cultural authority: it is logically a male character who provides the historical reference, even in a lesbian novel.[75]

Unfortunately, history did not offer any substantial solution to the limits imposed by the heterosexual plot on the narrative representation of lesbians. It is neither accidental or incidental that, in *The Well of Loneliness*, Stephen Gordon meets the love of her life, Mary Llewellyn, while they are both working in an ambulance corps in France during World War I. They meet in "history," as it were, rather than in the spaces of the private world. One advantage of history is that the heterosexual plot is at best marginal within its narratives. But this is because women are secondary subjects within history, still confined to a version of this now marginal plot. In *A Room of One's Own*, Virginia Woolf describes searching Trevelyan's *History of England* for information about the lives of Elizabethan women: her narrator discovers that "history" "meant—'The Manor Court and the Methods of Open-field Agriculture . . . The Cistercians and Sheep-farming . . . The Crusades . . . The University . . . The House of Commons,'" and so on (76–77). "Women" appear only in relation to marriage and male authority: there is a discussion of "wife-beating" "about 1470, soon after Chaucer's time," and "some two hundred years later, in the time of the Stuarts," the information that "It was still the exception for women of the upper and middle class to choose their own husbands, and when the husband had been assigned, he was lord and master, so far at least as law and custom could make him" (72–73).[76] In *The Ends of History*, Christina Crosby describes this exclusion of women as fundamental to the history of Trevelyan's *History of England*. History was "self-consciously embraced" in nineteenth-century England, "from the early and great popularity of Sir Walter Scott's historical novels, to the introduction of 'modern history' as a discipline in the universities," according to Crosby, "as man's truth."[77] This history could be constructed

> only if there is something other than history, something intrinsically unhistorical. . . . Producing "history" as the truth of man . . . necessarily entails constituting various categories which relate to history in quite different ways. "Women" is such a category, a collectivity that is positioned outside of history proper, identified rather with the immediacy and intimacy of social life. (1–2)

This identification of "history proper" with masculinity meant that modern lesbian writers who turned to history as a source of narrative alternative to the heterosexual plot were directed away from female subjects and towards male subjects. As Marguerite Yourcenar commented in her "Reflections on the Composition of *Memoirs of Hadrian*," (1963), "Another thing virtually impossible, to take a feminine character as a central figure, to make Plotina, for example, rather than Hadrian, the axis of my narrative. Women's lives are much too limited, or else too secret. If a woman does recount her own life she is promptly reproached for being no longer truly feminine."[78] "Women" cannot exist as central figures within such a history: if they were to be central, they would no longer be "women."[79] If the lesbian writers who turned to history wanted to regain access to female subjects, they had to reconfigure "history" as well as narrative. Those lesbian writers who engaged in narrative experimentation did develop more complex accounts of history. The more conventionally narrative the writer's work, the more conservative the understanding of history with which the writer was working, and the more likely it was that her subjects were male. The more narratively experimental the writer, the more complex her sense of history, and the more likely her subjects would be female. This pattern produced two striking outcomes: narratively and historically conservative lesbian writers focused consistently in their histories on male homosocial and homosexual relationships; "history" became a key element in the formal experiments of the lesbian modernists.

* * *

Critical discussions of lesbian writing about male homosociality/sexuality have so far foundered on expectations of lesbian writing still dominated by the lesbian novel. Eve Sedgwick has written about Willa Cather's "Paul's Case" and *The Professor's House* as part of "the rich tradition of cross-gender inventions of homosexuality of the past century."[80] Terry Castle objects to Sedgwick's "elevation of Cather, Yourcenar, Compton-Burnett and Renault . . . to an all-

new lesbian pantheon: of lesbians who enjoy writing about male-male eros ...
more than its female equivalent."[81] But both Sedgwick and Castle, alternatively "for" and "against" the interest of lesbian representations of male homosexuality, employ a rhetoric of choice that implies a freer field than exists
within the frame of narrative or social conventions. Moreover, both Sedgwick
and Castle still view the female couple as the privileged site of lesbian presence
in a text, whether this couple is, in Sedgwick's terms, visible "as itself," through
refractions onto hetero or male homosexual paradigms, or through its absence,
when "What become[s] visible . . . are the shadows of the brutal suppressions
by which a lesbian love did not . . . freely become visible as itself" (69). If lesbian writers could do what they wanted or would do what they should, both
Sedgwick and Castle imply, they would write about lesbian couples. However,
if there are neither so many choices nor an authentic lesbian representation,
there is less to praise or criticize in lesbian writing about male homosexuality.

Gay men appear in "lesbian novels" throughout the pre-Stonewall decades
of the twentieth century.[82] These figures—such as Jonathan Brockett in Hall's
*The Well of Loneliness*, Dr. Matthew-Mighty-Salt-of-the-Sea-Dante-O'Connor
in Barnes's *Nightwood*, and Jack Mann in Bannon's *I Am a Woman, Beebo
Brinker*, and so on—serve as guides to the (gay) underworld for the novels'
readers and their lesbian protagonists. Even "gay novels" of the period offered
one representative and guide, usually an extremely stereotypical—effeminate
and flamboyant—figure.[83] That the representative guide in lesbian novels
should be a man reflects the extent to which gay men rather than lesbians
served culturally as representative of homosexuality.

But gay men or male homosocial/sexual relationships are central to much
historical fiction by lesbian writers, especially the novels of Mary Renault, but
also those of Bryher, Willa Cather, and Marguerite Yourcenar. Although these
gay subjects are in part a product of the masculinity of history, how or why did
these novelists translate masculine history into male homosexual/social narratives?

One way of approaching the question of lesbians writing about gay men is,
again, via the heterosexual plot. Feminist critics have argued that the heterosexual plot itself is a subordinate element within a larger male homosocial, if
not homosexual, narrative structure that is fundamental to the novel as a literary form. Myra Jehlen proposes that the feminine (though not necessarily the
female) is the necessary victim of a patriarchal exchange which is the basis of
the novel.[84] Nancy Miller and Mary Jacobus both posit more explicitly a male
homoerotic exchange. Miller proposes: "that the founding contract of the
novel as it functions in the phallocentric (heterosexual) economies of representation is homoerotic: 'woman' is the legal fiction, the present absence that
allows the male bond of privilege and authority to constitute itself within the
laws of proper circulation."[85] This male-male discourse is not violated by the
heterosexual plot, that is, by the presence of a woman in the text: as Jacobus re-

iterates, "the function of the [female] object of desire is . . . to mediate relations between men."[86] The heterosexual plot—embodied in the image of a
woman—reinforces cultural conventions about female subordination and
compulsory heterosexuality, while disguising the fundamental exchanges of
power, authority, and attention between men. In *Between Men* Eve Sedgwick
has provided the fullest development of such analyses, turning critics' attention
to the representation of these exchanges between men, on the premise that "the
status of women, and the whole question of arrangements between genders, is
deeply and inescapably inscribed in the structure even of relationships that
seem to exclude women."[87]

Having turned to history in order to remain within narrative, lesbian writers were faced with a male exchange of the sign of women even more obvious
than that in the novel. The male homosocial/sexual romances in lesbian historical fictions can then be read as inversions, reversals of the male-female-male
narrative triangle supported by the heterosexual plot. Refusing to develop even
the token versions of the heterosexual plot required to obscure this exchange
between men, these lesbian writers took the body of the woman out of the
text. Instead, they drew in the male figures usually addressing each other across
the woman, refocusing on the speakers who have always been history's as well
as the novel's real subjects, and articulating the male exchange structuring conventional historical discourse as a sexual exchange. This might explain why the
more "conventional" the historical subject, that is, the more masculine, and
more conventional the literary form of a given text or writer, the more likely
it is that the focus will be male and homosexual.

Terry Castle has argued that male homosocial/sexual narratives and lesbian
narratives function in opposition to each other, in an analysis based on Sedgwick's development of the argument that male homosocial desire is the basis
of canonical narrative structures. Assuming that "lesbian desire" looks like female couples, "lesbian desire emerges" Castle proposes, only "in the absence
of male homosocial desire."[88] But the lesbian novel's narratives about love between women cannot be read as one of two possible versions of a generic homosexual narrative, because they are narratives about women as well as
narratives of desire. The relation between the male homosocial/sexual narratives Sedgwick describes and the lesbian narratives that the heterosexual plot
produces is mediated by the heterosexual plot. If lesbians are dependent for
narrative representation on the heterosexual plot, which simultaneously constructs "women" as subordinate while serving as a screen for ongoing exchanges of power and attention between men, then lesbians and gay men
occupy vastly unequal positions in relation to that plot. This inequality is
magnified insofar as, while central to the narrative representation of women,
the heterosexual plot plays a much smaller role in relation to narrative representation of men. Lesbian and gay male narrative interests cannot simply be
opposed in such an unbalanced setting.

Moreover, those lesbian writers who wrote about male homosocial/sexual relationships were able to represent a form of homosexuality that they did not necessarily understand as different from their own.[89] "History" even allowed these writers to represent same-sex relationships without the constraints of the heterosexual plot. But their gay men are not lesbians in drag—despite Yourcenar's Emperor Hadrian, who observed of his beloved Antinous, "how much a thoughtful young man resembles a virile Athena" (132)—because their histories are not lesbian novels in drag. The lesbian novel offers a privatized romantic narrative, focused on the problem of lesbianism. But whatever account of relationship that is offered within "history" is taken out of the private.

* * *

Those lesbian writers who pursued modernist experiments were in the meantime undoing narrative and history to change the terms of representation for lesbians, gay men, and everyone else. "Nothing escapes history," as Marianne DeKoven repeats,

> but literary modernism is often discussed as if it did. Depending on their
> political aesthetic stance, such discussions either rejoice in modernism's
> flight from a debased social reality to a realm rich in meaning, aesthetic joy,
> and pure freedom, or they regret modernism's retreat from accessibility
> into bristling difficulty, its isolation from the life of society on a rarefied,
> elitist aesthetic pinnacle. Such discussions assume the absence or margin-
> alization of explicit historical reference in most modernist fiction.[90]

Feminist critics have worked to historicize modernism, but primarily through interpreting literary modernism as a response to historical circumstances.[91] In *Rich and Strange*, DeKoven maps British and American literary modernism most broadly as an effect of rather than a retreat from historical changes, and most positively as a matter of attempts to represent and further some of those changes. But modernist women writers' understandings of history, the role of history as a formal element rather than a subject of their writings, and the presence of "explicit historical reference" at the center of their work, are rarely discussed.[92] Stein, Barnes, and Woolf present their work as responses to historical events. They also offer representations of contemporary history. But both of these aspects of their writings are inseparable from their uses of history in their literary experimentation and their construction of alternative histories through the literary forms they developed.

Literary self-consciousness could take lesbian writers through the contraints of the lesbian novel, as in H. D.'s *HERmione*. Literary self-consciousness could also take lesbian writers through the constraints of "history." While *HERmione*'s "crisis" is produced by realist plot dilemmas and narrative structures, a resolution can be reached through such a passage as Hermione's vision of the runner because narrative "action" is subordinated to speech, meditation, repetition, metaphor, and allusion.[93] But H. D. also created an alternative geographic and erotic topography from a history that was produced through speech, meditation, repetition, metaphor, and allusion rather than narrative action.[94] That the Greek messenger is desperate to keep faith in the possibility of Hermione's love for Fayne would have been apparent even if Hermione had not referred to Fayne, because of the "historical" setting of her vision. When, loving Fayne, Hermione sees "the fantasy of the world reversed," the new world that opens out before her is created from a reimagined classicism. Hermione admits, "Dealing with terms of antiquity became a sort of ritual. It was all out of reality. I mean reality was out of it precisely" (211). Greece offers an arena for relationship: the two women together, "Prophetess to prophetess on some Delphic headland" (180). Greece offers the image of Sappho, and also "conventional" associations with male homosexuality.[95] Greek sculpture gave permission and forms for H. D.'s representation of bodies; Fayne can be described as a statue: "A head . . . set on space of blue serge, shoulders rising beneath schoolgirl sort of blue serge one-piece dress. . . . The blue cloth was flung across marble nakedness but nakedness remained unclothed, remained pure beneath it. . . . a marble from some place (Heliopolis? Persepolis?) far and far and far" (162). The masculinity of "Greece" in particular and "history" in general gave H. D. scope for complex evocations of gender transgression, at a historical moment when masculine women were routinely read as lesbian: Hermione could be represented as a young warrior; the text's author could be represented as knowledgeable about classical history when the classics and history were both understood as masculine preserves.[96] And in *HERmione* H. D. mixes up her history—her Greek messengers are female—and uses this history to produce an interpretive frame rather than a setting. But *HERmione* only begins to suggest the range of possible relations to multiplied and divided, reconstructed and redefined histories achieved by her peers and herself in many other texts.

The productive energy of the responses to history of these twentieth-century lesbian writers, especially the modernists, derives in part from the complex and sometimes conflicted relation in which they found themselves to narrative history's imposition of a focus on men, its assumptions about women, its elitism and racism, its vision of the nation (whichever nation), and cultural value. If the value of history lay in its narrativity, the history that was narrative, "history proper," the history of the official record, could not be abandoned. But, as Hayden White has observed, narrativity "in factual story-telling" as much as in fiction, "is intimately related to, if not a function of, the impulse to moralize reality."[97] The moralizing of conventional historical narratives is not focused on personal lives. Nevertheless, the history that offered narrative was profoundly conservative in its assumptions about gender, class, race, national identities, and cultural value.

Fredric Jameson proposes, in *The Political Unconscious,* that

> the relationship of . . . historical situation to the text is not . . . causal
> (however that might be imagined) but rather . . . one of a limiting situa-
> tion; the historical moment . . . block[s] off or shut[s] down a certain num-
> ber of formal possibilities available before, and . . . opens up determinate
> new ones, which may or may not ever be realized in artistic practice.[98]

The historical situation of the writers I treat here sharply disrupted their access
to narrativity. "History," Jameson argues, "is what hurts," and "this alone . . .
forestall[s] its thematization . . . as one master code among many others"
(102). History is certainly "what hurts" in the context I am examining here.
But "history" also functions as a master code in twentieth-century Anglo-
American culture. This study assumes "hurt," but that is not my subject here.

* * *

There are of course ways of addressing the relationship between lesbianism
and the literary other than my focus on lesbian writing, and ways of addressing lesbian writing other than my focus on narrative or history. But to continue to focus our critical discussions on the lesbian novel, either explicitly or
implicitly, is to remain hostage to the heterosexual plot and to capitulate to the
spirit of the age. The writers I am concerned with turned to history for formal
solutions to a formal problem—when formal problems are inextricable from
social problems. My critical strategy replicates their literary strategy: as they
turned to history as a means of moving beyond the limits of the heterosexual
plot and the lesbian novel, I am turning to their turning to history to explore
the possibilities of reading lesbian writing beyond the limits of the heterosexual plot and the lesbian novel.

Insofar as the results of lesbian writers' turning to history were not representations of lesbianism in the fashion established by the lesbian novel, the
work I am going to discuss often does not immediately appear to be "lesbian."
Given their complex positions within a heterosexist and homophobic culture,
lesbian writers have and will produce texts in which lesbianism has a much
wider range of meanings and consequences, and representations of lesbianism
take a much wider range of forms, than the lesbian novel allows. At the same
time, the lesbian novel's signifying couple, and the questions of love and sexuality this couple is supposed to represent, can be found far beyond the limits of
the lesbian novel, and in many relations to the text other than subject or
source. The distinction between lesbian novels and lesbian writing—a distinction I am articulating rather than creating—has been effective in limiting the
ways in which lesbianism has been read. But it has always been arbitrary in the
interpretations it allows. If love might be writing, everything they told the Lacadaemonians deserves our careful reading.

# PART I

---

# "TELL THE LACADAEMONIANS"

"Oh, it's a grand bad story, and who says I'm a betrayer? I say, tell the story of the world to the world!"

——Djuna Barnes, *Nightwood* (1936)

# 1

## Willa Cather's
## New World Histories

### I. Love and Convention

Willa Cather dramatized her problematic relation to the heterosexual plot in
*O Pioneers!* (1913), her second novel but the one in which she first essayed her
characteristic methods and subjects.[1] Sharon O'Brien has traced Cather's rejection of "the 'one string' of female narrative—the often-repeated tale of
'women and love' she disliked in nineteenth-century women's writing." In
*O Pioneers!*, O'Brien observes, Cather "Refus[es] to give" her protagonist
Alexandra Bergson "the conventional romantic story that ends in marriage,"
and "also declines to punish her with death."[2] Alexandra, whose world is the
land she farms rather than the home that is supposed to be her province, ultimately but parenthetically achieves a heterosexual relationship based on friendship rather than passion. However, as I have already argued, lesbian writers
cannot easily abandon the heterosexual plot when it is the only basis for narrative representations of sexual relationships between women. In *O Pioneers!*
Cather shifts the "tale of 'women and love' " from Alexandra to her brother
Emil, who is obsessed with their married neighbor, Marie Shabata. She then
"punishes" these lovers, who are shot in a shocking moment of sudden violence
by Marie's enraged husband. O'Brien reads this bloody ending to the novel's
heterosexual subplot as part of Cather's exposure of "the insufficiency—even
the danger—of passion channeled into romantic love," in contrast to "the
grandeur of passion directed toward 'something complete and great,' " such as
Alexandra's creative bond with the land.[3] But the fate of these heterosexual
lovers has as much to do with the circumstances of lesbian writing as with the
dangers of romantic love.

The ambivalence of lesbian writers' responses to the heterosexual plot can be traced through Cather's representation of Emil and Marie. This adulterous heterosexual couple occupies a "homosexual" position. As if they were a lesbian pair, Emil's and Marie's love is represented through its contrast with a heterosexual plot, the "sunny, natural, happy" romantic narrative of Emil's best friend, Amédée.[4] Like a lesbian couple, they are unable to speak their love. While Amédée can celebrate his marriage, Emil is unable to acknowledge his passion: "He and Amédée had ridden and wrestled and larked together since they were lads of twelve. On Sundays and holidays they were always arm in arm. It seemed strange that now he should have to hide the thing that Amédée was so proud of, that the feeling that gave one of them such happiness should bring the other such despair" (163).[5] Moreover, Cather's opposite-sex pairs—Emil and Marie and Amédée and his wife—are framed by a same-sex pair, Emil and Amédée "always arm in arm." These opposite-sex and same-sex couples are interdependent. Both heterosexual relationships, Amédée's marriage and Emil's adultery, are ended by the ending of the male friendship; Emil's grief over Amédée's sudden death precipitates the crisis within the adulterous couple that ends in their deaths. But Emil and Amédée's heterosexual pairings had already disrupted their same-sex relationship. The same-sex pair undercuts the heterosexual pairing after the heterosexual pair undoes the same-sex relationship. The homosexual positioning of Emil and Marie is completed when their speech is fatal; Emil and Marie are killed when they admit their love for each other.

When the heterosexual couple made by Emil and Marie is destroyed, so is a "homosexual" couple—also Emil and Marie—who cannot speak their love. But when they reject the heterosexual plot, lesbian writers must also give up the possibility of representing their own experience of romantic love—insofar as it is the heterosexual plot which makes that possible. So the couple who cannot speak are always being destroyed alongside the couple that is endlessly spoken. If in *O Pioneers!* shotgun blasts are directed at the heterosexual couple to obliterate the heterosexual plot, they are also blasts this lesbian writer is turning on herself.

The violence of Emil's and Marie's fate suggests the violence of Cather's conflicts about her own relation to the heterosexual plot they represent. These conflicts can be traced in her comments on literary convention throughout her career. She insisted on her own commitment to new literary forms, a commitment she represented as inextricable from a commitment to new subjects. *O Pioneers!* was to be a new kind of story, "a slow-moving story, without 'action,' without 'humour,' without a 'hero,' " that allowed her to represent new subjects, "heavy farming people, with cornfields and pasture lands and pig yards, . . . [and] Nebraska, of all places!" (*On Writing*, 94–95). Two decades later, she was still emphasizing her interest in reaching beyond the artifice of the literary: *Death Comes for the Archbishop* was written, she explains, "in the style of legend, which is absolutely the reverse of dramatic treatment. . . . without accent, with none of the artificial elements of composition" (*On Writing*, 9); *Shadows on the Rock* (1931) was "more like an old song, incomplete but uncorrupted, than like a legend. . . . a prose composition not too conclusive, not too definite: a series of pictures remembered rather than experienced" (*On Writing*, 14–15). Cather rejected conventional terms for the discussion of her work: "I am amused," she observed condescendingly, "that so many of the reviews of [*Death Comes for the Archbishop* (1927)] begin with the statement: 'This book is hard to classify.' Then why bother? Many more assert vehemently that it is not a novel. Myself, I prefer to call it a narrative. In this case I think that term more appropriate" (*On Writing*, 12–13). But she could also be vehement about the value of the strict limits on form and subject matter that conventions impose. "The condition every art requires is not . . . freedom from restriction," she insisted.

> The great body of Russian literature was produced when the censorship was at its strictest. The art of Italy flowered when the painters were confined almost entirely to religious subjects. In the great age of Gothic architecture sculptors and stone-cutters told the same stories (with infinite variety and fresh invention) over and over, on the faces of all the cathedrals and churches of Europe. (*On Writing*, 26–27)

The contradiction in Cather's responses to literary convention—her simultaneous commitment to innovation and constraint—is mirrored in her use of "history" in her fiction. She sought in history new forms and new subjects, but also rigid structures and the imprimatur of higher authorities. Cather began to separate her narratives from the conventions of the novel in *O Pioneers!*, where she declared her commitment to "the history of every country [that] begins in the heart of a man or a woman" (65). This New World history is based among local people, and concerned with broad social and economic changes such as the transformation of the open Divide to prosperous farmlands, and the Americanization of immigrant families.[6] History provided Cather with narrative frames, as it would her realist counterpart Renault. Occasionally, however, in line with Cather's own modernist impulses—most notably in her portrait of a professional historian in *The Professor's House* (1925)—she also structured her narratives around ideas of history. But New World history was simultaneously advantageous to her, and problematic. The possibility of a "democratic history" offered Cather more flexibility but less security than the history of great men and great events she repeatedly identifies with Europe. A "democratic history" might allow for the representation of women, or immigrants, or day-laborers. But such a history did not offer unequivocal authority to many plots. In particular, New World history did not offer the same authority to the representation of same-sex relationships that the unequivocally authoritative if undemocratic history of great men and great events conferred.

Over the course of her career, the problems of Cather's American history came to outweigh the advantages. Especially as she moved toward more innovative literary forms, she moved toward European or European-identified historical subjects. So in *Death Comes for the Archbishop*, which she wanted to describe as a narrative rather than a novel, the history of the Southwest is told through the figures of Spanish Catholic missionaries.

This model of history increasingly produced male couples. Despite the series of powerful women characters Cather is known for—including Alexandra Bergson in *O Pioneers!*, Ántonia in *My Ántonia* (1918), and Thea Kronborg in *The Song of the Lark* (1915)—women were gradually rendered secondary in her fiction. Even when her men were primarily observers, Cather's novels were often framed by men gazing at other men, whether in the form of Jim Burden's blithe celebration of "Cusak's boys," who at the conclusion of *My Ántonia* have become the burden and the caretakers of "his" Ántonia, or Niel Herbert's belated recognition, in *A Lost Lady* (1923), that his own obsession with Marian Forrester was an obsession with her husband.[7] The closer Cather comes to "history proper," such as World War I (in *One of Ours* [1922]), the "Spanish adventurers" in North America (in *The Professor's House* [1925]), or Catholic missionary movements in the Southwest (in *Death Comes for the Archbishop* [1927]), the more likely it is that her protagonists will be male, and that male couples will be the emotional focus of her fiction: Claude Wheeler and his fellow officer David Gerhardt in *One of Ours*; Professor St. Peter and his student Tom Outland, and Tom and his working partner Rodney Blake in *The Professor's House*; Bishop Latour and his lieutenant in the armies of god, Father Joseph, in *Death Comes for the Archbishop*.[8]

In this chapter I am not going to focus on those of Cather's novels most frequently discussed, nor necessarily on the most "historical" of her writings, but rather on her work in the 1920s, *One of Ours* and *The Professor's House*, and two late accounts of female couples in history, "The Old Beauty" (1936) and *Sapphira and the Slave Girl* (1940). In these texts the anger expressed at self/other through the story of Emil and Marie in *O Pioneers!*, and the conflicts between experiment and convention in her accounts of her writing, are played out in conflicts over sexuality in same-sex relationships, in the intersections of homo- and heterosexual relationships, and in a pattern linking homosexuality through history with death.

## II. Americans Abroad

In *One of Ours*, a "world" history that is located in Europe offers escape from a stifling contemporary American landscape, freedom for "men friends," and death as the cost of significant relationships between men. When Cather introduces her protagonist, Claude Wheeler, as a boy, his intangible "difference" from his peers is cued as homosexuality from his "sissy" name to his extreme sensitivity to the beauties of nature. He is especially close to his mother, while unable to assert himself against his overbearing father. When he tellingly tries to resolve his sense of himself as a failure by marrying, he equally tellingly chooses a sexually disinterested woman. Claude's frustrated adolescence and young manhood are redeemed only on the French battlefields of World War I. When the war finally arrives, it is explicitly identified as "history": "History had condescended to such as he; this whole brilliant adventure had become the day's work."[9] History as "adventure" is identified with "freedom": "He awoke every morning with that sense of freedom and going forward, as if the world were growing bigger each day and he were growing with it. . . . Something was released that had been struggling for a long while, he told himself" (265).

That this history provides an escape from women is dramatized in the story of another soldier whose injuries have erased "his recollection of women. . . . He can remember his father, but not his mother; doesn't know if he has sisters or not" (287), and even more emphatically, "the women are clear wiped out, even the girl he was going to marry" (288). Claude's early friendship with his neighbor, Ernest Havel, his pleasure in the company of young men, and his lack of romantic fervor for women come together in the war. The figure of his new "freedom" is a fellow officer, David Gerhardt, an American but an Easterner, a violinist, who is identified with Europe through both his art and his having already lived in Paris. Gerhardt fulfills Claude's dreams of young manhood: "In the years when he went to school in Lincoln, he was always hunting for some one whom he could admire without reservations; some one he could envy, emulate, wish to be. Now he believed that even then he must have had some faint image of a man like Gerhardt in his mind" (350). Cather is emphatic that it is history that enables this relationship: "It was only in war times," Claude notes, "that their paths would have been likely to cross; or that they would have had anything to do together . . . any of the common interests that make men friends" (350). Cather's ellipsis is provocative. What they are likely "to do together" in wartime is kill or be killed. What they do is care for each other, which apparently cannot be observed.

In *One of Ours*, the clearly European and authoritative history of World War I liberates the homosocial but punishes the homosexual. The Western Front provides a setting for the most formally conventional reference to homosexuality in Cather's fiction. But this takes the form of a disavowal. The homosexual is literally an enemy, and dead. Claude finds a locket around the neck of a dead German officer. Inside the locket is a portrait of a young man, "pale as snow, with blurred forget-me-not eyes. Claude studied it, wondering. 'It looks like a poet, or something. Probably a kid brother, killed at the beginning of the war' " (367). But the more sophisticated David looks at the locket with a "disdainful expression." However, after his disengenuous explanation of the locket, "Claude noticed that David had looked at him as if he were very much pleased with him,—looked, indeed, as if something pleasant had happened . . . where, God knew, nothing had" (367). David's disdain for the sign of the dead German's sexuality and his pleasure at Claude's ignorance convey only hostility to homosexuality. Claude's lack of understanding guarantees his innocence and, by extension, that of all the men in their troop, where there are a series of devoted couples like Claude and David. This passage identifies that innocence with Claude's untainted Americanness. However, if ignorance of the possibility of homosexuality is the guarantee of innocence, David's understanding suggests his own complicity. The homosexual is fatal to the homosocial: before Claude's and David's men kill him, the German destroys one of the other male couples in their troop. And the homosocial is fatal to the homosexual: Claude's and David's troop have killed the German.

"One of ours" is a term of identification. *One of Ours* identifies male relationships and the adventure of history. But if Cather offers history as the location of love in this novel, that love must not be articulated. Claude Wheeler goes gladly to his death in Europe, in history, rather than live out his life in America. Although many of Cather's soldiers welcome the war as a means of escaping their small-town American lives, Claude conceals his pleasure: "Life was a secret, these days," he concludes (309). The secret recurs in the novel's highly conventionalized final battle scene, when "his" men lie to Claude after he has been fatally wounded, assuring him that David is on his way, although his friend is already dead.[10] Their keeping David's death a secret is a recognition of the two officers' bond, but it also serves to keep the connection unspoken— Claude cannot express any inappropriate grief if he does not know David is gone. The violent stricture of the system of permission and suppression is completed. The innocent and the "guilty," those who never articulate their connection, like Claude and David, as well as those who do, like the German officer, all die alike.

## III. The Professor's Boy

Cather's pivotal portrait of a professional historian, *The Professor's House*, also offers an American boy—the pivotal figure of Tom Outland—who exchanges the possibility of growing up to be an American man for a fixed place within a frame of male relationships, by exiting to death on the Western Front. Recent critical accounts of this novel, however, focus on one male couple, what Eve Sedgwick calls the "gorgeous homosocial romance" of Tom Outland and Rodney Blake.[11] But in fact *The Professor's House* traces two male couples and three "histories" to pursue questions raised by *One of Ours* about the possibility of sexuality in same-sex relationships, as well as questions raised by *O Pioneers!* about the relation between homosexual and heterosexual couples and narratives. When Cather's historian, Godfrey St. Peter, was writing his histories, we are told, "all the foolish conventions" fell away, and he was able "to do something quite different" while apparently "trying to do the usual thing."[12] At the same time, when he declares, "There were some advantages of being a writer of histories," the advantages are those of retreat: "The desk was a shelter one could hide behind, it was a hole one could creep into" (161). This paradoxical representation of history as a site of possibility and a space of withdrawal echoes throughout the novel.

The two male couples in *The Professor's House*, Tom Outland and Rodney Blake, and Tom and the Professor, are interdependent. Although Tom's and Roddy's story is formally embedded within the Professor's, in chronological terms Roddy has to leave before the Professor can play his part in Tom's life. Roddy is a less compromised version of both Tom and the Professor. Roddy is the real cowboy and man of the people, fixed in all the positions Tom will move beyond in his journey from life among the day laborers to life in the middle classes, from "life" to "the university," from history to science. At the same time, his devotion to Tom is more generous than the Professor's: Roddy saves Tom's life, and works beside him; the Professor teaches him and launches him on the path to middle-class heterosexual adulthood that he himself had taken. Between Roddy and the Professor, Tom is an unstable figure. His instability can be read in class terms: the father he never knew was a schoolteacher; he is always better educated than Roddy's laboring boy, always on his way to the Professor's professional status. But the fundamental source of his instability—and of his class mobility—is his deference to authority.

In this novel, Cather explores the narrative and sexual possibilities of three different histories. There is the European-oriented history of great men and events represented by Cather's Professor, the internationally recognized author of an eight-volume study of the *Spanish Adventurers in North America*. But there is also a native history of cliff-dwelling people whose presence predates the European "discovery" of the Americas, and whose abandoned world is discovered in a Southwestern mesa by Tom Outland. And there is a third, international, contemporary, political history that the quintessential laboring boy, Rodney Blake, brings into the novel through his newspaper reading.

Like the adventure of history in *One of Ours*, each of these histories is exclusively male. Professor Napoleon Godfrey St. Peter's first and last names locate him between two historically all-male institutions central to "history proper," the army and the church. The Spanish "adventurers" about whom he has written are referred to by his son-in-law as his sons. The Professor claims heterosexuality as the source of his histories: "the design of his life had been ... shaped by all the penalties and responsiblities of being and having been a lover. Because there was Lillian, there must be marriage and a salary. Because there was marriage, there were children. Because there were children, and fervour in the blood and brain, books were born as well as daughters" (265). But his histories consistently take him from the women in his life to exchanges with

other men. The idea for his great work comes to him when the family is traveling together in Europe. Immediately, he sends his wife and daughters home,
and turns to his half brothers for help. They provide not only a boat in which
he can travel to Spain but the company of sailors: "On the voyage everything
seemed to feed the plan of the work that was forming in St. Peter's mind; the
skipper, the old Catalan second mate, the sea itself" (106). Tom Outland becomes the chief intellectual and practical influence on his project. The fate of
St. Peter's histories in the world is determined by the dialogue they establish for
him with other men: "With the fourth volume he began to be aware that a few
young men, scattered about the United States and England, were intensely interested in his experiment. With the fifth and sixth, they began to express their
interest in lectures and in print." It is because of the interest of these young
men that "The last two volumes brought him a certain international reputation and what were called rewards" (33). If the Professor's history is a world of
men attending to men, the native history of the Blue Mesa provides the focus
for male exchanges as well; in "Tom Outland's Story" the discovery of the cliff
dwellings is framed by a narrative of Tom's and Roddy's relationship. And like
these other histories, all of the actors in Roddy's political record are male.

As in *One of Ours*, in *The Professor's House* history is not only a male preserve and the focus of relationships between men, but the medium of such relationships. Their explorations on the mesa give Tom and Roddy, as the
Spanish adventurers give Tom and the Professor, the something "to do together
. . . the common interests that make men friends," supplied to Claude and
David by the war (350). Tom Outland seeks out the Professor after reading an
article he has written on the history of the Southwest, and presents himself to
the Professor as a potential student. They become close through their discussions of the Professor's work: "the Professor began to take Tom up to the study
and talk over his work with him, and began to make a companion of him"
(172–173). They spend summers traveling together, working jointly on the
Professor's history.

But also as in *One of Ours*, in *The Professor's House* history destroys the relationships it fosters. History limits male relationships in *The Professor's House*
because, at the same time that it offers a setting for same-sex relationships, history raises the spectre of social authority. Tom and Roddy are undone by Tom's
desire for the kind of legitimation for the history of the mesa that the Professor's history enjoys. Tom wants the Smithsonian's help and imprimatur for his
and Roddy's work and for the native history they have recovered. But because
the American cultural and political authorities he approaches prefer to cultivate their ties to Europe, there is no official interest in the mesa. Roddy, who
does not understand Tom's approach to authority, and assumes they are seek-
ing payment for their work, then sells the pottery, tools, and other relics they
have recovered to a German collector looking for native artifacts. By the time
Tom discovers what has happened, the materials are on their way to Europe.

(The Europeans, with their apparent monopoly over historical authority, know historical value when they see it.) This transaction (sale and loss) produces a crisis between the two men.

The crisis occurs because they did not produce their own history, that is, they never articulated the nature of their work or their relationship. It produces an attempt at articulation that fails and destroys their connection. This attempt at articulation fails and fails destructively because it raises interconnected questions about their sexuality and their relation to history. As Sedgwick notes, when they part, Tom's desire is simultaneously imagined as physical and impossible: "There was an ache in my arms to reach out and detain him, but there was something else that made me absolutely powerless to do so" (247). The terms of their conflict are the terms of representations of homosexuality: silence, speech, and interpretation. Their interaction had been unspoken. Roddy in fact protests Tom's silence about his understanding of their activities: "You might have given me some of this Fourth of July talk a little earlier in the game. I didn't know you valued that stuff any different than anything else a fellow might run on to: a gold mine or a pocket of turquoise" (245). This silence sets the stage for their conflict. But as Tom makes clear, speech is also destructive: "I walked up and down the kitchen trying to make Blake understand the kind of value those objects had had for me. Unfortunately, I succeeded" (245).

Insofar as they are driven to interpret their relationship, the interpretation they produce is destructive. The only terms available are apparently the terms of class—Roddy's response to Tom's horror at his sale of history is to see himself as hired: "I supposed I had some share in the relics we dug up—you always spoke of it that way. But I see now I was working for you like a hired man, and while you were away I sold your property" (245). But Tom has already identified money with women, and by extension with sexuality: "I'd as soon have sold my own grandmother as Mother Eve—I'd have sold any living woman first," he protests (244); nevertheless "If it was my money you'd lost gambling, or my girl you'd made free with, we could fight it out, and maybe be friends again. But this is different" (246). This betrayal, figured in sexual/financial terms but inexplicably "different" and worse than a sexual/financial betrayal, can be read as the articulation of (homo)sexual possibilities in their relationship; Roddy exchanges the relics, (their) history, for money, and money is a sign of sexuality throughout the novel.

The sexual significance of money in *The Professor's House* can be traced through its different significance in heterosexual and same-sex relationships. Money secures heterosexual relationships. The Professor's wife brings a small inherited income to their marriage, which he remembers as crucial to the success of their life together. When a fortune is made from the scientific invention Tom leaves behind on his way to war, the money goes to the Professor's daughter Rosamond, whom Tom was engaged to marry, and to Louie Marsellus, the

man she goes on to marry. But money must not circulate through male relationships. The professor explicitly refuses any of the money made from Tom's
work, a refusal couched in terms of his insistence on the difference between his
relationship to Tom and a heterosexual relationship. "Your bond with him was
social," he insists to Rosamond, "it follows the laws of society, and they are
based on property. Mine wasn't, and there was no material clause in it" (63).
Money identifies heterosexuality with the social, with the realm of property
which is also the realm of the prescribed and the authorized.

That money/sexuality is a threat to male relationships is demonstrated
throughout "Tom Outland's Story." On the night when Tom and Roddy meet,
Tom saves the older man's money and body from vengeful opponents at cards.
Blake is introduced as he is winning hundreds of dollars, and as unaccountably
unsocialized; refusing to conform to local conventions, he comes from his job
to the card game without cleaning up after work. Tom will keep watch over
him while he sleeps, but refuses to share the money next morning, a refusal
that excludes sexuality from their relationship.[13] When Roddy later creates the
crisis of their relationship by selling the relics, he does so to raise money for
Tom's education. But this motive hardly mitigates Tom's anger. Tom refuses
that money as well.

The exchange of money between men, of money for history, is problematic because it raises questions about how Tom's and Roddy's partnership
should be interpreted, but also because it raises related questions about their
relation to history. Tom represents what Roddy has sold as *their* history when
he declares that the relics, "belonged to this country, to the State, and to all the
people. They belonged to boys like you and me, that have no other ancestors
to inherit from" (242). This history is theirs, Tom claims, because they lack a
history, because they "have no other ancestors to inherit from." But is this
enough to make the native history of the cliff dwellers theirs? Despite Tom's
claim, the country, as represented by the state, by the Smithsonian, does not
want this history. "The people," in other words, might be different from "boys
like you and me." These "boys" are defined implicitly in class terms: they have
no ancestors because they are "boys," that is laborers. But the novel pauses here
in its account of American history, pauses on the potential gap between "boys"
and "all the people," which is to say, pauses on the question of how else "boys
like you and me" might be identified.

The novel's third history, a contemporary social and political history of injustice and resistance, is foregrounded during Tom's and Roddy's crisis. By this
point in the narrative, Roddy has already been identified as "a conscientious
reader of newspapers. . . . [who] always wanted to know what was going on in
the world, though most of it displeased him. He brooded on the great injus-
tices of his time; the hanging of the Anarchists in Chicago, which he could just
remember, and the Dreyfus case" (187). Roddy's identification with Dreyfus,
an emblematic figure in late nineteenth-century European history whose name

raises broad questions of social justice, resonates in the gay and lesbian fiction of the first half of the twentieth century.[14] In their final exchanges, Tom declares, " 'You've gone and sold your country's secrets, like Dreyfus.' 'That man was innocent. It was a frame-up,' Blake murmured. It was a point he would never pass up" (243). Ostensibly, the secret that Roddy's sale of the relics reveals is the country's indifference to its own history. What it also reveals is that, from Tom's point of view, Roddy had the wrong interpretation of their work together, their history, their relationship. But that Roddy cannot let the charge against Dreyfus pass suggests that, like Dreyfus, he is innocent. He sold the relics because the country did not want them; his understanding of their history is as valid as Tom's. And via the identification of Roddy with Dreyfus, Cather identifies Roddy's secret as the country's secret. The history of his country that begins in Roddy's heart is love for Tom, which leads him to the secret his country wants to keep. But what constitutes this secret? Is it (as Claude's American innocence suggests) the fact that sexual love between men is possible? Or is this secret the attendant fact of social injustice, the fact that such love is attacked—just as the Anarchists are hanged and Dreyfus unjustly imprisoned? If this is a "frame-up," is Tom attacking Roddy or himself for trafficking in these secrets?

Tom's attack on Roddy as Dreyfus is amplified by the novel's account of anti-Semitism, and its identification of Tom with the victim of this anti-Semitism, Louie Marsellus. Marsellus is the man Tom does not grow up to be: he marries the Professor's daughter Tom was engaged to, develops Tom's scientific discovery, earns the fortune Tom would have earned from it, and with his wife and this money builds and occupies a house named Outland in memory of Tom. Marsellus is represented by Cather as effeminate: Louie is sensitive, emotional, and flamboyant, knowledgeable about aesthetics, objects, and women's clothes.[15] The identification of Tom and Louie, and Louie's implication in Tom's and Roddy's relationship, are underlined by Cather's use of an appreciative comment Marsellus makes about a bracelet made from turquoise from the Blue Mesa, Outland's gift to the woman who has become Marsellus's wife, as the novel's epigraph. Just as class difference—Roddy's understanding of himself as Tom's hired man—bears the interpretive burden of Tom's and Roddy's relationship, Louie need not be read as gay because there is another social difference in place—his Jewishness—to bear the burden of interpretation of his effeminacy. Insofar as Tom and Marsellus are paired figures, Tom's attack on Roddy as Dreyfus can be read as an attack on a version of himself—the secrets Roddy is accused of selling are Tom's secrets as well—and the history of injustice Roddy represents is also Tom's history.

After driving Roddy away, Tom moves on to establish a new pairing with the Professor. Cather suggests the sexual possibilities of the relationship between the Professor and Tom Outland—in the fashion of the lesbian novel— via their challenge to the heterosexual plot. The Professor considers his situation: "He had had two romances: one of the heart, which had filled his life for many years, and a second of the mind—of the imagination" (172). His wife is the subject of the first, and Outland is the subject of the second. But although he wants to assign each of them different qualities, these romances cannot coexist. "Lillian had been fiercely jealous of Tom Outland," he observes, "people who are intensely in love when they marry, and who go on being in love, always meet with something which suddenly or gradually makes a difference. . . . In their own case it had been, curiously enough, his pupil, Tom Outland" (49). But Lillian St. Peter's reaction is hardly curious. She sees that this boy threatens her marriage. And he does. The Professor leaves her even though he is still physically present.[16]

The Professor attempts to defuse the sexual implications of his personal and professional histories, of his relationship with Tom—and by implication to explain Tom and Rodney Blake—through reference to two different realms represented as presocial and by implication presexual, the world of childhood and the world of the working classes. He muses about the boy he once was, and claims to be returning in old age to that primary self, implying that the male couple he forms with Tom is only a secondary, external form of an internal relation between his adult and his boy selves. He also identifies Tom with the fantasy of a Whitmanesque democratic brotherhood, a "dream of self-sacrificing friendship and disinterested love down among the day-labourers, the men who run the railroad trains and boats and reapers and thrashers and mine-drills of the world" (151).

The Professor's "dream" of love among the day laborers converges with his musings about boyhood in the narratives of "self-sacrificing friendship," the boy's adventure stories Cather offers as a frame for her male couples. Tom first tells the story of himself and Roddy on the Blue Mesa to the Professor's children: "in the stories Tom told the children there were no shadows. . . . They loved to play at being Tom and Roddy. Roddy was the remarkable friend, ten years older than Tom, who knew everything about snakes and panthers and deserts and Indians" (123). The children insist to their father, " 'Roddy was proud.' . . . [and] 'he was noble. He was always noble, noble Roddy!' " (124). When the Professor first hears "Tom Outland's Story" he can dismiss it as a boy's story: "nothing very incriminating, nothing very remarkable; a story of youthful defeat, the sort of thing a boy is sensitive about—until he grows older" (176). "Day-labourers" and boys converge in Tom's reference to himself and Roddy as disenfranchised "boys like you and me." But Tom evokes homosexual possibilities through reference to boyhood when he observes of Rodney Blake that "He ought to have had boys of his own to look after" (185). He presents Roddy's care for him as a substitute for the father-son relationships heterosexuality would have produced, thus underlining Roddy's identification with male relationships and eliding heterosexuality completely. Tom continues, "Nature's full of such substitutions, but they always seem to me sad, even in botany" (185–186).[17] The presence of a controlling "Nature" suggests both the "unnatural" in whatever substitution Nature has made here, and Tom's anxiety about same-sex relations.

Although the patterns of reference to boys and day laborers seem to divert, they actually broadcast sexual suspicion. To identify the novel's male bonds with boyhood or working men is to diffuse the possibility of homosexuality through the childhoods of all boys, and the lives of all day laborers, and thus perhaps to defuse the sexual threat. But does this diffusion of homosexual possibilities defuse the sexual threat? Or does it defuse the idea of homosexual difference, making it possible to imagine a "homosexuality" that might encompass such upstanding citizens as Professor St. Peter and the young man, ex-student and protégé, who is loved by one of his daughters and engaged to marry the other? Cather once observed about boy's adventure stories that *Treasure Island*, for example, offers "an atmosphere of adventure and romance that gratifies the eternal boy in us."[18] If there is an "*eternal* boy in *us*" then boyhood—with its homosexual overtones—is neither relegated to the past nor confined to men.

If one set of anxieties played out in the novel is about sexuality in same-sex relationships, another is about the relation of heterosexual and homosexual relationships. Sedgwick sees in *The Professor's House* "the crossing of the upstairs/downstairs vertical axis of heterosexual domesticity *by* the space-clearing dash of a male-male romance" (69). But Tom and Roddy establish a series of extremely domestic settings. And although they live outside the hierarchy of gender, their relationship is constructed precisely along an upstairs-downstairs axis; Tom and Roddy's pairing is unbalanced by class difference, a difference prefigured by Tom's desire for validation by the Smithsonian, and eventually confirmed by Tom's movement toward the middle class. Moreover, Tom's betrayal—Roddy comments as he leaves, "I'm glad it's you that's doing this to me, Tom; not me that's doing it to you" (247–248)—fits Tom's and Roddy's relationship into the sequence of (hetero)sexual betrayals in the novel.

History does not erase women from the Professor's life, as it erased them from the memory of the shell-shocked soldier in *One of Ours*. But women are repetitively represented as sources of betrayal. The Professor's wife transfers her attention from her husband to her sons-in-law; St. Peter assuages the pang of having lost her attention by developing a disdain for her ability to attend at all. His disappointment in his wife is repeated in his relations with his daughters: Rosamund is preoccupied by the opportunities for acquisition afforded by newfound wealth, and Kathleen is increasingly taken up with jealousy of her sister. The Professor thinks, as he says "absently" to his wife, "about Euripides; how, when he was an old man, he went and lived in a cave by the sea, and it was thought queer, at the time. It seems that houses had become insupportable to him. I wonder whether it was because he had observed women so closely all his life" (156).[19]

Cather dramatizes the Professor's conviction that he has been failed by women through the figures of the two sewing dummies that grace the attic workroom in which he produces his histories. In particular "the bust"—"a headless, armless female torso, covered with strong black cotton" (17):

> looked so ample and billowy (as if you might lay your head upon its deep-breathing softness and rest safe forever), [but] if you touched it you suffered a severe shock. . . . It presented the most unsympathetic surface imaginable. Its hardness was not that of wood, which responds to concussion with living vibration and is stimulating to the hand, nor that of felt, which drinks something from the fingers. It was a dead, opaque, lumpy solidity, like chunks of putty, or tightly packed sawdust—very disappointing to the tactile sense, yet somehow always fooling you again. For no matter how often you had bumped up against that torso, you could never believe that contact with it would be as bad as it was. (18)[20]

The fantasy of laying one's "head upon . . . deep-breathing softness and rest[ing] safe forever," which repeated disappointment does not allay, suggests fixed expectations that no actual woman could meet, supporting Sedgwick's argument that the Professor's is an old story of the husband's resentment. But the figure of a betraying woman is also central to the history of the Blue Mesa. Tom Outland and Rodney Blake find "Mother Eve," the body of a woman mummified by nature, among the cliff villages. The name they give her identifies her as the first and generic woman, and identifies her with betrayal. Mother Eve has to be dead in order to enter the novel's masculine histories. But she was murdered into history—she has a wound in her side, and an expression of horror frozen on her face—and the narrative given to her death is a narrative of female betrayal and its punishment. Father Duchene, the Catholic priest who presides over Tom Outland's life, concludes that "Mother Eve" was killed by her husband because she had committed adultery.[21]

Not only are the betrayals of this novel both homosexual and heterosexual, but the homo- and heterosexual betrayals are emotionally and narratively interlocked. The Professor turns from his wife to Tom Outland. Subsequently, Lillian St. Peter turns from her husband to her son-in-law, Louie Marsellus. But by then, Marsellus has become a figure of Tom Outland. "Mother Eve" is supposed to have been punished for heterosexual adultery. But Roddy's sale of "Mother Eve" undoes his potentially homosexual relationship with Tom. The doubling, and doubling back, of terms in these sequences suggest more than formal interrelationships produced by the dependence of same-sex narratives on heterosexual plots. They imply that it is betrayal across homo/heterosexual lines that is particularly at issue, with conflict between homo- and heterosexuality at the core of all the betrayals, and betrayal at the center of the relation between homo- and heterosexuality.

The backwash of money within the narrative suggests the inescapable taint of (homo)sexuality. The Professor cannot finally escape selling his own histories. As a professional he is selling history at one remove. But not only does he make his living by trading in history; the honors he has garnered include a financial award, even though he resists moving into the new house this money has built. Moreover, he cannot completely escape Tom's money: that is what Louie uses to pay for his trip to deliver a prestigious series of lectures at the University of Chicago. And in yet another acknowledgment of Tom's, Roddy's, and Marsellus's ambiguous sexuality, Marsellus is left advertising in the newspapers—his history of record—for Rodney Blake, because, as both he and the Professor agree, Blake has a primary claim on the money made from Tom Outland's invention.

Like Tom Outland, the Professor betrays himself. In one version of self-betrayal, the Professor begins to induct Tom into his own experience of heterosexual middle-class adulthood, a world in which he "would have had to 'manage' a great deal of money, to be the instrument of a woman who would grow always more exacting" (261). In the other version, the Professor sends Tom back to history, to the authoritative history he himself represents in contrast to stories of lost peoples and modern anarchists: Tom dies after he is led off by a Catholic priest, surely another version of Napoleon Godfrey *St. Peter*, to a European war easily identified with the Europe-oriented historian *Napoleon* Godfrey St. Peter. Tom is fixed within history as well as within the frame of male relationships—as the Professor's boy—at the cost of his life.[22]

*The Professor's House* is about the betrayal of history as well as betrayal by history. After his battle with Tom, the noble but unnatural Rodney Blake climbs down from the mesa and disappears from the text. What disappears with Roddy are, significantly combined, both the questions of social justice his history offered and the sexual possibility he embodied. The histories that remain, the Professor's account of the Spanish adventurers and Tom's commitment to the story of the vanished cliff dwellers of the Blue Mesa, are a perfect match. The Professor never mentions who the Spanish adventured against. The extinction of the people of the mesa, while finally inexplicable, is certainly not the work of European invaders, even though the Spanish succeeded the cliff dwellers in time. So the European displacement of native people that produced the Professor's and Tom's North America, like the sexual possibility of male relationships, remains suspended for both Tom and the Professor in the realm of implication.

## IV. Old and New Women

In the last part of her career, in the second half of the 1930s, Cather finally produced out of history two narratives of female relationship—a female couple established in Europe and out of World War I in "The Old Beauty," and a monstrous variation on female coupling, located within the system of slavery in antebellum Virginia, in *Sapphira and the Slave Girl*.[23] In both of these narratives, sex is associated with violence and shame. In both, female couples are to be feared.

"The Old Beauty"—Cather's pairing of the old beauty, Gabrielle Longstreet, a confidante of those "great men" who governed their late Victorian empire from the London of the 1890s, and Chetty Beamish, famous in her own day on both sides of the Atlantic in the "boy parts" of the music hall stage—is set in 1922 but explicitly presented as a product of history.[24] "It must seem," Chetty comments, "the queerest partnership that war and desolation have made."[25] Gabrielle Longstreet and Chetty Beamish meet on a war relief committee in Paris, rather than on the Western front.[26] Nevertheless this fading beauty and her aged musical hall boy recall the other queer partnerships shaped by war in Cather's fiction: Claude Wheeler and David Gerhardt joined by World War I at the conclusion of *One of Ours*; the Professor and Tom Outland, separated by the same war in *The Professor's House*. "It's a beautiful friendship" (40) Cather's narrator observes of the two women, but also a "strange" one (45).

However, as it is for Cather's male couples, history is as destructive as it is enabling of these women's relationship. History divides these queer partners: Gabrielle Longstreet remains bound to the prewar world in which she was beautiful; Chetty Beamish has adapted to change and lives in the present. But if their differing relations to history make their relationship vulnerable, so too does the fact that the model of women's relationship they exemplify belongs to the earlier period, which is to say that it is socially unremarkable. Chetty's stage history allows us to see them as a masculine/feminine pair, but they are both "Mrs." (though their marriages were brief). When observers question their interaction, the question is economic; they want to know whether Chetty's companionship is paid for. Only Lady Longstreet's past relations to her great men prompt sexual speculations.

Cather represented different male couples in conflict in *One of Ours* and *The Professor's House*, their conflicts framed by history. In "The Old Beauty" the conflict is itself historical. The story's setting, "the Hôtel Splendide at Aix-les-Bains," and its male observer, an elderly Englishman, the dapper bachelor Henry Seabury, evoke Cather's reliance on Jamesian paradigms in her earliest stories and first novel. But here Henry James meets Radclyffe Hall, the nineteenth century meets the twentieth century, and is defeated. The story's narrative crisis is produced when a car the two older women are riding in is almost run off the road by another, driven by two young women, "Americans; bobbed, hatless, clad in dirty white knickers and sweaters. They addressed each other as 'Marge' and 'Jim' " (66). Gabrielle and Chetty's "queer partnership" cannot withstand this vision of the modern female couple. The accident leaves Lady Longstreet "lying back in her seat, pale, her eyes closed, something very wrong with her breathing" (66). But "The two girls who had caused all the trouble"—" 'those creatures' " (67), "the two intruders" (67)— "had lit cigarettes and were swaggering about with their hands in their trousers pockets, giving advice to the driver about his wheel" (66). Gabrielle later alludes to the "shock. Oh, I don't mean the bruises we got! I mean the white breeches" (68).

History is, in fact, fatal for the older female couple, as it is so often for Cather's men and boys. This generational shock is so great that it leads to the frail Lady Longstreet's death, in her sleep that night, a death understood as a return to her "great men," as a restoration to heterosexuality. While the older "queer" partnership has been framed by a larger allegiance to great men, and excused by the historical circumstances of the war, which removed the last men from the old beauty's life as well as introducing her to Chetty, the young couple is unaccompanied, unexplained, and unapologetic. Before the war Chetty wore breeches, but only on the stage, where her performance was applauded as a comedy. These women wear breeches in the world, and dirty white ones, suggesting at the least virginity lost. Moreover, if Gabrielle and Chetty's partnership has been justified by models and events that have become history, what is to be found in history—in the past—is sexual shame. Decades earlier, the last time Seabury, the story's male narrator, had seen Gabrielle, he had rescued her from another man's attempt at rape. In the story's present, it is he who "dispose[s]" of Marge and Jim. His presence then links these two occasions, and that link clarifies the "frightfulness" of the more recent scene. The younger couple signifies for Gabrielle the violation and sexual shame signified by rape. In the postwar world, the male narrator Seabury's presence, and the Jamesian literary model he represents, cannot really shield the older couple from the meaning of the younger. Again in Cather's fiction the introduction of sexuality disrupts/destroys the same-sex couple.[27]

But only half of the older couple is defeated by or even dependent on history; Chetty Beamish remains. Chetty recalls two women from Cather's early stories, Thomasina/"Tommy" from "Tommy the Unsentimental" and Jemima/"Jimmy," another comedy actress particularly successful in boy roles, from "Flavia and Her Artists."[28] Both of these downright, scrubbed, and boyish figures suggest the downright, scrubbed, and boyish figure of the adolescent Willa Cather, who sometimes signed herself "William." Chetty Beamish is also evocative, in her boyish sturdiness, of the noble but unnatural Rodney Blake. Chetty does not comment on "Marge" and "Jim." Her "boy parts" have been abandoned to history as well as to age by 1922. But her continuing interest in the world, in contrast to Gabrielle's withdrawal, suggests a refusal of the great men and the sexual shame of this story's history, a commitment to the future—even the future represented by Marge and Jim—that persists in tension with her admiration for and grief over her loss of the old beauty.[29]

## V. Family Histories

In *One of Ours* and "The Old Beauty," Cather merges individual and historical narratives: Claude's story offers a commentary on the values of prewar
American culture before it ends in the war; Gabrielle and Chetty are posed
against changes in the social implications of women's relationships. In contrast,
the narrative of *The Professor's House* is organized around understandings of
history and the possibilities of writing history. The stories of individuals "subject" to history, and the issues of power and social justice that disappear from
*The Professor's House* with Rodney Blake, reappear in Cather's final novel, *Sapphira and the Slave Girl*. The terms of the relation between individual and historical circumstances in this novel are, inseparably, racial and sexual injustice.
When the female couple constituted through history, the female couple as a
threat and the female couple as a sign of sexual shame sketched in "The Old
Beauty," reappear, the effect is monstrous.

In *Sapphira and the Slave Girl*, Cather produced a portrait of ruthless female
power shadowed by complete powerlessness. As an aristocratic white woman,
Sapphira Dodderidge Colbert's race and class are more significant than her
gender. But her exercise of authority is nonetheless treated as transgressive: her
husband insists that she is the "master," refusing to recognize her as a powerful woman. The powerlessness behind her power, and the monstrousness of a
powerful woman, are both reflected in her illness, a "dropsy" that has swollen
her legs and feet, rendering her immobile: she cannot walk and can barely
stand.

Sapphira's monstrosity is identified with the possibility of a woman's sexual
designs on another woman, when she tries to arrange for the rape of another
woman, Nancy, the "slave girl" of the novel's title. Sapphira and Nancy's in-
terchanges are initially triangulated through a heterosexual plot—the story of
Sapphira's marriage (Sapphira thinks Nancy has taken her place in her husband's bed)—and are to be brought to an end by a man (Sapphira's licentious
nephew Martin, whom she invites to visit her Back Creek home assuming that
he will attack Nancy). These triangulations are a sign of sexuality. In *Sapphira*
the casting of sexual possibility between women as rape can also be read back
through Sapphira's monstrosity to lesbianism. Rape and lesbianism are linked
by sexual shame in "The Old Beauty." But that the lower half of Sapphira's
body should be both swollen and immobile suggests the conventional figura-
tion of lesbian sexuality as both masculine and powerless.

*Sapphira's* tortuous narrative is dependent on Cather's return, in this novel,
to a completely American history, to the history of slavery in the United States.
Cather's use of the history of slavery makes possible the female pairing of the
novel's title; the interactions of Nancy and Sapphira are given a social structure
without a familial form. The history of slavery, with its institutionalization of
white men's sexual access to black women, "explains" Sapphira's suspicion of

her husband, and thus provides an ostensible motive for her attack on Nancy. The novel's setting within the social structures of the antebellum South makes Sapphira's attack on Nancy possible. She herself can claim absolute rights over the younger woman, as she assumes Martin will. Moreover, Sapphira is able to order Nancy into situations in which she will be most vulnerable to him.

*Sapphira and the Slave Girl's* historical setting allows Cather to situate the personal within the historical in a fashion parallel to her invocation of Dreyfus in *The Professor's House*. The alternatives of Cather's previous fictions—the division between North America and Europe in *One of Ours* and *The Professor's House*, between the world and the mesa in *The Professor's House*, or between pre- and postwar worlds in "The Old Beauty"—can be represented in terms of oppression and freedom. The secrets abundant in Cather's writing—Claude's secret happiness; the Professor's two lives, Tom's "secret" narrative—can be institutionalized and overtly politicized in the division between slaveholders on the one hand and slaves and abolitionists on the other. There are rhetorical structures—in slave narratives and in abolitionist literature—that legitimize in *Sapphira* the desire for escape familiar from Cather's earliest fiction. The abolition movement and the underground railway offered social structures through which an oppressive system could be explicitly and actively contested.

In particular, the social control of sexuality and its consequences can be made explicit within a representation of slavery. Sapphira's attempted attack on Nancy is the central instance of an elaborate pattern of white attempts to control black sexuality: "Tansy Dave" goes crazy when he is separated from the woman he loves, because her "owners" move away; Sapphira marries her housekeeper, Till, to Jeff, a "capon man," so that Till will not be distracted from her service by children.

But *Sapphira and the Slave Girl's* account of oppression and escape is extremely problematic. On the axis of sexuality, Cather privatizes oppression within this historical frame. Nancy needs to escape from Sapphira as much as from slavery. She in fact escapes from Sapphira with the help of another woman, Sapphira's abolitionist daughter Rachel, who literally puts her on the underground railroad. This completes an alternative and female triangulation of Sapphira's and Nancy's interactions, and offers a model of a woman caring for another woman and a woman opposing slavery, to set against Sapphira's monstrosity. But it also completes a pattern in which the white characters engage in all of the significant actions of the novel. In the novel's epilogue, Nancy returns twenty-five years later as a beautiful and authoritative matron. But Nancy's successful escape is muddied: she made a free life for herself working as she would have worked as a slave, as a housekeeper to a white family; all that is represented of her life after she escapes Sapphira's control is her return; and she is shown returning to see her mother who, despite Sapphira's viciousness, the Civil War, and Reconstruction, has remained faithful to the white family at Back Creek.

Just as, in *The Professor's House*, Louie's effeminacy is explained by his Jew-ishness, just as Tom and Roddy's partnership can be defensively as well as de-structively dissolved into a matter of money, in *Sapphira*, Nancy's vulnerability to female sexual threat is explained by racial difference. But the question re-mains as to whether Cather can only offer Nancy a compromised escape be-cause her own imagination is compromised by racism, or because Nancy's escape from racism is inseparable from an escape from sexual control. Perhaps Cather can only represent a compromised escape from sexual control, and from the twin horrors of female sexual power and female sexual powerlessness.

In a move unprecedented in her fiction, Cather presents herself within *Sap-phira*, identifying its history with her own childhood. This novel has a double ending: first the epilogue, a post-Civil War racial and generational reconcilia-tion scene observed by a child whom narrator Cather claims as "I"; and then an additional paragraph in which she insists on the family "truth" of this fic-tion, which is signed separately "Willa Cather." Here Cather aligns her own childhood with *Sapphira*'s history of sexual control and female sexual threat. She also suggests that this monstrous history was the context in which her child self developed a fascination for names and was, consequently, the place where her writing began. *One of Ours*, *The Professor's House*, and "The Old Beauty" suggest that European history offered no space to escape the sexuality of same-sex relationships, or no space to escape and survive. *Sapphira* suggests Cather's late recognition of the impossibility of escaping her own American history. This New World history, represented finally as a family story, at the same time that it generalizes and displaces, identifies same-sex sexuality as a threat, identifies same-sex sexuality with women, and brings the threat home.

# 2

# Mary Renault's Greek Drama

## I. "The Whole Point of the Story"

Mary Renault did not begin to publish until the late 1930s, after *The Well of Loneliness* and its trial had established the parameters of the "lesbian novel" and the understanding of the relation between lesbianism and literature that the lesbian novel represents.[1] She was dismissive of Hall's work.[2] Nevertheless, she was as committed as the lesbian novel was to the conventions of realist fiction and to love and sexuality as subjects. However, Renault not only occupied the lesbian writer's problematic narrative position, but she was interested in representations of relationship as well as romance. Consequently, she needed to write beyond the ending of the heterosexual plot as well as the lesbian novel. Instead of pursuing new literary forms, she used "history" as a basis for writing novels about homosexual relationships that were much more conventional in form than Cather's texts. But her difficulties with the official historical record's assumptions about gender became dramatic.

Renault's conflict with the limits of the lesbian novel and her path towards gay male subjects and "history" are laid out in the two contemporary novels with gay subjects that she produced before she began her historical novels: her only lesbian novel, *The Friendly Young Ladies* (1944), and *The Charioteer* (1953). The extent to which she understood her writing as shaped by her lesbianism is suggested by the fact that her only "lesbian novel" was also her only novel about writers. The three different literary options *The Friendly Young Ladies* offers are even all forms of the novel. Renault begins her lesbian novel with references to the interchangeable heterosexual romances, with titles such as *Beau Brocade*, that the adolescent Elsie reads over and over. They so shape her vision of the world that she cannot understand the relationships between the men and women surrounding her, neither her parents' manipulativeness, nor the egotism of Dr. Peter Bracknell, the man she thinks she adores. When she sets off, with only the suggestion of scandal to guide her, in search of the sister who had escaped the family years before, Elsie can only imagine Leonora as the muse and mistress posing "in a Chinese shawl or (for one must not run away) naked on silk cushions" for an eminent male artist.[3] When she finds a boyish Leo living with a perfectly feminine Helen—who rather than producing great art, draws illustrations for medical textbooks—Elsie cannot read their relationship at all.

Her education in heterosexual romance has also left her unable to read either of the other two literary modes represented within this novel. Leo supports herself by churning out masculine genre fiction—Westerns—under a comic male pseudonym and for a readership consisting chiefly of young boys. Renault takes the opportunity these horse operas offer to draw attention to conventional narrative requirements. Even in such gender-specific genre writing, Leo's publishers require that she add an "obligatory girl" to every adventure. But her loud complaints about this requirement are not based on literary principle. She makes no claims for the literary value of her efforts. Nevertheless she is very impressed by the serious novels about "real life" produced every few years, after contemplation and great spiritual labor, by Joe Flint, the obligatory boy in Renault's own narrative. Elsie finds Leo's and Joe's fictions equally alien, but it is Joe, the real man, and not the butch Leo, who is the real writer.

As a lesbian novel, *The Friendly Young Ladies* is structured around a series of heterosexual plots. The central triangle is that established among Leo and Helen and Joe. The novel concludes with the apparent disruption of the lesbian couple in favor of the union of Leo and Joe, the genre hack and the real writer. That union presages Renault's eventual literary course on two counts. The masculine/masculine couple made by Leo and Joe will be obsessively replicated in her later historical fiction. And as the pair plan to leave England for Arizona, the site of Leo's cowboy fantasies, they plot Renault's own escape from contemporary literary realism to a masculine genre fiction world. Meanwhile the "real" lesbian, Helen, is to be left behind by this resolution of the literary and sexual stories, as the lesbian character will be left behind in Renault's later work.

But within the narrative of *The Friendly Young Ladies*, Renault connects lesbianism with writing through a story Leo tells Elsie in an attempt to explain her life. Leo describes her first meeting with Helen. Helen, a nurse, arrived at Leo's hospital bedside when she was suffering from acute appendicitis, and offered to read a recently arrived letter that turned out to be Leo's first offer of publication. "I didn't know you were a writer," Helen comments. "Nor did I," Leo responds (88). With Helen's entry into her life, Leo becomes simultaneously a lesbian and a writer. Now she will also recover from the threat to her life. But Elsie cannot interpret the autobiography Leo has offered her. She does not even realise that Helen is present in the narrative, that she is the nurse in question, prompting Leo to underline at the conclusion of this scene that her meeting with Helen "was really the whole point of the story" (89). As she does throughout this novel, Renault uses Elsie's naïveté here to underscore what Elsie does not see. "The whole point of the story" might be the very thing Elsie never understands: that Leo and Helen are lovers. But the point of this story is also that the lesbian and the writer are indivisible. And this sequence contains a warning. We should not assume that "the whole point" of any of Renault's stories is a lesbianism that could be predictably expressed.

Even the partial "point" of this particular novel is hard to determine. Is this a story of naïveté or sophistication, the sentimental educations of Elsie and/or Leo, the disruption of the lesbian couple, or the literary dilemma of a lesbian writer? *The Friendly Young Ladies'* conclusion is ambiguous. The reader is not shown Leo's departure with Joe, but that is the least of it. We are told that Leo, who was a "boy," has now become a woman, after a night of passion with a man. At the same time the expected relationships among gender, biological sex, and sexual behavior are all undermined. Throughout the novel Renault has undercut her heterosexual triangulation by presenting her apparently opposed couples so as to leave unclear which is heterosexual and which homosexual, or whether the terms can be separated: the lesbian couple, Helen and Leo, look like a feminine-masculine pair, while the heterosexual pairing, Leo and Joe, look like a masculine-masculine couple. It is not clear, then, whether Leo's butch persona is the basis of her lesbian relationship with Helen (the butch-femme couple secured by its approximation of the heterosexual plot), or the source of that relationship's instability (insofar as Leo as butch suggests her underlying insecurity with a female-female/same-sex paradigm). Will Leo's newly discovered femininity guarantee a new commitment to heterosexuality, or make her departure with Joe impossible (as their connection, to this point, has consisted of masculine bonding), thus ensuring that she stays with Helen?

Renault's lesbian writer-protagonist is situated not between homo- and heterosexuality but between two possible models of homosexuality—the same-sex paradigm of Helen and Leo and the same-gender paradigm of Leo and Joe—and two models of heterosexuality—the cross-gender paradigm of Helen and Leo, and the cross-sex paradigm of Leo and Joe.[4] Not only is the reader not given the potentially comforting vision of Leo leaving on Joe's arm, but whether Leo stays with Helen or goes with Joe, the meaning of the ending is left open. Either might be heterosexual conclusions, and either might be gay. The connection between writing and homosexuality marked in the story Leo tells Elsie about her origins as a lesbian and a writer would be maintained by either of the novel's possible endings. So is Helen abandoned after all? Or what would the abandonment of the lesbian character signify? Certainly not the end of gay texts. But that leaves open a range of questions. Can a woman be a real writer? Could a real writer produce genre fiction? Would a real writer produce gay texts?

## II. "An Army . . . Made Up Only of Lovers and Their Beloved"

In her subsequent historical novels, Mary Renault's particular achievement was a merger of domestic and public narrative—romance and history—constructed out of the interrelations of individual and group identities, male homosexuality and the dominant culture, and lesbians and cultural discourses about male homosexuality.[5] At the conclusion of her career, in her only non-fictional statement about homosexuality, Renault explicitly rejected gay activism in favor of individualism. "Conventions change," she admitted:

> but defensive stridency is not, on the whole, much more attractive than self-pity. Congregated homosexuals waving banners are really not conducive to a goodnatured "*Vive la difference!*" Certainly they will not bring back the tolerant individualism of Macedon or Athens, where they would have attracted as much amazement as demonstrations of persons willing to drink wine. Distinguished homosexuals like Solon, Epaminondas or Plato would have withdrawn the hem of their garments; Alexander and his friends would have dined out on the joke. Greeks asked what a man was good for; and the Greeks were right. People who do not consider themselves to be, primarily, human beings among their fellow-humans, deserve to be discriminated against, and ought not to make a meal of it.

The focus of her objections is the "congregation" of homosexuals as much as the banner-waving, group identity as much as activism. But to invoke the "tolerant individualism of Macedon or Athens" is anything but individual. Her championing of "tolerant individualism" is based on the most conventional resource of writing on gay subjects, history, particularly "Macedon or Athens." Mary Renault's most accomplished fiction is also based on this convention of classical reference—giving substance to Socrates' passion for Alcibiades and the image of Alexander and his Hephaistion.

In both *The Friendly Young Ladies* and Renault's contemporary gay male novel, *The Charioteer*, individual lesbian and gay characters are validated at the expense of the group. In *The Friendly Young Ladies*, Leo declares her preference for the "ordinary":

> "I don't feel separate from . . . ordinary people. . . . I like them. Why should they pamper oddities, anyway? It's they who are in charge of evo-

lution. They think it's better not to be odd, as far as they bother to think at all, and they're quite right. There are shoals of women made up pretty much like me, but a lot haven't noticed and most of the rest prefer to look the other way, and it's probably very sensible of them. If you do happen to have had your attention drawn to it, the thing to do is to like and be liked by as many ordinary people as possible, to make yourself as good a life as you can in your own frame, and to keep your oddities for the few people who are likely to be interested." (178)

Similar conflicts between individual identity and a gay group identity are central to Laurie Odell's process of coming to terms with his homosexuality in *The Charioteer*. That novel's heroes are explicitly distanced from the gay subculture, which is characterized by male effeminacy, "bracelets and eye-shadow."[7] Laurie accepts himself when he realizes he does not have to be like the men he met during his brief prewar stint at Oxford: "He kept telling me I was queer, and I'd never heard it called that before and didn't like it. The word, I mean. Shutting you away, somehow; roping you off with a lot of people you don't feel much in common with, half of whom hate the other half anyway, and just keep together so that they can lean up against each other for support" (152–153). Instead he finds Ralph Lanyon, who upholds "the obligations of men" in his relationships and is scathing about people "looking for bluebirds in a fun-fair" (200): "we all have to use the network sometime. Don't let it use you, that's all. Ours isn't a horizontal society, it's a vertical one. . . . [and] there isn't any bottom" (178).[8] Like Leo, Laurie also does not want to be shut out of the straight world: "He was overcome by a sudden, stifling claustrophobia. Charles's and Sandy's [gay] friends had tried to lock the door on him from inside. Now [heterosexual] Reg was doing it from out in the street. There was a difference: he liked Reg much better" (212). And like Leo, Laurie and Ralph both accept the authority of the "normal": Ralph says, "They've got children and they want grandchildren. . . . They've learned to leave us in peace unless we make public exhibitions of ourselves" (200).

But in *The Charioteer*, Renault does not finally accept the authority of the "normal." Through Ralph's warnings, as well as through the development of a range of other gay characters, Renault invokes the possibility of "our . . . society," for which she claims Plato, Michelangelo, Shakespeare. From within the rejected gay subculture, Alec insists: "I'm not prepared to accept a standard which puts the whole of my emotional life on the plane of immorality. I've never involved a normal person or a minor or anyone who wasn't in a position to exercise a free choice. I'm not prepared to let myself be classified with dope-peddlers and prostitutes. . . . I'm not a criminal" (199). Renault also demonstrates the suffering caused by heterosexual hostility: the subject of homosexuality is introduced into the novel when Ralph is abruptly expelled from school in disgrace for being gay; Laurie, Ralph, and the other gay men

they interact with avoid being recognized as gay; Laurie is shamed and isolated after his fellow soldiers realize he is gay, even though some of them make
efforts at support and friendliness. As a result of his experiences, Laurie leaves
Andrew, whom he loves, to the possibility of a "normal" life. But after a close
brush with the suicide that so often ended gay novels in this period, another
male couple, Laurie and Ralph, is affirmed.

However, *The Charioteer's* individual solution leaves Renault's gay lovers
with only their couple as a refuge against the sense Laurie expresses of being a
"citizen of nowhere" (255). And the course of Renault's career suggests—paradoxically, given her rejections of collective gay identity—that to be a "citizen
of nowhere" was intolerable. Although the "Greeks asked what a man was
good for; and the Greeks were right," or as Ralph Lanyon protests, "God . . .
what are any of us? . . . It's not what one is, it's what one does with it" (131),
Renault went on after *The Charioteer* to create a country in which gays could
be citizens. Having grasped at individualism as the only basis for gay self-
respect in a society that stigmatized gays as a group, her best efforts as a novelist were dedicated to the construction of a gay society. In *The Charioteer*,
"Greece" already offers a middle way between Ralph's bitterness and Alec's
fledgling gay pride. Laurie invokes "Greece" to resolve their argument. Ralph
insists drunkenly, "A lot of bull is talked about Greece by people who'd just
have been a dirty laugh there," but nevertheless concedes, "They were tolerant in Greece and it worked," even if only because, "There was a standard; they
showed the normal citizen something" (200). In Renault's subsequent novels,
"Greece" resolved the pressure contemporary heterosexual culture imposed on
her individual solution. Love and sex between men were permitted, even celebrated. Not only did their homosexuality not bar her characters from citizenship, it could be integral to their citizenship. For better and for worse, the
politics of sexuality could be absorbed into the prerogatives of masculinity.

* * *

Nevertheless, adopting history as a source of narrative—but in marked contrast to Cather, however romantic the male relationships she represented—Renault shaped her historical narratives around the narrative structure most
identified with women, the romance, executing a double movement exemplified by the vision of an "army . . . of lovers." In *The Charioteer*, Ralph Lanyon,
the ideal beloved, quotes from *The Symposium*, "If a city or an army could be
made up only of lovers and their beloved, it would excel all others. For they
would refrain from everything shameful, rivalling one another in honor; and
men like these, fighting at each other's side, might well conquer the world. For
the lover would rather be seen by anyone than by his beloved, flying or throw-
ing away his arms; rather he would be ready a thousand times to die" (301).
Like *The Friendly Young Ladies*, *The Charioteer* prefigures Renault's historical
novels. *The Charioteer* is paradigmatic not only in its gay male protagonists

and abundant classical allusions, but in its setting, England during World War II, in which the war provides a public frame for her fiction of personal life. *The Charioteer* was representative in that it was, in this sense, both her first gay novel and her first historical novel, and insofar as it is a historical novel, in that it is a war novel about the home front. In her later novels, whatever real and metaphoric distinctions might be drawn between home front and battlefield dissolve. "Love" is the basis of all of Renault's armies.

Renault's historical novels—international best-sellers during her lifetime, and still going into new editions a decade after her death—are all about "gay" men: Alexias in *The Last of the Wine* (1956), Nikeratos in *The Mask of Apollo* (1966), Alexander in *Fire From Heaven* (1969), and Bagoas in *The Persian Boy* (1972). When her protagonist is heterosexual, as is Simonides in *The Praise Singer* (1978), the action nevertheless turns on homosexual relationships, in this case the love of Harmodios and Aristogeiton. She also wrote about other famous male couples: Socrates and Alcibiades in *The Last of the Wine*; Plato and Diôn in *The Mask of Apollo*. The only exceptions to these patterns are the two novels based on the legend of Theseus, *The King Must Die* (1958) and *The Bull From the Sea* (1962). But in *The Bull From the Sea*, Theseus' great love, for the Amazon leader Hippolyta, is cast as gay. The manly Hippolyta is treated by Theseus's supporters as "if she had been a youth . . . like a boy of some kingly house over whom I had lost my head."[9] They appear so much like a homosexual couple that some of his people are hostile; she is attacked as a "freak of nature" (163). They defend their relationship in modern gay terms: "We are what we are, love," Hippolyta tells Theseus as they prepare to go into battle side by side, "Let us keep our pride" (219).[10]

The gay terms of Theseus's relationship with Hippolyta, the most important heterosexual romance in her historical fiction, suggest that Renault does not write about gay men simply because she writes about Greece. Nor does she write about Greece simply in order to write about gay men. Rather, her Greek historical novels allowed her to write about relationships not based on heterosexual hierarchies and not short-circuited by the heterosexual plot. In fact, it is her commitment to the subject of relationship as much as to homosexuality that drives her historical narratives, for there the question resonant in gay fiction of the period—David's demand of Giovanni, "What kind of life can two men have together, anyway?" in James Baldwin's *Giovanni's Room* (1956)—can be answered.[11]

"Greece" offered Renault a context for the representation of homosexual relationships, within which individual rather than representative gay stories could be developed. These relationships could be worked out in relation to the kind of complex cultural expectations and social responsibilities represented by "citizenship," rather than organized around an overdetermined conflict with dominant mores, or limited to the conflicted gay social world that could be represented in the fiction of the period. "Greece" offered a social form for homosexual relationships. This was, as Renault interpreted it, a pattern of stylized inequality—"lovers and their beloved." But this inequality was organized around age or status rather than gender difference, which meant that the anxiety about masculinity and femininity prevalent in gay fiction of the period— the question of who is the girl—could be dispensed with. At the same time, Renault's lovers always share a fundamental class equality; whatever difference of status divides her central couples is neutralized by the gulf separating her patrician or at least citizen protagonists from most of the other inhabitants of their social worlds. Their relationships are also given structure by their shared participation at the center of the "great events" that would become the history of their days.

The possibilities Renault found for the narrative representation of relationship in Greece/history are, however, all based on gender. The social, cultural, and political activities of Renault's protagonists are conditional on their status as men. So Renault's access to the fictional world she created depended on her acceptance of conservative understandings of gender and gender hierarchy, and the conventions of mainstream historiography. In Renault's novels, history is unitary: there is no conflict like that between New World experience and professional historians in Cather's *The Professor's House*; and no attempt, such as was made by a writer like Bryher, to represent the events of the conventional historical record from the periphery or from multiple perspectives. Masculinity and the state are both central to Renault's histories, which deal with "great" battles, "great" leaders, "great" thinkers and artists. This is an understanding of history within which Greece itself is a privileged site.

The only significant relationships within this history could be male. That the terms of Renault's narrative choices are masculine is confirmed when the very few lesbians who enter these histories do so as gay men. Hippolyta has a female partner when she is the leader of the Amazons, before she becomes Theseus's boy/consort. Axiothea, an athlete as well as a student of Plato, first appears in *The Mask of Apollo* as a young man the protagonist Nikeratos admires from afar, before he discovers not only that she is a woman, but that she has a female lover. To ensure her safety among the chaos of the novel's dramatic climax, the fall of Syracuse, she has to agree to pose as Nikeratos's male lover. Axiothea's story also illustrates the subordination of gender to homosexuality in Renault's fiction.[12]

## III. "A Memory. . . . a Dream of Mystery and of Command"

In her historical fictions, Renault identified the history of Western culture as gay. But like Cather, Renault drew on cultural images of childhood and youth, as well as on the classics. Homosexuality was identified with the history of childhood as well as the history of the culture. And the childhood of the individual and the history of the culture were identified. If then, the history of the culture is gay, the history/childhood of every individual might be gay. Or, to put it another way, if all the boys' stories might be homosexual, then all the boys might be homosexual too, at least in their childhoods. The childhood and youth mirroring Renault's childhood of the culture is an imperial boyhood.

These patterns are established in *The Charioteer*, through references, as in Cather's *The Professor's House*, to boys' adventure stories. In the course of a long, drunken, birthday party that is the reader's introduction to gay society (which includes a series of flaming rows and one attempted suicide), Laurie, sitting in a corner, pulls a familiar-looking book off a shelf. He finds himself reading about "cool drafts of air" and "the sea lying blue and sunny to the horizon," off *Treasure Island*:

> A young man sat down beside him on the divan and, without any kind of preliminary, said, "Is it a queer book?"
> "No," said Laurie.
> "Oh," said the young man, on a note of utter deflation. He got up and went away. (129)

*Treasure Island* is offered as a welcome respite from the scene that surrounds Laurie, in implicit contrast to a "queer book." *Treasure Island* is specific—it has a title and is familiar—while "queer books" are generic.[13] "Queer books" might be counters in a system of male sexual exchange. The implication is that her book is not going to be "queer." Nevertheless, through such use of childhood fictions she made extensive connections between her queer books and "treasure island."

Allusions to schoolboy adventure stories are almost as pervasive in *The Charioteer* as invocations of classical literature. Laurie reacts to Ralph with

> a sharp stirring of some very old, romantic memory; perhaps of some book illustration he had known as a young boy, of which his very first glimpse of Ralph at school had reminded him before he had even known his name. So strong was this sense of the past that his own feeling, caught up in it, seemed like a memory. He stood looking at Ralph in startled admiration, moved by a dream of mystery and of command. (226)

"Memory" and "dream" suggest a state before consciousness of sexuality, and a natural or at least unconscious and uncontrollable origin for adult sexuality. The "mystery" of Laurie's boyhood is homosexuality, as it is of all of the boys' childhoods in twentieth-century gay fictions, from E. M. Forster's *Maurice* (1913) to Andrew Holleran's *Nights in Aruba* (1983). The possibility of "command" is inherent in these boys' stories, because boys should grow up to be men. But "command" is also a dream. Renault's gay men are not only men but members of the upper classes. They go to public schools, to Oxbridge; in the services they are the captains of their ships or fighter pilots; and if out of uniform they are doctors or medical students. Yet while these men are central to, they are not of their culture. Ralph for example, represented as the quintessence of honorable masculinity, embodying strength, authority, and order, is a *Treasure Island* hero. He does not cease to be so because he is gay. But as the sign of childhood, Treasure Island becomes the dream of the novel, the possibility of a space of innocence.[14]

The "dream" quality of Laurie's childhood vision of Ralph presages both the glamour and the nostalgia that are fundamental to Renault's "Greece." As well as freeing herself from the demands of heterosexual plots, Renault's choice of "history" gave her love(r)s the gravity of world-historical events, of the politics of cities and states and empires and the ideals of Western culture in their images. But she also gave them a glamour beyond even that which the rhetoric of "Western culture" habitually bestows on its "classics." Her portrait of Alexander, in *Fire From Heaven* and *The Persian Boy*, is the highest pitch of this glamour: Alexander as a figure of beauty and charm, strength, intelligence, skill, and magic. But the quality of romance is apparent throughout her writing, and clings particularly to her gay male heroes. "Great Alexander" is already apparent, however muted, in the limping soldier Laurie.

This glamour is, however, inseparable from nostalgia and even grief. Renault simultaneously builds and destroys her fictions. In *The Charioteer*, childhood is the location of loss. When Laurie sits at Ralph's knee, listening to his sea stories, his

> whole being seemed to relax in a sigh of mysterious contentment. . . .
> All the tangles of his life seemed looser and easier to resolve. He didn't want to take his mind from the story, or disturb with analysis this fragile happiness and security, which were what one might feel if some legend, dear to one's childhood but long abandoned, were marvellously proved true. (229)

But childhood is not a haven in Renault's fiction. The central event of Laurie's childhood is his father's abandonment of his mother and himself, with which the novel begins. This abandonment is echoed by his loss of his mother to her second husband, which takes place in the course of the novel, as he is "coming to terms" with his homosexuality. Mary Renault's Greece is constructed of legends "dear to one's childhood" that in her fiction can be momentarily, "marvellously proved true." But even in childhood, "happiness and security" are a "legend." Stevenson's *Treasure Island* is about an innocent boy battling adult greed, betrayal, and violence.

In Renault's subsequent historical fiction, the personal loss of *The Charioteer* is transposed into a sense of public loss in which the beloved and the state are merged. These novels' narrative structures, their preoccupation with historical defeats, and the fact that because they are "history" even the brightest promises of these worlds are past, all contribute to their nostalgia. But these factors do not explain why elegy is their fundamental mode. Renault's histories always offer a country of old as well as young men. These novels are first-person narratives of lives told retrospectively—by Alexias, Theseus, Nikeratos, Bagoas, and Simonides, as old men, recalling what is lost, whether the glory of Athens or the love of Alexander. But the Athenian ideal, for Alexias, is inextricably connected to his love for Lysis, and the image of Alexander, for Bagoas, cannot be separated from his glory. Insofar as Renault's Greece is an exploration of love, these histories are inseparable from love. When the beloved is lost, the battle, the city, the ideal, or youth are lost. And the battle, the city, the ideal, or youth are always lost.

The glamour, the nostalgia, and the sense of loss are inseparable from questions of gender as well as sexuality. *The Last of the Wine* inaugurates Renault's historical cycle with the death of an ideal pair of male lovers who perish while trying to save one another. Death is, of course, a routine presence in gay male novels of the period at which Renault began writing her own. Baldwin's *Giovanni's Room*, James Barr's *Quatrefoil* (1950), and Christopher Isherwood's *A Single Man* (1964) all end with death, and both Baldwin's and Isherwood's works also begin with reference to death. We know we are in another world in Renault's novel by virtue of the honor accorded her dead couple: their mutual devotion inspires a memorial plaque in the city wall; the novel's protagonist, Alexias, whose birth coincides with their deaths, will be named after one of them, his uncle.[15] But even in the historical fiction, we are still in a world in which the possibility of same-sex love is introduced via mortality. Any reading of this mortality, however, must also consider that this mortality is not confined to gay men. At this beginning of Renault's historical cycle a woman also dies; Alexias's mother expires while giving birth to the new gay protagonist. Renault's choice of historical fiction was a choice between female and gay subjects. Historical fiction freed her from conflicts over the representation of women apparent in her earlier fiction.[16] Yet at her entry into history with *The Last of the Wine*, the death of the mother as well as the male lovers suggests anxiety at the abandonment of female subjects as well as anxiety about the representation of homosexuality.

## IV. "The Right of a Man"

The nostalgia of Renault's historical fiction is not finally nostalgia for the failed securities or authorities of childhood or of Greece, or for the possibilities of citizenship somewhere. It is about masculinity itself, where (in "history" and in "Greece") masculinity is the basis of subject status. Renault attempted to reverse the double exclusion of being a woman in a universe in which subjects are masculine, and gay in a universe in which homosexuality is male.[17] She tried to convert her own homosexuality into access to subject status, which required that she identify homosexuality with masculinity, and lesbians with/as gay men. This is why in her last contemporary and her first historical novels, *The Charioteer* and *The Last of the Wine*, her first two "gay" texts, she stresses the masculinity of her protagonists and rejects femininity so emphatically. But Renault's bid for subjectivity did not succeed; masculinity remained a dream, or a fiction. While her historical project began with the promise of glamour and order, it ended in grief and chaos. The chaos was a consequence of the grief, and the grief was ultimately about gender. As the novels succeed one another, their glamorous images are increasingly hedged, challenged and/or undermined by the feminine, sometimes in conjunction with racial differences.

The authority of the masculine is gradually eroded in Renault's fiction through challenges to the masculinity of her Greeks, and to their identification with "Greece." In *The Last of the Wine*, the lovers, Alexias and Lysis, who go into battle side by side in defense of Athens, are defined in contrast to other, less manly men. By *The Mask of Apollo*, the protagonist can be an actor rather than a soldier. Onstage Nikeratos plays both male and female roles, developing his own "feminine" qualities; offstage he establishes a friendship with Axiothea once he realizes she is disqualified as a potential lover. The still-later *Persian Boy* begins with the blood and pain of the hero's castration. Bagoas is a victim of the warriors' history—his father betrayed, his family killed, himself as a child taken prisoner and sold rather than slaughtered only because of his good looks. As a slave and a eunuch, he will neither be trained for battle, nor grow up to be a man. Bagoas's gender disruption is mirrored by his racial otherness as a Persian. Race becomes an issue in the Theseus novels, which offer accounts of the Hellene domination of the Cretans. But racism is personalized in *The Mask of Apollo* through the character of Menekrates, Nikeratos's guest-friend and fellow actor, when Nikeratos observes the slights Menekrates is subjected to even in the multiracial world of Syracuse and from his own family, for being the darkest skinned among them. By *The Persian Boy*, there are suggestions that the emperor Alexander himself may not be racially "proper," not the Hellenic ideal of the earlier novels. His love for Bagoas, which crosses caste/class and racial lines, is mirrored by his battles against racism among the Greeks, and his desire for unity between Greeks and Persians.

These challenges to masculine and Hellenic ideals fissure the profound conservatism about what constitutes "history"—the interlocking assumptions about the necessary masculinity of the subject and the necessary coherence of narratives—that underlies Renault's early historical novels. As the masculinity of Renault's subjects is eroded, so is the coherence of her narratives. The early historical fictions are most often first-person stories focused on the life of the narrator and events in which he has been centrally concerned. But *The Praise Singer* is as much about events of which the protagonist, Simonides, another artist rather than warrior, is only an observer, as about his character and life. As the narrator of *The Persian Boy*, Bagoas gives the story of Alexander's conquests entirely from the perspective of his lover. In Renault's final novel, *Funeral Games*, which begins with the death of "Great Alexander," there is neither a protagonist nor a central narrative. The novel is as fractured as the "world" after the emperor's death.

These narrative breakdowns are accompanied by a progressive reworking of "Greece" as a source of authority or validation. In *Fire From Heaven* (1969), the first part of the Alexandriad, Alexander self-consciously compares his love for Hephaistion with the heroic cultural and historical images of Achilles and Patroclus, Harmodios, and Aristogeiton. By *The Persian Boy*, Bagoas has never heard of Achilles and Patroclus, Harmodios or Aristogeiton. He listens to what Alexander tells him about them with deference to his lover's interest, but is unmoved. He knows that many of the stories in the manuscripts Alexander studies are not true, certainly when they claim to record the history of his own people. *Funeral Games* concludes with battles over Alexander's corpse and his history: conflicting narratives are produced by those who loved and those who hated him, those who want to legitimate their own succession and those who want to discredit others', some who knew him and others who did not. History has fragmented with the fragmented world.

In this sequence of Renault's novels, the breakdown of gender and racial/ cultural ideals, the fragmentation of narrative forms, and increasing skepticism about the authority of classical literature and finally of "history" itself are all accompanied by an increasing emphasis on sex. The army of lovers with which Renault began her historical fictions was a collectivity of couples, lovers and their beloveds, its strength based on the solidity of those relationships— these men are expected to be longtime companions if they do not die together. Moreover, their proof of love is the steadfastness with which they "fight . . . at each other's side." But this containment of sexuality within the army of lovers—the couple and the battlefield—does not hold. The couples and the armies are sexualized. In *The Last of the Wine*, although Alexias's relationship with Lysis becomes sexual, this is seen as a retreat from an earlier ideal dedication; neither ever has another male lover. But by *The Mask of Apollo*, Nikeratos progresses through a series of relationships, always sexual but not always monogamous, rather than clinging to a single ideal passion that might justify his homosexuality. *The Persian Boy* not only gives us Alexander's conquests of the world through his lover's eyes, but Bagoas's trade is sexual pleasure, so that sex is foregrounded in the narrative and in their relationship. Alexander himself is claimed, in *Fire From Heaven*, by an Athenian courtesan who declares, "He's one of us, you know, at heart. . . . like the great, the famous ones; like Lais or Rhodope or Theodotis they tell tales of in those old days. They don't live for love, you know; but they live upon it."[18] Later Bagoas describes Alexander's relation to war and to his army as that of a lover, repeating the reference to prostitution; he has "seen the great courtesans of Babylon and Susa. . . . the cream from Corinth," but, he insists, "the crown" belongs to Alexander.[19]

Nevertheless, Renault always identifies sex with grief; a tension between sexuality and subjectivity recurs throughout these histories, developed through a shifting pattern of references to sex, love, boys, and bodies. The difference between the homosocial world of schoolboy fiction and the homosexual world of "queer books" is sex; sexuality would turn *Treasure Island* into a queer book. So the initial containment of sexuality in Renault's gay/historical fiction could be read as a protective or apologetic gesture, and her increasing emphasis on sex as a sign of her decreasing anxiety about queer books. In *The Charioteer*, Laurie's conviction that his unconsummated love for Andrew is superior to his sexual relationship with Ralph appears to be an effect of homophobia. But within the relationship between Laurie and Ralph, Ralph is, at least initially, the lover, and Laurie both wants to be the beloved and fears that the fulfillment of his childhood dreams will keep him a child. If masculinity is the basis of subjectivity, sex is, for Laurie, potentially in conflict with both masculinity and subjectivity, a source of subjection instead. Sex is always more available to the less powerful, potentially more subject characters in Renault's fiction than to her "great" men.

The sexual freedom of Renault's protagonists increases as their social positions become more marginal. Renault insists on the bisexuality of her soldier-citizen heroes in *The Last of the Wine*. Lysis eventually marries, with Alexias standing beside him and his bride at the ceremony, although when Lysis is killed in battle at the novel's conclusion, Alexias then marries her, so that this "marriage" is completely subordinated to the male couple. By *The Mask of Apollo*, Nikeratos—who, as an actor, is both marginal and central in a warrior culture that values the theater as a precinct of the sacred—has only male lovers.

While sex becomes less threatening, "love" remains the crucial term in Renault's histories. So the pivotal narrative element in *The Mask of Apollo* is Nikeratos' love for Dion, although there is no possibility of a sexual relationship between the two, and even their meetings remain formal and rare. Similarly, Alexander's love for Hephaistion continues long after their sexual relationship has ended. And even when Alexander is described as a courtesan, his seductions are all justified by love: "He needed love as a palm tree needs water, all his life long: from armies, from cities, from conquered enemies, nothing was enough" (*Persian Boy*, 157).

The "Persian boy," Bagoas, literally embodies Renault's fictional negotiations among sex and subjectivity, and sex and love. Alec declares angrily, in *The Charioteer*, "I'm not prepared to let myself be classified with dope-peddlers and prostitutes" (199). But the subjection to sexuality Laurie fears in that novel is literalized in the body of Bagoas, who has been castrated so that he will remain boyish, and then carefully taught rituals of sexual service. Through Bagoas, sex is identified again with the loss of masculinity and subjectivity. As a eunuch, he is a slave and an object: "I was to be enjoyed, like the flame and crimson birds, the fountain and the lutes. . . . the perfect vase or the polished gem" (31).[20]

But if, in *The Persian Boy*, sexuality recurs as a threat, love becomes a basis for subjectivity that is alternative to masculinity. Through love—his love for, and the love of Alexander—Bagoas is transformed from an object into a subject significant enough to be the narrator of his own and the emperor's stories. Nevertheless, although love allows Bagoas to challenge masculine/feminine distinctions, and demonstrate the power of sexuality, he cannot escape identifications of authority with masculinity and sexuality with weakness. Great Alexander's love for Hephaistion is challenged by his love for Bagoas. But ultimately Hephaistion, whom Alexander had known from boyhood and who does become a man, is unassailed. In fact, it is Hephaistion's dying that sets the stage for Alexander's death only two months later. And Alexander's death marks the end of Bagoas's narrative. The story he can tell of himself is only of himself in relation to Alexander.

Of all of Renault's historical characters, Bagoas is presented in terms that most clearly evoke the gay figure of modern fiction. He fulfills the subliminal identification of homosexuality with boyhood in *The Charioteer*. He is also presented in the image of the "third sex": "There are eunuchs who become women, and those who do not; we are something by ourselves, and must make of it what we can" (43). He loses the social position and the family into which he was born, and is unable to create a new family, "People like me . . . having lost part of our lives" (184). And he is as often as not dismissed by those around him, other than Alexander, when he is not treated with outright hostility.

The limitations of Bagoas's agency indicate that despite the possibilities of love, it is the body that is finally definitive in Renault's fiction, and that what the body defines is gender. In her later novels, Alexander holds his empire together, and Renault bridges the growing contradictions in her own fictional world, through his combination of masculine and feminine qualities. Bagoas and Alexander are paired figures—both boyish looking, both performers, both courtesans, both dependent on love. At the same time, Bagoas's presence masks Alexander's beauty, grace, and empathy; Bagoas ensures Alexander's manhood by being his "boy." So when, in *Funeral Games*, the hero-king is reduced to his body, the "world" he has conquered and Renault's fictional universe both implode, because the balancing act made possible by Alexander and Bagoas's relationship is ended. Alexander as a body demonstrates that the body is finally inescapable, and inescapable as a site of difficulty. In dying, Alexander becomes

Bagoas, insofar as Bagoas is an object, and not-Bagoas, insofar as Alexander's is still a male body. Renault cannot write about the nonsubject, the boy Bagoas, beyond the circumference of his relation to a man. She can also no longer write about "real" men.

But women could only ever be secondary subjects. In *The Mask of Apollo*, Nikeratos, who spends his childhood listening to his actor father rehearse, learns that "it was the right of a man to have seven voices; only women made do with one."[21] Eventually he changes gender routinely on stage, by changing his clothing, his masks, and his voice. The possibility of splitting voice and body represented by Nikeratos's masks is identified with art: "When I put on a woman's mask I am a woman," he says, "I could do nothing if I were not. There are two natures in most of us who serve the god" (77–78). But his body can cease to signify only because he is male, in a theatrical tradition in which women could not perform. Women could not put on masks, serve the god, or become men. Although the men in Renault's later fictions are less constrained by gender conventions, and more sexually active, these developments do not translate into increased access to subjectivity for women, even if they mimic these men. Her increasing interest in the volatility of sexuality and gender is ultimately constrained by the disqualification of the female, within history if not within her own imagination as well.

The sign of female disqualification becomes Renault's women's inability to escape their bodies, and the sign of the female body is female bleeding. At the climactic moment of *The Mask of Apollo*, as Syracuse is being destroyed around them, Renault's rare historical lesbian, Axiothea, accepts the protective fiction that she is male and Nikeratos's lover, and they take refuge together in a theater. Nikeratos defends them from the army looting the city through a performance, using his voice in combination with the theater's machinery to create deafening thunders that drive the soldiers away in fear. He literally performs the masculine role, using his acting skills rather than the military skills he lacks. Caught up in the fear and relief of the moment, Nikeratos and Axiothea have sex. Axiothea's loss of her heterosexual virginity to a gay man could serve as a confirmation of her gay/male status, an initiation into subjectivity that mirrors the terms of Renault's entire project. It was, after all, Axiothea's desire to escape the limits of "female" experience that brought her to the dangers of Syracuse. That desire carries through the morning after to her willingness to witness the devastation of the city. But she bleeds, and is therefore identified with the raped and murdered women, their bodies stiffening in pools of blood, that she and Nikeratos encounter as soon as they venture out of their refuge. Her disqualification is confirmed when she disappears from the narrative almost immediately thereafter. Women bleed again in *Funeral Games*, where the blood again produces exclusion. It is Alexander's cousin Eurydike, of all those contending for some remnant of his power, who most resembles the dead leader and would be his fittest successor: "She was wearing her man's tunic, and all her armor except her helmet. She was uplifted, glowing; her skin was clear and transparent; her hair shone; the vitality of great daring flowed through her and rayed out of her. . . . Alexander had glowed like this on his great days."[22] But despite her assumption of armor, she cannot assume the role of king, for unlike Nikeratos she cannot separate her voice from her female body. At the crucial moment in her bid for power, she is unable to stand to argue her cause before the assembled troops, because she has unexpectedly begun to menstruate, staining her robes with blood. Her menstrual blood serves simultaneously as an nonnegotiable sign of the female and of the impossibility of female authority.

In *Funeral Games*, Renault's most bloody and bitter text, Eurydike's story reverses Renault's fictional romances as the novel records the reversal of Alexander's empire. She reaches the verge of power only through her willingness to marry Alexander's half brother, Phillip Arridaos: as a woman alone she has no claim. And this Phillip is the last boy in Renault's fiction. But, although he is crowned by men who also hope to gain power indirectly, he is a man with the mental age of a small child. There is neither love nor sex in this novel: Eurydike and Phillip are the only couple, and on their wedding night the uncomprehending Phillip is goaded into an epileptic fit by the taunts of the men who are supposed to be his lieutenants. Renault's literary career ends with Eurydike, a would-be woman warrior unable to escape her body, and Phillip, a boy-man unable to escape his childhood, immured alive and left to die together. The manly woman and the boy are joined in their destruction, as the manly men (Alexander's less successful subordinates), and the feminine women (willing to rule through their children), tear his empire apart.

Mary Renault could not inhabit her own fictional universe. As the epigraph to *The Mask of Apollo*, she offered in Greek (and in translation), Plato's epitaph for Diôn:

> Tears were for Hekabê, friend, and for Ilion's women,
> Spun into the dark Web on the day of their birth,
> But for you our hopes were great, and great the triumph,
> Cancelled alike by the gods at the point of glory.
> Now you lie in your own land, now all men honor you—
>
> But I loved you, O Diôn![23]

Grief is felt by and for women, love and honor by and for men. But the grief underlying these fictions, the grief that wells up in the final bitterness of the story of Phillip and Eurydike, is for exclusion: love can be expressed honorably between men, but love and honor are only for men. Her heroes are more and less manly, more and less feminine. But to be female is an inescapable disqualification that is finally not mitigated by lesbianism. Renault cannot have her own fictional universe and inhabit it. Or she cannot inhabit her own fictional universe without also bringing grief and chaos. Like Bagoas, she can only tell Alexander's story. Or like Bagoas, she can only tell her own stories, whatever they might be, by telling Alexander's.

# PART II

# "LOVE IS WRITING"

A novel is do not fancy that everybody knows do not fancy that they have to go do not fancy that they build what is there do not fancy that parts of it are different, do not fancy that they do not look alike, do not fancy that they please us, do not fancy that they should object, do not fancy that they call when or as they come do not fancy that this place is not a place for that do not fancy that they should spoil that do not fancy that they have this do not fancy what they like.

A novel may not be theirs anymore.

———Gertrude Stein, *Four in America* (1933)

# 3

## Washington, James, (Toklas), and Stein

### I. War and Representation

Gertrude Stein liked to talk about modern art—her own writings and the paintings of others—by talking about camouflaged cannon and trucks. She returned again and again, for example, to a memory of World War I. In *The Autobiography of Alice B. Toklas* (1932), it was

> The first year of the war, [when] Picasso and Eve, with whom he was living then, Gertrude Stein and myself, were walking down the boulevard Raspail a cold winter evening. There is nothing in the world colder than the Raspail on a cold winter evening, we used to call it the retreat from Moscow. All of a sudden down the street came some big cannon, the first any of us had seen painted, that is camouflaged. Pablo stopped, he was spell-bound. C'est nous qui avons fait ça, he said, it is we that have created that, he said. And he was right, he had. From Cézanne through him they had come to that. His foresight was justified.[1]

In *Picasso* (1938), she wrote, "I very well remember at the beginning of the war being with Picasso on the boulevard Raspail when the first camouflaged truck passed. It was at night, we had heard of camouflage but we had not yet seen it and Picasso amazed looked at it and then cried out, yes it is we who made it, that is cubism."[2] And as she reported in a "Transatlantic Interview" in 1946, "I remember one day in the rue Raspail I was walking with Picasso. There came down the street a camouflaged truck, and he stood absolutely still and stared at it and said, 'That is what you and I have been doing for years.' . . . He had known for fifteen years before they knew that it was contemporary."[3]

Between the early 1930s and the mid-1940s, Stein revised this account of her work in accord with both world events and her personal history. She stops claiming causal responsibility: instead of their "creating" the cannon, it becomes a product of what she and Picasso "have been doing." Moreover, the cannon become trucks—less sinister, less violent, even given the trappings of twentieth-century warfare. This reduced assumption of responsibility is obviously a response to the horrors of the intervening years. The chief change in Stein's personal history between 1932 and 1946 was her entry into public history, a change which enabled her to assert her self with increasing confidence. Cézanne disappears, and her identification of herself with Picasso is clarified: "we" become, only and explicitly, "you and I." And there is another change in the cast. Eve and Alice also disappear. In *The Autobiography of Alice B. Toklas*, Stein's relationship to Alice is in part established through such anecdotes as this about the cannon, as a parallel to the heterosexual pattern represented here by Pablo and Eve. But "Alice"'s narration of the *Autobiography* established Alice herself within Gertrude Stein's personal history at the same time that the *Autobiography* established Stein personally within the public history of her own century.[4] By the mid-1940s, Toklas's place in Stein's life could be assumed. Gertrude and Alice, Pablo and Eve, become simply Picasso and I.

Despite these variations over time, this anecdote continued to serve multiple purposes. The story confirms Stein's peer relation to Picasso ("you and I"), and hence her role in the cultural history of the twentieth century, of which, in her accounts, he is the chief representative. It connects that cultural history (the history of representation, in this instance painting) to the "history proper" represented by war. It illustrates her use of "history" in her accounts of art and in discussions of her own work. The telling of the story itself turns a moment of personal life—Gertrude and Alice, Pablo and Eve, walking down the rue Raspail—into a moment in history (a history at the same time both cultural and political). Thus this anecdote also illustrates the significance of history in Stein's writings about her life as well as her work, and especially her merging of autobiography and history.

Stein connects autobiography and history proper, the narratives of arts and states, via the camouflaged cannon and trucks—that is, by reference to war. This choice reflects the significance of war as a structuring principle within her histories. She invokes war in this case through representation: it is the camouflage—"painting"—that alone identifies the trucks with battle. Moreover, it is the camouflage which marks the cannon as an instrument of modern warfare, which serves to identify its war with the twentieth century—"painting" that locates this image of war in history. Within Stein's histories, in this often repeated anecdote, "war" is then identified with representation: the camouflaged cannon and trucks embody both painting and war—art (representation/writing) and history. The double status of the camouflaged cannon and trucks as both instruments and representations of war suggests the double role of "history" within Stein's later work, as both a subject and an instrument of representation, of writing.

## II. "Not a Simple Novel with a Plot and Conversations"

Gertrude Stein began her literary career by rejecting literary convention, especially plot, and embracing history.[5] In the first draft of *The Making of Americans* (1903), Stein declares, "the thing I mean to write here is not a simple novel with a plot and conversations but a record of a family progress respectably lived and to be carefully set down. . . . I take a simple interest in family history."[6] The idea of "history," in varying forms, recurs throughout the early narrative phase of her work that ended with the final version of the *Making*.[7] *Fernhurst* (1904–1905) was subtitled "The History of Phillip Redfern, A Student of the Nature of Women" (1). While she was subsequently casting around for a new project, she persisted in including "history" in at least the titles of the works she was proposing to herself: "The Making of an Author being a History of one woman and many others"; "The Progress of Jane Sands, being a History."[8] Her next work, *Three Lives* (1905–1906), would, but for a publisher's decision, have been "Three Histories."[9] Although the term "histories" had appeared in the course of *Three Lives* as a synonym for "stories," Stein did not develop her idea of history until, in 1906, she returned to her original project, and began again with *The Making of Americans being a history of a family's progress*. "History" was the fundamental structural category of that work. "Soon there will be a history of every kind of men and women and of all the mixtures in them," she announces, "sometime there will be a history of every man and every woman who ever were or are or will be living and of the kind of nature in them and the way it comes out from them from their beginning to their ending . . . there will be a history of them and now there is here a beginning."[10]

Stein's history, however, had only an idiosyncratic relation to conventional understandings of history. History as a record of public events, which might encompass the nineteenth-century European immigration to the United States, is present as an assumed but unexplored background to *The Making of Americans* and two of the *Three Lives*. The history of slavery and racism are implicit behind the middle-class strivings of Jeff Campbell in "Melanctha," the third of the *Lives*. Autobiography was the unstated basis of *Q.E.D.*, and *Three Lives* also contained unacknowledged autobiographical elements: Stein herself as the second mistress of "The Good Anna"; and as Jeff Campbell in her recasting of *Q.E.D.*'s triangle in "Melanctha."[11] But in the *Making*, Stein declared overtly that her subjects were "real," her stories biographies which, despite being accounts of individual lives, she would present as "history." Because its compendium of personal histories (everybody's biographies) is grounded by a framework of more conventional ideas of history, *The Making of Americans* presages Stein's later use of conventional history as a framework for unconventional interpretations of "history," and the merging of history and auto/biography which served as the basis for many of her later writings. Although she did not pursue these projects until she returned to narrative in the 1930s, it was her first major break with literary convention that made possible her first extensive experiments with history and auto/biography.[12]

Within the experimental context of *The Making of Americans*, Stein offers auto/biography as history as a source of validation: "Sometime there will be then such a history of every one who ever was or is or will be living, and this is not for anybody's reading, this is to give to everybody in their living the last end to being, it makes it so of them real being, it makes for each one who ever is or was or can be living a real continuing" (177). In particular, "every one will have in them the last touch of being a history of any one can give to them" (180). This hope of a "last touch of being" provides a key to the sense of "will"—willed writing (the book will be written) and willed history (everyone will have their history)—that pervades the whole work. But such a determination for "the last touch of being" most powerfully implies need. Both of these presences, will and need, behind the "histories" of *The Making of Americans*, point to absences. There is no easy assumption of the possession of history here, and there is no sense of a "right" to history. Stein herself had already written one history that was "not for anybody's reading," in the lesbian auto-biographical *Q.E.D.*[13]

*The Making of Americans* illustrates the early connections in her work among literary possibility, "history" and sexuality—or the question, as she describes it, of "ways of loving"—and in particular between "ways of loving" and a need for the "last touch of being" history could confer. The *Making*'s histories are in part histories of "ways of loving":

> There are many kinds of loving in men, more and more this will be a history of them, there are many ways for women to have loving in them this will come out more and more in the history of women as it is here to be written. . . . There are many ways of having loving in them in men, there are many ways of having loving in them in women, more and more there will be a history of them, sometime there will be a history of all of them. (158)

What might be references to lesbianism appeared in Stein's earliest writing, in *Fernhurst* (the relation between the college president, Miss Thornton, and the teacher Janet Bruce) and in *Three Lives* (Mrs. Lehntman as the "romance" of the good Anna's life, and the "knowing" between Melanctha and Jane Harden), as well as in *Q.E.D.* But the experimental histories of the *Making*, which allowed Stein to incorporate first-person discussions of her purposes and her progress, also allowed her to make personal statements, including declarations of the "difference" of her own loving, and references to her developing relationship with Alice Toklas: "A very considerable number of men and women have different ways of having loving in them. I have different ways of having loving feeling in me I am certain; I am loving just now very much all loving. I am realizing just now with lightness and delight and conviction and acquiescing and curious feeling all the ways anybody can be having loving feeling" (605). The form of the *Making* also allowed her to record her sense of prohibitions against lesbianism:

> A very great many have very many prejudices concerning loving. . . . This is very common. Not very many are very well pleased with other people's ways in having loving in them. Some are very much pleased with some ways of having loving and not with other ways of having loving. . . . Some are pretty well ready to let most people do the kind of loving they have naturally in them but are not ready to let all people do the loving the way loving naturally comes to be in them. (605)

### III. "Wishes Guessed Expressed and Gratified"

The connections established in Stein's early work among literary possibilities, history, and sexuality were maintained throughout her refusal of narrative in subsequent decades. As she later commented of her experimental writings of the 1910s and twenties, "I could have begun with Chapter 1 but anybody even I have had enough of that."[14] But "history" continued to be identified with sexuality. Stein tells us, "Do not forget the Romans." Critics working on Stein's sexual languages, Linda Simon and Richard Bridgman among others, have shown that "Caesar" was an integral part of her sexual vocabulary, as in the orgasmic passages of "Lifting Belly" (1915–1917):

> I say lifting belly and then I say lifting belly and Caesars. I say lifting belly gently and Caesars gently. I say lifting belly again and Caesars again. I say lifting belly and I say Caesars and I say lifting belly Caesars and cow come out. I say lifting belly and Caesars and cow come out.
>     Can you read my print.
>     Lifting belly say can you see the Caesars. I can see what I kiss.[15]

These are American Caesars: she alludes to the "The Star-Spangled Banner" with "say can you see."[16]

The project of creating histories of ways of loving recurs in "Didn't Nelly and Lilly Love You," Stein's 1922 account of her proposal to Alice Toklas. "If

fishes were wishes the ocean would be all of our desire. But they are not,"
Stein writes. "We wish for land and sea and for a birthday and for cows and
flowers. Our wishes have been expressed. We may say that the history of
Didn't Nelly and Lilly love you is the history of wishes guessed expressed and
gratified." The history of "Didn't Nelly and Lilly Love You" is Alice Toklas's
personal history, a story of failed courtship (Nelly and Lilly were earlier suit-
ors) and of Stein's successful courtship, resulting as it did in "wishes guessed
expressed and gratified."[17]

   "History," in a variety of senses, could also be central to the method of
recording love in Stein's experimental writings. In "Didn't Nelly and Lilly Love
You," "history" is the location of love in a double sense. First, as the medium
of the expression of love, this "history of wishes guessed expressed and gratified"; second, as a source of the ongoing possibility of a "last touch of being,"
the resistant exteriority on or against which love could be proven, inscribed, or
otherwise established. "How can you remain extraordinarily permanent. I have
always been fond of permanent" (245), Stein writes, and "The history of establishment is a history of bliss" (232). But to achieve this permanence, the
"establishment" that history might confer, it is necessary to battle the social
conventions that "history" can also represent: "Now in fighting history we find
acknowledgements. I acknowledge that you are often precious" (232). To engage in this battle with history is both to produce history and to love. But to
have a "history" is also the sign of love:

> Now I wish to tell what she resembles I wish to tell this very well.
>    She resembles at the same time everything I have mentioned. In the
> historical sense there is nearly every satisfaction and in this particular we
> are not deceived. I know my history.
>    A historical novel is one which enriches all who bore colors and stones
> and fires. To be fierce and tender to be warm and established, to have cel-
> ebrations and to lean closely all these establish a past a present and a fu-
> ture. The history of establishment is a history of bliss. (231–232)

And this "history of establishment" takes an explicitly literary form, as "a historical novel."

   At the same time that sexuality and love continued to be identified with history in Stein's experimental writing, they were also linked to questions of language. In "Lifting Belly," quoted above, Stein asks, "Can you read my print,"
which becomes "say can you see the Caesars." The answer is, "I can see"—implying also "I can read"—"what I kiss." In "Nelly and Lilly" the question is,
"How can you control weddings. When all is said one is wedded to bed. She
came and saw and seeing cried I am your bride. And I said. I understand the
language. Don't Nelly and Lilly love you. Didn't Nelly and Lilly love you"
(223). Instead of coming, seeing, and conquering, the Caesar implied here sur-

renders: "She came and saw and seeing cried I am your bride." But the response is not a declaration of love. It is rather an affirmation offered through reference to words: "I understand the language." Such statements, at once about both love and language, could also be more directly about writing. In "Pay Me" (1930), for example, Stein writes, "She is my wife. That is what a paragraph is. Always at home. A paragraph hopes for houses. We have a house two houses. My wife and I are at home."[18] Here writing confers the security in loving—the possibilities of "houses," of being "at home" with "my wife"—elsewhere found in history.

"Love" assumed an integral role in the new form, the literary "explanation," Stein developed in the 1920s and early thirties as she began to write about her writing in "Composition as Explanation" (1926), *How To Write* (1931), *Lectures in America* (1934), *Narration* (1935), and "How Writing is Written" (1935). In his discussion of one of Stein's earliest explanations, *How To Write*, Bridgman observes, "If nouns were people and things, then sentences expressed the possibility of their union. 'A sentence is their wedding' (123). Therefore, when Gertrude Stein spoke of the sentence, she was likely to be making symbolic formulations that referred to human relationships as well as to verbal ones. Sometimes a sentence was a verbal fulfillment, evidence of a subtle joining. 'A sentence says you know what I mean. Dear do I well I guess I do' (34)."[19] "Love," Stein argues in "Poetry and Grammar" (the last of the *Lectures in America*), is the basis of poetry and the difference between poetry and prose. In prose,

> a noun is a name of anything by definition that is what it is and a name of anything is not interesting because once you know its name the enjoyment of naming it is over and therefore in writing prose names that is nouns are completely uninteresting. But and that is a thing to be remembered you can love a name and if you love a name then saying that name any number of times only makes you love it more, more violently more persistently more tormentedly. Anybody knows how anybody calls out the name of anybody one loves. And so that is poetry really loving the name of anything and that is not prose.[20]

When love becomes the basis for explanations of writing, discussing writing becomes a way of discussing "the way they do when they are in love," as in another of Stein's descriptions of nouns: "As I say a noun is a name of a thing, and therefore slowly if you feel what is inside that thing you do not call it by the name by which it is known. Everybody knows that by the way they do when they are in love and a writer should always have that intensity of emotion about whatever is the object about which he writes" (*Lectures*, 210).[21]

These discussions of writing, to which "love" was integral, were accompanied by a reconsideration of history (in "We Came. A History" [1930] and

"History or Messages from History" [1930], for example), preparing the way for Stein's return to narrative in the 1930s. History was still tied to writing practice: "What is historical. Sentences are historical."[22] It also retained the emotional promise of a record, the hope of a "last touch of being": "Those who make history=Cannot be overtaken=As they will make=History which they do=Because it is necessary=That every one will=Begin to know that=They must know that=History is what it is" ("We Came," 149). To "make history" was still to extend the reach of history, to demonstrate that "history is what it is."

Stein's writing on history in the early 1930s was focused by her renewed concern with questions of what history had been, was, and might be over time. She produced two versions of history. Her answers include a very rigid sense of the history of the official record, the history of wars, authority, and "importance": "There is no history in gentleness."[23] In this history, "one does not mention dahlias mushrooms or hortensias" ("Messages," 228); "Better have sepoys than lovely ladies sepoys are hindoo soldiers in revolt" ("Messages," 227). If it "is not description it is not authority it is not history," she declares ("Messages," 228). In "We Came" she insists, "History must be distinguished=From mistakes.=History must not be what is=Happening. . . . History must=Be the occasion of having=In every way established a=Precedent history must=Be all there is of importance. . . . History is made by a very=Few who are important" (148–149). This history will later be identified with the official "historian" who cannot deal with complexity: "I would rather not know than know anything of the confusion between any one doing anything and something happening. So says the historian" (*Geographical History*, 105).

But Stein always described this restricted view of history—the official version that necessarily denies "the confusion between any one doing anything and something happening"—with irony, and opposed it with a vision of the possibilities of profusion and pleasure, and insubordination. She insists, "History is made and=Preserved by heliotrope=Lavender and tube-roses" ("We Came," 149), and "They may mention dogs and geraniums and verbena also acacia lavender and apricots. Apples and pears and now birds and flowers and clouds and distance. History is placed where it is and hope is full of wishes" ("Messages," 228). Authoritarian "history" "must . . . be" subordinated to new and subversive authorial authorities: "History must again be=Caught and taught" ("We Came," 149). The fundamental lesson remains that "History is this anything that they say and that they do and anything that is made for them by them. . . . This is historical" ("We Came," 148). "They" are the ones who like and tell, or whose telling as well as liking might matter, as it matters for example to lesbians: "What did they do. They were willing to like them and to tell it of them in telling everything" ("We Came," 148). These are emphatically not the "very=Few who are important" in terms of the conventional record. They are then, perhaps, Stein and Toklas themselves.

## IV. "Events" and "Daily Living"

By the mid-1930s, in *Narration* (1935), history has entered the literary "explanations," and Stein is declaring the triumph of profusion. History can no longer be contained by the official record. Even the security of repetition has been lost: "Of course if you like anything does happen again but when one does know as the historian now does know all the things that happened every day while it was happening then for the purpose of the historian history is no longer repeating and so the historian has now no comfort really none left to him."[24] History as authority and order, the history represented by the historian, has been defeated by the history of the twentieth century.[25] This defeat becomes one justification of her own literary experiments, as she explains in *The Geographical History of America*: "There is no reason why chapters should succeed each other, since nothing succeeds another, not now any more. . . . Every body knows just now how nothing succeeds anything" (54).[26]

Stein described the gulf between the history of the historian and the history of the twentieth century as it was being lived in terms of an opposition between the history of "events" and the history of "daily living." In "How Writing is Written," she dismisses the history of events: "For our purposes, for our contemporary purposes, events have no importance. I merely say that for the last thirty years events are of no importance. They make a great many people unhappy, they may cause convulsions in history, but from the standpoint of excitement, the kind of excitement the Nineteenth Century got out of events doesn't exist."[27] In contrast, Stein embraces daily living. "Each generation has to do with what you would call the daily life: and a writer, painter, or any sort of creative artist, is not at all ahead of his time," she explains. "He is contemporary. He can't live in the past, because it is gone. He can't live in the future because no one knows what it is. He can live only in the present of his daily life." Not only must a writer be contemporary, he must express the contemporary in the form of the quotidian: "He is expressing the thing that is being expressed by everybody else in their daily lives. The thing you have to remember is that everybody lives a contemporary daily life. The writer lives it, too, and expresses it imperceptibly" ("How Writing," 151). "Events," which are identified with "story," share the limitations of plot. So she comments, in a 1935 interview, "What [Thomas] Wolfe is writing is his autobiography, but he has chosen to tell it as a story and an autobiography is never a story because life does not take place in events."[28] Stein reiterated her rejection of the trappings of conventional narrative in terms of her own daily life, as in a discussion of *The Making of Americans* in *Narration*, in which she explains, "dimly I felt that I had to know what I knew and I knew that the beginning and middle and ending was not where I began" (24).

However, Stein returned to narrative in the 1930s, and the basis for that return was a redefined history that included—even depended upon—the history of "events" as well as the history of "daily living." This leaves us with a doubled set of contradictions: Stein rejected the history of events even as she exploited it; and she dismissed narrative as she reclaimed it, "because of course most literature is narrative that is in one way or in another way the telling of how anybody how everybody does anything and everything" (*Narration,* 2).

These contradictions can be explained through the third term already routinely yoked to history and writing—"ways of loving." When she was asked, "What has passion got to do with choosing an art form?" she answered, "Everything. There is nothing else that determines form."[29] In *The Geographical History of America*, she identifies the relations between representations and their subjects with human relationships:

> There is always a relation between one thing and any other thing such as human nature and the human mind, between painting and what you paint. . . .
>     Being a relation is one thing.
>     Just to-day I said is she a mother or a daughter.
>     Well anyway it might be thought that anyway she would have had to have been a daughter.
>     But not at all she might have been a granddaughter.
>     Being a relation is not a necessary thing. (61)

Her questioning of human relationships—of the nature of a given relationship ("is she a mother or a daughter") and of the necessity for formal connection ("Being a relation is not a necessary thing")—suggests that the connection "between painting and what you paint," or presumably writing and what you write (about), is also problematic. The connection between representations and their subjects is difficult to define in the ways that human relationships are difficult to define. From the possible relationships of two women within a recognized family structure Stein goes on to ask about her and Toklas's friends:

> Jo Alsop is he a relation.
> Perhaps not.
> René Crevel was.
> Thornton Wilder is.
> Sometimes some one is as if he were an only son.
> But is he a son at all.
> May be he never has been. (61)

These questions are not only about positions within a family structure but about the limits of family, that is, the limits of socially recognized relationships. Because "there is always a relation between one thing and any other thing," so, she seems to be insisting, there will always be a relation between this problem of indefinable human relationships and the relations between representations and their subjects.

While Stein claims that her rejection of the history of events was based on the defeat of that history by the profusion of the twentieth century, her prototypical rejection of "the beginning and middle and ending" of narrative was obviously based in part on the difficulties of translating her own passion, her own relationship, her own daily living, into literary form. Not only did her lesbianism produce problems in relation to literary form, but insofar as her lesbianism was one of the factors shaping her experiments, it also created difficulties within her project of explanation. The "great many" who "have very many prejudices concerning loving" had hardly declined in the two decades since she recorded her awareness of their existence in *The Making of Americans* (605). And what Stein was doing in the 1920s and thirties was offering a brief for the historical and personal (emotional/sexual) referentiality of her own writing, which was complicated enough. She could hardly offer lesbianism as an explanation for her formal choices.

In *Narration* and other explanations of the mid-1930s, she negotiated this dilemma by emphasizing her identity as an American, representing her personal and literary dilemma in the language of cultures, states, and history. She could then explain her rejection of conventional narrative form as quintessentially American. She argues that

> it was right and quite a natural thing that the book I wrote in which I was escaping from the inevitable narrative of anything of everything succeeding something of needing to be succeeding that is following anything of anything of everything consisting that is the emotional and actual value of anything counting in anything having beginning and middle and ending it was natural that the book I wrote in which I was escaping from all this inevitably in narrative writing I should have called The Making of Americans [*sic*]. . . . [because] American writing has been an escaping not an escaping but an existing without the necessary feeling of one thing succeeding another thing of anything having a beginning and a middle and an ending. (*Narration*, 25)

But it is certainly not only as an American that Stein was "escaping from the inevitable narrative of . . . everything . . . needing to be succeeding" and "the emotional and actual value of anything counting," that is, depending for its value on, "beginning and middle and ending" (25). It was the lesbian Stein who knew that there might be "emotional and actual value" outside of the confines of "a simple novel with a plot and conversations."

However, as a lesbian, Stein lacked a narratable daily life: lesbian lives do not take place in (personal but socially recognized) events. Her use of "America" here serves as a model of her larger practice whereby, in the 1930s and early 1940s, she resolved her narrative dilemma by adopting the history of events as a frame for more or less narrative accounts of her daily life. By continuing to publicly disavow the history of events, and by continuing to reject "beginnings, middles and endings" as such very explicitly, she could disavow the narrative structures that excluded her.

Passion—her daily living—was not merely the source of the contradictions between Stein's statements and the narratives, but also another source—in conjunction with history—of her narrative solution. In the course of her 1930s explanations of her writing, Stein repeatedly announced, "I love my love with a b." This phrase marks the integral role of her relationship with Toklas in the resumption of narrative, the new histories of the 1930s and 1940s, which began with *The Autobiography of Alice B. Toklas*. These new narratives had two bases—"history" but also "love"—each of which was represented by a specific term in her writing: "war" and "marriage." Love and history continued, as in the earlier work, to be interwoven. But in their later, more elaborated public forms, "war" and "marriage" ultimately exchange narrative values.

## V. War

When she resumed her early interest in narrative in the 1930s, Stein began a double project she would carry on for the rest of her life: an increasingly detailed exploration of autobiography as the history of daily life, grounded in an increasingly detailed invocation of the history of events.[30] The history of events provided broad narrative frameworks. Although it may be about "My Twenty-five Years With Gertrude Stein" (237), *The Autobiography of Alice B. Toklas* begins, in its explanation of Alice, with reference to American forty-niners, moves backwards in time to call up Napoleonic armies, and forward again to the barricades of 1848. World War I provides the text's narrative shape: after introductory chapters about Toklas's and Stein's separate journeys to and then arrivals in Paris, the story of their life together is organized around this "event," divided into the prewar period (1907 to 1914), the climactic chapter on "The War," and the postwar years (1919 to 1932, the year of the text's composition).

Important characters and occasions in the *Autobiography* and in Stein's other late narratives are frequently presented in terms of the history of events: in the *Autobiography*, Picasso and Stein are introduced to the reader, via Picasso's conceit that he resembles Abraham Lincoln and Stein's idea of herself as a Civil War general (15). The relation between these two, which will be so important for this narrative, is established in terms of their joint interest in Civil War photographs; the tensions in their relationship are subsequently forecast with reference to their opposing identifications in discussions of the Spanish-American War.

Stein engaged in a detailed patterning of her own life against the cultural events of her time. So in the *Autobiography*, and later in *Everybody's Autobiography*, she discusses her early interests and education in terms of "the nineteenth century," giving her own development a public trajectory: Radcliffe to Johns Hopkins; Darwin to William James. "I began then when evolution was still exciting very exciting. . . . Science meant everything," she announced (*EA*, 242). "I was of course very interested in psychology. I was interested in biology and I was interested in psychology and philosophy and history, that was all natural enough, I came out of the nineteenth century you had to be interested in evolution and biology" (*EA*, 264). Moreover, as is widely noted, she located the development of her writing within the development of the modern in the history of art. In the *Autobiography*, she claimed Cézanne's painting as the inspiration for her literary innovations in *Three Lives*.[31] She described the afternoons she sat for Picasso while he painted her portrait as the occasion when she and he thought through and discussed the fundamental propositions that resulted for both in the beginning of their revolutionary work: Picasso's cubism and her "Melanctha" (46–50). That a portrait of herself should be presented as the instrument of this shared breakthrough only underlines the connections Stein is making between her own work and the larger patterns of cultural history.

Stein routinely used autobiographical anecdotes to locate herself in history. Other examples include the episode of Picasso and the cannons in the rue Raspail. Even the two "earliest memories" that she records are fitted into this pattern. She claims to remember, of her first trip to Paris, swinging on the chains that then—after the German defeat of the French in the Franco-Prussian War of 1870—spanned the base of the Arc de Triomphe, placed there to ensure that no other victorious enemy army would pass through. This story, of a three-year-old Stein in the company of her governess (a potentially Jamesian child precociously observing historical detail rather than adult morality), is told in *The Autobiography of Alice B. Toklas*, and repeated in *Paris France* and *Wars I Have Seen*.[32] It offers a primary connection between Stein and Paris—the later location of her writing (and her love)—via a connection between Stein and history. The other early memory that, beginning with the *Autobiography*, she offered repeatedly, was of the experience of seeing her first oil painting.[33] The object of this first encounter with painting, the art that would shape her personal and literary history, was a panorama of the Battle of Waterloo; Stein's first understanding of the difference between representation and reality was the result of being surrounded by oil painting and history.

Stein invoked various forms of historical writing as significant intertexts from the *Autobiography* onward. "Alice" comments on Stein's childhood reading, "She read a tremendous amount of history, she often laughs and says she is one of the few people of her generation that has read every line of Carlyle's *Frederick the Great* and Lecky's *Constitutional History of England*" [*sic*] (70).

References to "historical novels" appear throughout the autobiography/histories of the 1930s and 1940s, and references to Shakespeare's histories assume a significant presence in *Wars I Have Seen*.[34] These histories are linked to questions of aesthetic form. She explains, for example, in the "Pictures" lecture of *Lectures in America*, that it was her reading of histories and historical novels that enabled her to understand and respond to her first oil painting.[35]

The history of events was inescapable in the period at which Stein resumed narrative. In *Everybody's Autobiography*, Stein observed that "Every time I go out I meet some one and we talk together of revolutions and the weather" (121). This awareness of the history of events was also unavoidably of war. Stein's use of the history of events and especially "war" can be read as both responses to the moment and a way of managing her responses. The "history and fears" of the 1930s are reflected in *The Geographical History of America* (1936), where she insists anxiously that "The newspapers tell about events but what have events to do with anything nothing. . . . now everybody knows about the events but really nobody tells them they are still only interested in the weather and money./ Sure that is the way it is" (103). Nevertheless, "history and propaganda and government" are terms that keep recurring in this text: "politics and geography and government and propaganda, well and what of it what of politics and geography and government and money and propaganda, do they make you nervous. Do they" (60). War is also the subject of rhetorical questions: "Why is Europe too small to wage war because war has to be waged on too large a scale to be contained in a small country therefore as they think about war they know that they can only think and not do" (33). Stein expresses a desire for a "history" that would be securely past: "I wish I knew a history was a history./ And tears./ I wish I knew a history as a history which is not which is not there are no fears" (36–37). A "history" which "was a history" would not produce "fears."

Stein's emphatic and detailed location of herself in history, begun in the *Autobiography* and continued through the 1930s and 1940s, drew on assumptions about the interrelation of personal and public, auto/biography and history, the family and the nation, implicit in her writing from the beginning of her career: *The Making of Americans'* story of a nation was after all the "history of a family's progress," and that family was her own. By *Everybody's Autobiography*, Stein was admitting the autobiographical basis of her histories. She comments retrospectively on the *Making*: "We had a mother and a father and I tell all about that in The Making of Americans [*sic*], which is a history of our family" (135). She also develops the earlier implicit parallels between the family and the nation, family history and world history. In *Everybody's Autobiography*, fathers become the rulers of the world: "Sometimes barons and dukes are fathers and then kings come to be fathers and churchmen come to be fathers and then comes a period like the eighteenth century a nice period when everybody has had enough of anybody being a father to them and then gradually

capitalists and trade unionists become fathers and which goes on to commu-
nists and dictators, just now everybody has a father" (143). Contemporary politics, the history of events, could then be represented in personalized terms, as
an excess of fathering: "Everybody nowadays is a father, there is father Mussolini and father Hitler and father Roosevelt and father Stalin and father Lewis
and father Blum and father Franco is just commencing now and there are ever
so many more ready to be one" (133). Not only is "There . . . too much fathering going on now," but "there is no doubt about it fathers are depressing.
. . . The periods of the world's history that have always been most dismal ones
are the ones where fathers were looming and filling up everything" (133).

* * *

But while she was responding to the threat of her historical moment, and
drawing on assumptions long present in her writing, Stein's location of herself
within history during the 1930s was also based on her understanding of the relations between literature and history. For Stein, to locate herself in history was
to emphasize the contemporary quality of her own work, an emphasis which
was essential if she was to be understood to be a "great writer." From her earliest public literary theorizing, "Composition as Explanation" (1926), to
"Transatlantic Interview 1946," her account of art was founded in history, on
the conviction that the creative artist must be contemporary. In "Composition
as Explanation" she argued, "There is singularly nothing that makes a difference a difference in beginning and in the middle and in ending except that
each generation has something different at which they are all looking. . . .
Nothing changes from generation to generation except the thing seen and that
makes a composition."[36] She elaborated, in "How Writing is Written":

> If he doesn't put down the contemporary thing, he isn't a great writer, for
> he has to live in the past. That is what I mean by "everything is contem-
> porary." The minor poets of the period, or the precious poets of the pe-
> riod, are all people who are under the shadow of the past. A man who is
> making a revolution has to be contemporary. A minor person can live
> in the imagination. (158)

Moreover, if composition is determined by "what is being looked at from
generation to generation," by what is contemporary, then the explanation of
composition is history. "The progress of my conceptions was the natural
progress entirely in accordance with my epoch as I am sure is to be quite easily realised if you think over the scene that was before us all from year to year,"
Stein writes in "Composition as Explanation" (520). For Stein to locate herself
in the histories of events and daily living then was also (implicitly but automatically) to explain her work as well as herself.[37] This effect explains the centrality of references to the histories of events and daily living in her literary

"explanations." The story of Picasso, the cannon, and the rue Raspail recurs. Autobiographical narratives appear in the initial "Composition as Explanation," as well as in "What Are Master-pieces," *Narration,* and the *Lectures in America.* In *Lectures in America,* in "Portraits and Repetition," she explains her developing understanding of repetition, an understanding which led her to the form of *The Making of Americans,* through an account of her early years and, in particular, the storytelling habits of her Baltimore aunts (168); in "Pictures" she gives a history of her own interest in painting, including descriptions of summer vacations in Europe spent sleeping in front of the pictures in Italian museums (70).

Stein's grounding of her accounts of writing both in personal narratives and in the history of events can be traced historically and intellectually to her first venture into explanation. In "Composition as Explanation," Stein focuses her own narrative of explanation on World War I. According to her account of the history of culture, contemporary art can never be valued in its own time because a culture is always a generation behind itself in its perceptions of reality. Hence the relative obscurity of her first decades as a writer. But, she goes on to argue, for her, as for the other creative artists of her generation, the cataclysm of World War I functioned as a catalyst that brought Western culture to the unusual position of being able to recognize the work of contemporary artists. Stein thus self-consciously dates the beginning of her own public career to the war.

Creating the possibility of public recognition of her writing, the war made it possible for Stein not only to enter the history of events but to write her own kind of history. Public recognition gave permission for her particular combination of accounts of her own daily living with the history of events: the early narrative of "Composition as Explanation," as well as the more developed forms of autobiography and explanation heralded by *The Autobiography of Alice B. Toklas.* Consequently, when, in the *Autobiography,* she includes the story of herself and Picasso (and Alice and Eve) in the rue Raspail, watching the cannon go by, her claim that she and Picasso are responsible is part of a circular pattern of meaning. If the war was an effect of the modern she had been attempting to represent for years before, as she claims, it was also a cause of the entry into history of her attempts to represent the modern, and so also of the entry into history of the different narratives (beginning with the *Autobiography*) in which her interpretation of the war's effect is embedded. She and Picasso are responsible for the cannon/the modern, but the cannon are also responsible for them. As she explains in *Picasso*:

> the war is only a publicity agent which makes every one know what has happened, yes, it is that.
> So then the public recognises a creator who has seen the change which has been accomplished before a war and which has been expressed

by the war, and by the war the world is forced to recognise the entire change in everything, they are forced to look at the creator who, before any one, knew it and expressed it. (30)

Because of the cannon, she is recognized as a creator. The presence of such conventional historical tropes as World War I in Stein's accounts of her writings as well as of her life is an indication of her own understanding—that history made Gertrude Stein as Gertrude Stein made, in the modern, history.

## VI. "Henry James Being a General"

But the significance of "history" and specifically "war" to Stein's later writing, her histories as well as her explanations, was finally as much formal as a matter of literary or political history or autobiography. In the 1930s, Stein's literary explanations revolved around her conclusion that there were two kinds of writing. She begins this discussion in the "Henry James" section of *Four in America*:

> There are so many ways of writing and yet after all there are perhaps only two ways of writing.
> Perhaps so.
> Perhaps no.
> Perhaps so.
> There is one way the common way of writing that is writing what you are writing. That is the one way of writing, oh yes that is one way of writing.
> The other way is an equally common way. It is writing, that is writing what you are going to be writing. Of course this is a common way a common way of writing. Now do you or how do you make a choice. And how do you or do you know that there are two common ways of writing and that there is a difference between.
> It is true that there is a difference between the one way and the other way. There is a difference between writing the way you are writing and writing the way you are going to be writing. And there is also choosing. There may be a choosing of one way or of the other way.[38]

The first, "writing what you are writing," is easily identified with Stein's own individual and deliberately unconventional work of the preceding decades: that "is the writing which is being written because the writing and the writer look alike" (*Four*, 124–125). The second, "writing what you are going to be writing," is writing to expectations, fulfilling conventions: "You write what has always been intended, by any one, to be written. . . . You write what some one

[else] has intended to write" (*Four*, 124), "what some other one would have written if they had been writing" (*Four*, 127). In that case, "the . . . writer writes and the writing and the writer look alike but they do not look alike" (*Four*, 125). This was the manner of writing Stein had explicitly repudiated with her rejection of beginnings and middles and endings.

Stein's mid-1930s articulation of a distinction between these two kinds of writing was specifically the result of her new understanding of narrative. In her 1946 interview, she explained retrospectively her realization that

> most narrative is based not about your opinions but upon someone else's.
>
> Therefore narrative has a different concept than poetry or even exposition, because, you see, the narrative in itself is not what is in your mind but what is in somebody else's. . . . so I did a tour de force with the Autobiography of Alice Toklas. . . . But still I had done what I saw, what you do in translation or in a narrative. I had recreated the point of view of somebody else. ("Transatlantic Interview," 19)

Emphasizing again the difference between conventional narratives ("what some other would have written"), and her own more experimental work ("writing what you are writing"), she concluded, "If it is your own feeling, one's words will have a fullness and violence," whereas when she was writing to a pattern, producing narrative, "I had recreated the point of view of somebody else. Therefore the words ran with a certain smoothness" ("Transatlantic Interview," 19).

Marking this distinction between two kinds of writing, which was finally a distinction between conventional narrative and formal innovation, offered Stein an opportunity to (re)introduce the first kind of writing—conventional narrative—into her literary discussions. She needed to reintroduce conventional narrative, because by the 1930s she was interested in "choosing" between these two possibilities again. But the "choosing" of the 1930s would not involve the rejection of one option for another. In *Four in America*, after establishing these distinctions, she went on to praise James as a writer who chose both options. Moreover, Stein spoke of James specifically as a general, and it was in those terms that she could describe him as choosing both literary options, and so winning a battle and a war:

> Remember that there are two ways of writing and Henry James being a general has selected both, any general has selected both otherwise he is not a general and Henry James is a general and he has selected both. Neither either or or nor.
>
> It was a glorious victory oh yes it was, for which it was, for which oh yes it was. (138)

By writing about writing as the practice of generals, she places James and her literary questions into the history of events, without having to invoke a specific event. She goes on to conclude *Four in America* with a discussion of George Washington as a novelist. James and Washington have exchanged their "values," but most importantly, the terms novelist and general are presented as interchangeable.

This emphasis on the connection between writing and history is reflected in the conclusion of *Narration*, where both the opposition between literature and history that she poses at the beginning of that work, and her own decades of repudiation of narrative, are jointly reconciled in Stein's final elliptical declaration of her own intention of writing history:

> We talked a great deal all this time we talked a great deal how hard it is to tell anything anything that has been anything that is, and that makes a narrative and that makes history and that makes literature and is history literature. . . .
>
> What can the historian do, well I do hope he will do something, I almost would like to be an historian myself to perhaps do something. You see that is why making it the Autobiography of Alice B. Toklas made it do something, it made it be a recognition by never before that writing having it be existing. It is a natural thing to do if writing is to be writing, but after all it ought to be able to be done as history as a mystery story. I am certain so certain so more than certain that it ought to be able to be done. I know so well all the causes why it cannot be done and yet if it cannot be done cannot it be done it would be so very much more interesting than anything if it could be done even if it cannot be done. (58, 62)

Writing "to be writing" should "never before be existing," but "after all it ought to be able to be done as history as a mystery story," that is, as a narrative. To combine writing that "never before" was "existing" with narrative "would be so very much more interesting than anything if it could be done even if it cannot be done," that is, even if it does not succeed. This project has already been described in the course of *Narration* as an attempt to record the profusion of material reality, the history of daily living, without losing the quality of writing that is "writing what you are writing." Despite "how hard it is to tell anything that has been anything that is," Stein declares, "I almost would like to be an historian myself," a desire expressed more forcefully when she says, "I wish it could be done and if it could be done all these reasons for its not having been done would be of no importance because it will have been done./ That is what makes anything everything that it has been done and so perhaps history will not repeat itself and it will come to be done" (62). Paradoxically, this new form of writing history will be achieved only if history does "not repeat itself" and enforce the same old patterns.

From the point at which she began discussing Henry James as a general in *Four in America*, on into the lectures of *Narration*, Stein was marking the formal intention behind her narratives of the 1930s and 1940s. As she declared in *Four in America*, she, too, is a general like James: "I did not choose to use either one of two ways but two ways as one way" (123). She would achieve her new choice of both kinds of writing at once through a literary sleight of hand—substituting "history" for literary convention as the source of the expectations that structure "writing what you are going to be writing." Exchanging the expectations of literature for the expectations of "history," she could combine the two kinds of writing she had identified while still bypassing conventional plot altogether to achieve a history that was literature and a literature that was narrative.

Stein's desire and ability to create narrative on the basis of history depended in part on her 1930s redefinition of history to include the "history of daily living." But that, in turn, depended on her experience of the diminished authority of "events" in the fragmented and particularized history of the twentieth century. As she observed over and over again, "One must never forget that the reality of the twentieth-century is not the reality of the nineteenth century, not at all" (*Picasso*, 22). To the extent that this modern history lacked the rigidity—beginning, middle, and end—of literary convention, it could be combined with literary experimentation, to provide a minimal structure for a twentieth-century narrative. Stein claims history as one half of a formula of which the other half remains a deliberate commitment to literary unconventionality, "writing as you are writing." As Marianne DeKoven has argued, "Most of her work in the thirties is, or is almost, conventionally readable, but it does not represent a repudiation of or release from experimental writing . . . [but a] rapprochement of the experimental with the conventional."[39]

At the same time, Stein's decision to use history as a substitute for literary convention depended on her sense of the strength of "history" itself as a convention. For Stein, "history" signified "narrative" rather than narrative being understood as an attribute of history, as it was for Cather and Renault. Consequently, when she invokes "history" (or even "history as autobiography"), the conventional rules or attributes of narrative are considered automatically accounted for. So the narratives of her "histories"—*The Autobiography of Alice B. Toklas*, *Everybody's Autobiography*, *Paris France*, *Wars I Have Seen*, and even *Four in America* (which she refers to as a narrative) and *The Geographical History of America*—can be attenuated, antichronological, and lacking, in part or entirely, beginnings, middles, and endings.

Stein's history not only contained both events and daily living, but also combined in itself options analogous to the two kinds of writing she distinguished. This mirroring of history and writing becomes apparent in her discussions of World War I in "Composition as Explanation":

Lord Grey remarked that when the generals before the war talked about the war they talked about it as a nineteenth century war although to be fought with twentieth century weapons. That is because war is a thing that decides how it is to be when it is to be done. It is prepared and to that degree it is like all academies it is not a thing made by being made it is a thing prepared. Writing and painting and all that, is like that, for those who occupy themselves with it and don't make it as it is made. Now the few who make it as it is made, and it is to be remarked that the most decided of them usually are prepared just as the world around them is preparing, do it in this way. (513–514)

Here preparations for war function like literary conventions, necessarily limiting when it comes to the crises of battle or creative possibility ("making it as it is made"). And yet these preparations are necessary, even for those who can follow when "war" or writing "decides how it is to be when it is to be done." This sense of doubling within history is the source of her later image of James as a general combining both kinds of writing. She would later use the same language to describe the double qualities of war/history:

Do not forget that there are two ways to write, you remember two ways to write and that Henry James chose both. Also you must remember that in a battle or a war everything has been prepared which is what has been called begun and then everything happens at once which is what is called done and then a battle or a war is either not or won. Which is as frequently as one, one, one.

You can see that he chose both Henry James, you can see that he was a general Henry James, you can see that a war or a battle may or may not be won or both or one, one, one.

I like Henry James as that. (*Four*, 139)

If "history" combines the qualities of those two writings within itself—"may or may not be won or both or one, one, one"—for Stein to have assumed the role of the historian is also proleptically to have achieved the double literary choice she was otherwise working toward.

As these passages from "Composition as Explanation" and *Four in America* illustrate, "war" is the specific element that embodies "history's" potential for the combination of convention and experimentation, and so, for Stein, the possibility of narrative. War is a recurring element in many of Stein's "historical" anecdotes and examples. Her own history began, by her own account, with earliest memories connected with the Battle of Waterloo and the Franco-Prussian War; it ended with *Wars I Have Seen* (the most personal of her autobiographical histories) and "Reflections on the Atomic Bomb." This recurring presence of war is not only an accident of history or biography. In her lecture on "Pictures," she bases her modernist conviction of the gap between representation and "reality," and her argument for the effectiveness of representation in and for itself, on a description of her first oil painting. That this original painting was, as I have noted, a historical illustration, a panorama of the Battle of Waterloo, might seem simply circumstantial, but for her use of an ongoing discussion of battlefields she has seen and the difference between battlefields and paintings of battles in order to develop a distinction between art and reality. Stein comes to imply that the historical quality of the battlefields themselves is as necessary to their representations as the oil paintings; she describes a visit to a particular French site (the field of the battle of Metz), during which she claims that the battlefield itself almost looked like "an oil painting," because it was "so historical."[40] The battlefield, presented as the subject of the primary distinction between reality and art, becomes itself somehow a crucial link between the two states of "reality" and "art." Similarly, war serves as a condition of representation for Stein, within the histories of events and of daily living.

## VII. Washington "Wrote a Novel"

The history of daily living on its own lacks the "convention" that Stein needs from "history" if it is going to be possible to substitute "history" for the conventions of literature as a basis for narrative. Despite the fact that she repudiates the history of events—its lack of confusion, its comforting repetition, its exclusionary authority, and consequently its narrativity—that narrative quality remains an absolutely necessary part of her choice of history. And it is "war" in particular which gives to the history of events the necessary narrative line, providing, in Stein's analysis, at the very least beginnings and endings.

War gives definition and form to the histories that Stein records. They have different beginnings: the Napoleonic Wars and Waterloo, which "begin" her own history of looking at art; the American Civil War, which she repeatedly declares marked the beginning of the twentieth century in America, and hence in the world; the Spanish-American War, "the first to me modern war" (*Wars*, 30); and World War I, the prerequisite for contemporary interest in her own work and therefore her role in twentieth-century history. As she says at the beginning of *Narration*, about wars and the form of centuries,

> it just does take about a hundred years for things to cease to have the same meaning that they had before. . . . a hundred years does more or less make a century and this is determined by the fact that it includes a grandparent to a grandchild and that that is what makes it definitely different one time from another time and usually there is a war or a catastrophe to emphasize it so that any one can know it. . . . The eighteenth

century finished with the French revolution and the Napoleonic wars
the nineteenth century with the world war. (1)

The beginnings and endings of historical periods are not marked by dates on
calendars but by upheaval, wars, and revolutions that lead to wars. War is, for
Stein, the punctuation in the grammar of history—the convention of the history of events, the basis of history's narrative possibilities.

"War" is also a source of structure within Stein's "histories" because, in the
twentieth century, war not only orders the history of events, it also anchors the
history of daily living to the history of events. So she can argue for the importance of the history of daily living, in opposition to the history of events, while
taking her examples of both from a memory of World War I. "I always remember during the war," she writes,

> being so interested in one thing in seeing the American soldiers standing,
> standing and doing nothing standing for a long time not even talking
> but just standing and being watched by the whole French population
> and their feeling the feeling of the whole population that the American
> soldier standing there and doing nothing impressed them as the Ameri-
> can soldier as no soldier could impress by doing anything. It is a much
> more impressive thing to any one to see any one standing, that is not in
> action than acting or doing anything doing anything being a successive
> thing, standing not being a successive thing but being something exist-
> ing. (*Narration*, 19–20)

Soldiers themselves always experience a doubled history—"standing . . . not in
action"—living daily lives that are not particularly narrative, "not being . . .
successive," in the midst of the narrative history of events. But Stein argues
against conventional distinctions between the experiences of soldiers and civil-
ians:

> The eighteenth century knew that soldiers were soldiers that is to say
> they were different from others.
> The nineteenth century said soldiers were soldiers but after all soldiers
> were men.
> And we, U.S. we, us, in the nineteenth century discovered the twen-
> tieth century because we discovered there were no such thing as soldiers
> even in a war. (*Four*, 26)

In modern wars entire populations live daily through the history of events: "I
did not raise my boy to be a soldier. No of course not but if not why not since
at any rate that has nothing to do with this that anybody is a soldier as I say"
(*Four*, 61). There are "no such thing as soldiers" because "anybody is a soldier."

This quality of "war"—that it bridges and connects the histories, personal and public, of the twentieth century, in such a way that the history of daily life cannot be separate from the history of events—allows Stein to use the convention represented by events while she repudiates events.

* * *

"War" becomes a doubled axis. Connecting the two histories, "war" is the ordering principle of Stein's "history." But she was also using that "history" as the framework, the substitute convention on which she could base her combination of both kinds of writing, and create narratives without literary plot. So "war" becomes the pivot on which both Stein's "history" and her narratives turned, the sign of the possibility of narrative in literature as well as in history.

As a function of both her own construction of the place of war in history and her own use of history in her narratives, Stein also bestows the qualities of art, and particularly literary qualities, on war: war as representation, war as (potentially) writing. Her identification of "war" as the image of both forms of writing combined, and war as the punctuation of history; her beginning her explanation of narrative and the work in which she declares her intention of writing history, *Narration*, with a discussion of this role of war in history; the *Four in America* exchange between James and Washington of the roles of writer and general—all point to an alignment of war and writing. This connection is confirmed by Stein's discussions of war as an effect rather than a cause within history. As an effect, war functions like an illustration, a representation even within history. In the "Grant" section of *Four in America* she explains:

> The funny things I wish to say about war is first how war only says what everybody knows.
>     Everybody likes to see pictures, pictures of what everybody knows. Pictures of what everybody knows that that is a war.
>     Everybody knows which side has won before there is a war, everybody knows it, but nobody likes to believe it, and then they make a war. (26)[41]

As a picture, a representation, war has two dimensions. War fulfills expectations, shows people an already known, and that is reassuring: "Everybody likes to see pictures, pictures of what everybody knows. Pictures of what everybody knows that that is a war." Or, as Stein wrote in *Everybody's Autobiography* about the relation of World War I to changes in her own life: "The war had nothing to do with that of course not. Wars never do, they only make anybody know what has already happened it has happened already the war only makes it public makes those who like illustrations of anything see that it has been happening" (74).[42] This effect is conservative. As "pictures of what everybody knows," war is representational in the strictly conventional sense of nineteenth-century realism. In *Paris France* she observed, "War is more like a novel than it is like real life and that is its eternal fascination. It is a thing based on reality but invented, it is a dream made real, all the things that make a novel but not really life."[43] This is the novel of the nineteenth century rather than the twentieth, the literary equivalent of "pictures of what everybody knows." This is the war that is described in *Four in America* as a refuge from "lonesomeness." By *Brewsie and Willie* (1946), her portrait of the American soldier in Europe, she had developed this idea of war as a refuge from reality to the point where that reality includes not only "lonesomeness" but also jobs and women. As a conservative form of representation, war is allied, in Stein's final work, with Hollywood movies and "pin-up girls":

> Well, said Ed, anyway you look at it girls, well we have to have them, an American soldier has to have wine women and song, he just is made that way. Oh is he, said Willie, you just listen to Brewsie. Well what of it, it's true anyway. Not so true, said Brewsie, not so true, kind of true but not so true. Pin-up girls, not so true, said Brewsie, wait till you get home and have to treat girls in an ordinary way, not so much wine women and song. You think you're soldiers and you make yourselves up like soldiers and soldiers have to have wine women and song, and so all American soldiers just are so sure they have to have wine women and song, American soldiers think life is a movie and they got to dream the parts in their feelings.[44]

The skeptical Brewsie points to the self-delusions of their army experience: "You think you're soldiers and you make yourselves up like soldiers." But he has to acknowledge the power of this collective mystification—"American soldiers think life is a movie"—as well as the loss, if "they got to dream the parts in their feelings." (The references to "pin-up girls" and "movies" also suggest larger cultural/political patterns, sources of responsibility beyond the soldiers themselves.)

War provides a refuge, Stein observed, because of the authority of its combination of imperative and simplicity:

> in wars nothing is happening that has not to do with back and forward and forward and back, and that is the reason that wars are interesting. Anybody and everybody is interested in forward and back and back and forth and back and forward and this is something that is completely occupying the attention and everybody likes their attention to be completely occupied that is the way not to be lonesome and so that is the reason why war is interesting, there is no time wasted and so nobody is lonesome. Yes you do see. How can you waste time how can time be wasted when forward and back and back and forward is everything and it is always going on as it is a war. (*Four*, 51–52)

War offers a collective structure and purpose, and hence value, to individual lives. She contrasts this collective value with individual experience. In peacetime,

> something or nothing is happening until there is no more to happen. Everybody likes that, it is their life just like that and it is interesting but not as occupying to the attention as forward and back and back and forward. It is not at all likely that it could be as interesting as naturally it does not hold the attention and so naturally it can be lonesome. Most naturally.
>
> Peace has its victories as well as war. Sure. But it takes more time to go back and forward and forward and back in peace than in war and so most everybody stops looking. That is it. Most everybody stops looking. (*Four*, 52)

Commanding and conveying attention, form and meaning, war is then finally like literary convention, like plot. Stein explicitly connects as she contrasts the narrative authority of war with that of the heterosexual plot: "There is more back and forth in war than there is even in dancing or in kissing and so war is interesting" (50).

At the same time, the seductive order of war is conjoined with a disturbing, radical effect: war is described as forcing people to see fundamental changes already accomplished, or to admit what they may already know but do not want to recognize: "Everybody knows which side has won before there is a war, everybody knows it, but nobody likes to believe it, and then they make a war. Dogs bark, that is war, but they all already know some one was coming./ Everybody knows what most everybody knew, but now to show it they make a war and after the war is over they believe it" (*Four*, 26). War forces knowledge by forcing changes in appearance: "The spirit of everybody is changed, of a whole people is changed, but mostly nobody knows it and a war forces them to recognise it because during a war the appearance of everything changes very much quicker" (*Picasso*, 30). War is therefore potentially revolutionary. This revolutionary potential can be expressed through formal analogies. Stein describes World War I as a modern art work:

> Really the composition of this war, 1914–18, was not the composition of all previous wars, the composition was not a composition in which there was one man in the center surrounded by a lot of other men but a composition that had neither a beginning nor an end, a composition of which one corner was as important as another corner, in fact the composition of cubism. (*Picasso*, 11)[45]

From this perspective, the function of war as representation is similar to Stein's own stated goal: "I have of course always been struggling with this thing, to say what you nor I nor nobody knows, but what is really what you and I and everybody knows" (*Lectures in America*, "Plays," 121).

As she observed the development of European fascism through the 1930s, Stein voiced an acute awareness of the seductions of the order promised by increasingly militarized cultures. But war as representation has a doubled aspect—conservative and revolutionary. Stein uses this most "conventional" manifestation of the history of events as the basis for fundamentally anticonventional writing. In this way, the figure of war in Stein's writing of the 1930s and 1940s reflects the acknowledged paradox of her own literary practice at that period. As she observed in *The Geographical History of America*, "Whether they write or whether they do not they could not write if anything did or did not resemble any other thing. This is very important and no one can disturb anybody or anything./ Resemble and disturb" (63). Admitting both a new sense of the necessity of resemblance and of the difficulty of disruption ("no one can disturb anybody or anything"), Stein is nevertheless determined always to "resemble and disturb."

## VIII. Marriage

When Stein brought "I love my love with a b" into her literary explanations of the 1930s, she was referring back specifically to the work in which versions of that line first appeared, "Before the Flowers of Friendship Faded Friendship Faded" (1930).[46] Stein wrote there, "I love my love with a v/ Because it is like that/ I love myself with a b/ Because I am beside that/ A king./ I love my love with an a/ Because she is a queen./ I love my love and a a is the best of then." In her explanations, she identified the experience of writing that piece, begun as an attempt at a translation of her friend George Hugnet's poetry, as crucial to the development of her new interest in and understanding of narrative. She learned, as I have already noted, that

> most narrative is based not about your opinions but upon someone else's.
>
> Therefore narrative has a different concept than poetry or even exposition, because, you see, the narrative in itself is not what is in your mind but what is in somebody else's. . . . I did a tour de force with the Autobiography of Alice Toklas. . . . But still I had done what I saw, what you do in translation or in a narrative. I had recreated the point of view of somebody else. Therefore the words ran with a certain smoothness. . . .
>
> Then I became more and more interested in the subject of narration, and my work since this, the bulk of my work since then, has been largely narration. ("Transatlantic Interview," 19)

The line, "I love my love with a b," also, of course, refers to Alice B. Toklas and the relationship between the two women. In the context of the literary explanations, it invokes the structural significance of that relationship to Stein's writing. Toklas's life, and particularly her "twenty-five years with Gertrude Stein," provided the premise as well as the content of Stein's first attempt at narrative after her translation, the *Autobiography*, which could be read as a translation of Alice Toklas. Toklas became the requisite "somebody else," and her relationship to Toklas gave Stein access to the "point of view of somebody else," enabling her to construct her first narrative since *Three Lives*, twenty-six years before.[47] If Toklas could enable the second of the two kinds of writing, the writing to convention, by herself providing the structuring expectations, then the relationship between the two women could bring the two kinds of writing together, could bring Stein to narrative. This is why the incorporation of someone else's opinions, which is achieved in the *Autobiography*'s narrative, can be described in *Four in America* as a "caress":

> But it is true that there are two ways of writing.
>
> There is the way when you write what you are writing and there is the way when you write what you are going to be writing or what some other would have written if they had been writing. And in a way this can be a caress. It can not be tenderness. Well well. Of course you can understand and imagine. (127)

The contradiction ("It can not be tenderness") is obligatory, if the underlying relation is one between two women, which should not be acknowledged so directly. But Stein cannot resist adding, "Of course you can understand and imagine."[48]

Although Stein moved beyond her use of Toklas's point of view, their relationship continued to be the basis of her narrative experiments. As Stein tells us, "A great deal has to do with everything. And marrying" (*Four*, 145). As early as "Ada," her 1908 portrait of Toklas, Stein had made a positive connection between love and narrative: "Someone who was living was almost always listening. Some one who was loving was almost always listening. . . . The one who was loving was telling about being one then listening. That one being loving was then telling stories having a beginning and a middle and an ending."[49] By the 1930s, their relationship could provide the conceptual paradigm of "marriage" that made it seem possible to return to beginnings and middles and endings, to choose both kinds of writing and lose neither.

Stein takes over the heterosexual plot, remaking "marriage," the dominant trope hostile to her literary as well as social existence, in the image of her own experience, for her own literary purposes. By the conclusion of *Narration*, Stein was describing the problem of narrative as the problem of whether communication between the writer and her reader/audience was possible. That question was identified with the larger question of communication between individuals, and both were focused on the possibility of writing history, Stein's recently chosen form of narrative:

> After all can [history] be written.
>     It is certain that any man that is any human being at no time has the same feeling about anything as anyone can have who tells them or to whom they tell anything, any one who is alone is alone but no one can have that thing happen and go on living that is continue to be alone and so any one that is every one is always telling any one anything or something. (57–58)

While "any human being at no time has the same feeling about anything as anyone can have who tells them," and therefore, "any one," or perhaps everyone, "is alone," it is not possible to "go on living" alone. "Telling any one anything or something" is necessary for life itself. Stein resolves this tension between the impossibility and the necessity of communication in an image of marriage:

> That is what mysticism is, that is what the Trinity is, that is what marriage is, the absolute conviction that in spite of knowing anything about everything about how any one is never really feeling what any other one is really feeling that after all after all three are one and two are one. . . . and it never is happening, the one is not one, the two are not one, the three are not one, and still in violent living, in the thing that makes history what it is in the telling, the two although they are not one still again are not two and the three although they are not one are again not three. (*Narration*, 57–58)

This description of marriage contradicts the theological traditions Stein invokes with her references to the "Trinity," as well as most Western social and legal history (Blackstone's *Commentaries*, for example, and the Napoleonic Code). As these interpretations would have it, in marriage two do become one—the husband—and there is no space for questions or doubt. The value of Stein's image of marriage lies exactly in its reversal of the conventional; it signifies intermediacy, the possibility of suspension between two absolutes: "after all after all three are one and two are one . . . [but] the two are not one, the three are not one." Stein's image of marriage reflects the social state of an illegitimate relationship of the kind, as a lesbian couple, she and Toklas lived. Never legally and socially "one," given their life together they also were not socially or personally "two." (The social situation may of course also have reflected her personal experience of the relationship: "that is what marriage is . . . the two although they are not one still again are not two.") And that intermediacy, that suspension is clarified in moments of crisis, "in violent living," arguably in the course of a convulsive event such as war, which was for Stein "the thing that makes history what it is in the telling."

"Marriage," the paradigm provided by her relationship to Toklas, thus provides Stein with both faith in the possibility of communication and a means of conceiving of that communication. When Stein distinguishes, then, between the two kinds of writing in *Four in America*, and declares her decision to choose both, she uses this language of "marriage": "Two ways two ways of writing are not more than one way. They are two ways and that has nothing to do with being more than one way. Yes you all begin to see that. There can not be any one who can not begin to see that" (123).

"Marriage" appears to function in a manner parallel to that of "war," insofar as they are both terms which represent the possibility of achieving narrative through choosing both kinds of writing at once. Marriage and war could also be seen as the primary events of their respective discursive domains, literature (certainly fiction) and history. But the relation between these two terms in Stein's work is more complex. Marriage is the fundamental "explanation," because marriage—redefined as a contradiction constantly dissolving and renewed—is the interpretive key to the balancings of Stein's later work (convention and experimentation, literature and history, narrative and not-narrative, public/historical and private/personal, via the history of events and the history of daily living). There is not convention *or* experimentation, the historical *or* the personal, or alternatively convention *plus* experimentation, the historical *plus* the personal. Both terms are always chosen, and although "two ways of writing are not more than one way," nevertheless "the two although they are not one still again are not two."[50] Stein's "marriage" is then a precondition of her "war," which is finally writing. History can only be written if the general is married.

"War" is history is writing. In *Four in America*, James is a general and Washington is a novelist. But James is a general because he is a novelist: "Henry James is a combination of the two ways of writing and that makes him a general a general who does something" (137). Washington is a novelist simply by virtue of being:

> George Washington made no mistake. He made no mistake in writing anything or more than anything which he did. He did not make that mistake.
>     What did he do.
>     He wrote a novel.
>     And not only one but more.
>     And what kind of a novel did he write.
>     He wrote several novels some of the same kind and some of different kinds.

He wrote historical novels and natural novels and artificial novels.
And he prepared novels.
And he concluded novels.
And he wished for novels. (170)

Stein admits, "Of course he did anybody can and does wish for novels./ Nevertheless." She draws attention to the contrast between her version of Washington and what might be expected: "Everybody knows his life./ He knew his life and he wished for novels. And he did not confine himself to wishing for novels he wrote novels. He certainly did" (*Four*, 170). But perhaps there is no contrast. What "everybody" is likely to "know" of Washington's life are stories of his political and military achievements. What can we conclude but that these are his "novels"? That is, that war/history is writing.

Marriage is key. Stein introduced her two kinds of writing, along with the conceit of the writer as general, in a subsection titled "Duet," at the beginning of the third, the "Henry James" section, of *Four in America*. But duality has already been the key aspect of the first and second portraits in this text, "Grant" and "Wilbur Wright": Grant is doubled on the basis of having changed his name, into both Hiram Ulysses Grant and Ulysses Simpson Grant; Wilbur Wright is described as always both single and double because he shared responsibility with his brother Orville for the invention that brought them together into history. In these early portraits Stein also discusses relationships; an encomium on the subject of wives suddenly appears in the "Wright" section, where she asks whether Wright was married:

Just here I can introduce this about a wife.
There is no use in denying a wife is not only pleasant but useful. Never never do you want not to be grateful for having a wife. It is a thing for which always there is to be an expressed gratitude. And why. Because a wife is irremediably what is necessary not only with and will but in season and in out. There is no out season. No out season in a wife. (100)

"Wright" also includes a discussion of the experience of being paired that might refer as well to Stein and Toklas as to the famous brothers:

And so not quietly if you like but really if you like, yes really if you like as well as not quietly if you do not like, he was one, and almost then he was one, and not one of two. But he was one of two. Exactly so.
When they were with them they were not without them neither one of either one of them. . . .
He had lived the life he lived the two of them either one of either of them so that when it was done it was not only done but smoothly done

and either one of them knew which one. If they did not nobody suf-
fered.

What is suffering.

Suffering is certain is being certain that some time later if anything is
lost, that is to say if it is difficult to go on nobody will join in. That is
suffering.

That never happened to them. No indeed that did not happen to
them. (114–115)[51]

As through the 1930s Stein and Toklas were less and less "quietly"—more and
more publicly—a couple, the question of whether they were "really" a couple
remained. The evidence is the life they lived. They did not suffer from being
alone.

Marriage of this kind is established as necessary to writing and to war in
"Henry James." As soon as James is identified as a general because of his ability to combine both kinds of writing, Stein raises the question of his marital
status: "There are two things to be said. He was not married, to be said and
he was a general, to be said" (142). But his unmarried state is immediately
problematized:

May they recognise being married as yes and no in marriage.

Henry James had no marriage as he was not married. They were
obliged to give this answer. Not when they heard him. Or even after they
heard him. . . .

Why can marriage be made away.

Henry James was not married. By this they mean what they say. (144)

The question of whether James, the general, was married, has three elements.
Stein challenges the hegemony of marriage as a sign of relationship. Is the one
who is not married necessarily alone? "If he were not married and lived alone
he would live as if he were not married and lived alone but really not he would
live as if he were not married. If they are not married do they live as if they live
alone. Think about this a Henry James and think about this a general and then
think about this as this" (144). Marriage is presented as the basis for receiving
help in war/writing, providing access to another person's perspective and expectations, and so making it possible to combine both kinds of writing:

What did he make him do when he wrote what did it make him do
when he had it to do to help with a battle or help with a war or help with
whatever he ordered that he should help. He would of course never help
himself. Any one who is not married and who lives as if he is not married does not help himself. He can not help himself. And this makes him
write as he does, does or was. (144)

Because the general is the writer who combines both kinds of writing, the general must be married—hence, the possibility of arranged marriages for generals: "In many instances marriages are arranged in many instances of generals" (144). If the writer/general is married, then war/writing can occur, that is, history can be written. Narrative history is being written—the general is married. But not married. But not alone. As a lesbian can be not married but not alone—not one but not two. As *Four in America* is neither narrative nor history in any familiar sense.

"Marriage" then becomes a literary term in Stein's later writing. Paradoxically, given its identification with convention, it marks the continuing problematization inherent in her histories, and the continuing experimentation of her later writings. Her consistent problematization of "marriage" itself—is this character married or not married—refers back always to the challenging definition of marriage on which her use of the term is based, and without which she could not put it to any of the uses she does. And this problematized "marriage" points back in turn, beyond the literary structures, to the socially problematized marriage of the life.

The term "marriage" recurs throughout Stein's later writings, accompanied by references to war, dualities, and the question of whether or not a character is married, or whether or not a particular marriage is valid. *Ida* (1941), for example, contains a complex of references to doubling, twins, marriage, and soldiers.[52] Both of her final histories, *Brewsie and Willie* and *The Mother of Us All* (1945), contain characters who are not sure whether or not they are married. In *Brewsie and Willie*, there is Brock, the soldier who "although he had been married . . . did not know whether he was married now or not" (5). In *The Mother of Us All*, it is Jo the Loiterer's marriage that is at issue. The problem of Jo's marital status is produced by some difficulty in "telling":

| | |
|---|---|
| Jo the Loiterer. | I want to tell. |
| Chris the Citizen. | Very well. |
| Jo the Loiterer. | I want to tell oh hell. |
| Chris the Citizen. | Oh very well. |
| Jo the Loiterer. | I want to tell oh hell I want to tell about my wife. |
| Chris the Citizen. | And have you got one. |
| Jo the Loiterer. | No not one. |
| Chris the Citizen. | Two then. |
| Jo the Loiterer. | No not two. |
| Chris the Citizen. | How many then. |
| Jo the Loiterer. | I haven't got one. I want to tell oh hell about my wife I haven't got one. |
| Chris the Citizen. | Well. |
| Jo the Loiterer. | My wife, she had a garden. |

. . . . . . . . . . . . . . . . . . . . .

And was she your wife said Chris, yes said Jo
when she was funny, How funny said Chris. Very
funny said Jo. Very funny said Jo. To be funny
you have to take everything in the kitchen and
put it on the floor, you have to take all your
money and all your jewels and put them near the
door you have to go to bed then and leave the
door ajar. That is the way you do when you are
funny.

Chris the Citizen.    Was she funny.
Jo the Loiterer.    Yes she was funny.
(Chris and Jo put their arms around each other)[53]

The difficulty of telling about this relationship suggests homosexuality. The
wife/marriage that Jo does want to tell about, although the telling is so difficult, both is and is not real, as in a lesbian or gay partnership. She or it (the
relationship) is "funny" (queer?) in a way that is connected with risking all that
is valuable when you go to bed. And the sequence ends with the homosocial if
not the sexual embrace of two male characters.

## IX. "The Last Touch of Being": *Wars I Have Seen*

This marriage remade in the image of lesbian experience, instead of the conclusion of domestic/personal narratives, becomes the premise of public/histor-
ical narratives that express the domestic and personal in a way that would not
otherwise have been possible. As I have already discussed, for narrative purposes the lesbian Stein had no daily life. Neither the conventions governing the
representation of daily life in realist fiction, nor the assumptions of a conventional (auto)biography, would have been possible vehicles for a narrative that
encompassed her emotional and sexual as well as her literary and social experiences, much less the connections among them all. But, premising her narratives on a history (her relationship with Alice Toklas) that could itself have no
"events" in any conventional sense, she gave their relationship the events of
"history." Biography that was also history could take its form from impersonal
events that justified an account of their daily living. That account, as a record
of the structure of their relationship, offered at the least a "negative" image of
their love, an image of its effects and public forms that resembles and disturbs
perhaps both their private experiences and readers' expectations. Even as a negative, that account, both because of the way it is written *vis-à-vis* conventional
history, and because of its achievement of narrative, could then be brought
into history, bringing their shared lives into history. *The Autobiography of Alice
B. Toklas* was Stein's great popular success.

Paradoxically, the most public had become the setting for the representation of the most private. From the first history, the *Autobiography*, through the rest of her narratives, the indications of intimacy between Stein and Toklas are invariably located within an "historical" moment. The first hint of the intimacy on which the *Autobiography* is founded appears in the form of "Alice's" admission, in the course of describing her first dinner party with the Steins, that she would later "tease" Gertrude about her identification of herself as a Civil War general.[54] In the course of the *Autobiography*, the rare references to physical contact between the women all have historically significant settings. Stein places her hand on Toklas's shoulder as Toklas sits puzzled before paintings by Braque and Derain at her first *vernissage*, in 1907, unaware that this exhibition of work by his followers marked Picasso's entry into the history of twentieth-century culture (17). Stein and Toklas are represented as crying with relief together after they hear in November 1914 that the German advance has been halted and Paris saved; Stein describes herself, later in that war, waking Toklas in the night in their Paris home, and taking her hand to lead her downstairs in the dark during an air raid (148).

Stein's late narratives and personal histories culminate in *Wars I Have Seen*, with its combination of journal, memoir, and meditation. Entirely structured by the public history of the war years, it offers a record of daily experience—Stein's life with Alice Toklas just outside the French villages of Belley and then Culoz, from 1943 to 1946. Stein interweaves observations about history and literature, foraging for food, and the activities of the local *Maquis*. Narrative tension is provided by the hope for Allied victory (as German and Italian soldiers move through the countryside and the house); a narrative climax by the liberation of France; a narrative conclusion by Stein's observations of the American army. But war ties daily life to the history of events even more intimately in this work, in that war finally provides a paradigm for understanding daily life as well as history. Stein begins by retelling the story of her life, beginning with her birth, in terms of war, the wars she has seen being both external (although sometimes the seeing was metaphorical)—the Civil War, the Spanish-American war, the Boer War—and internal, as she observes of the period after her family settled in California, "Such wars as there were were inside in me, and naturally although I was a very happy child there were quite a number of such wars" (6).[55] Yet to complete the paradox set up in *The Autobiography of Alice B. Toklas*, whereby the most public is the setting of the most private, *Wars I Have Seen* is the most personal of Stein's histories, finally her own autobiography.

Stein's capacity to tell her own life story in this text, in more detail and in a more straightforward narrative voice than ever before, depends on its complete merger of daily life and events. In earlier works, Stein's construction of connections between the lesbian couple and history/culture were necessary for representation. In *Wars I Have Seen*, connection is also necessary for survival. Stein and Toklas survived the war as aliens (American, Jewish, lesbian) in enemy territory because of their integration into histories of daily life at this moment in the history of events.[56] *The Autobiography of Alice B. Toklas* placed Stein and Toklas at the center of a Parisian artistic elite and of the cultural history of the twentieth century; they move through *Everybody's Autobiography* (an account of their subsequent U.S. lecture tour) within the overlapping realms of American celebrity and intellectual life. But *Wars I Have Seen* demonstrates Stein's and Toklas's place in the daily lives of French villagers and American GIs. Stein's conversations with local people—young men who must choose between going to Germany under orders or escaping to the mountain; children remembering bananas; the baker dreaming of the restaurant he will open when the war is over; the lawyer who warns them they are in danger; old women going to visit their daughters or worrying about their sons; the mayor's wife refusing to be intimidated by the occupying army—form a large part of her text. These conversations have material consequences. "As Madame Pierlot said, you do not buy now-a-days only with money you buy with your personality," Stein notes. "Nothing is sadder these days than people who never make friends, they poor dears have nothing to eat, neither do the indiscreet" (45–46).

But even in these circumstances, Stein insists on their anomalous status, a difference tied to the world of events. She describes them as dependent also on their difference: when, in 1943, they are advised that they must leave immediately for Switzerland, they decide, after much anxiety, to remain where they are, because "it is better to go regularly wherever we are sent than to go irregularly where nobody can help us if we are in trouble" (50), and when the fighting is over and they meet their first member of the Resistance, "we are Americans we said, yes we know he said" (233). The narrative's conclusion with the Liberation of France is played out through a series of encounters in which Stein and Toklas recover their status as "known," as different. So for example when they find their first American soldiers, "I said in a loud voice are there any Americans here and three men stood up and they were Americans God bless them and were we pleased. . . . and I told them who we were, and they knew, I always take it for granted that people will know who I am and at the same time at the last moment I kind of doubt, but they knew of course they knew" (245).

In *Wars I Have Seen*, the difference that Stein reclaims as the urgency of events recedes is that she is an American, and in particular an American writer. So after the D-Day invasion, "glory be, and we are singing glory hallelujah, and feeling very nicely, and everybody has been telephoning to us congratulatory messages upon my birthday which it isn't but we know what they mean" (194). The connection between the American and the writer is underlined by one of many replays of the "recognition by American soldiers" scene. A trainload of GIs were waiting at a local siding, strolling along and standing about and I said Hello to the first group and they said Hello and I said I am an American and they laughed and said so were they . . . and I told them who I was thinking some one of them might have heard of me but lots of them had and they crowded around and we talked and we talked. . . . and one of them told me that they knew about me because they study my poems along with other American poetry in the public schools and that did please me immensely it most certainly did. (251)[57]

Nevertheless the "kind of doubt" of recognition Stein also voices suggests an underlying anxiety, perhaps explained by the shift from scene to scene between "who we were" and "who I am." "They knew of course they knew," but who is this American writer Gertrude Stein who depends on war in her writing, but is only known again when the war is over? And who is the woman with her?

Stein's other potential identities are present in *Wars I Have Seen*, and also represented through reference to historical events. At the beginning of her narrative, Stein describes her young self as impressed not only by wars but also by "the famous Oscar Wilde trial and the question of public opinion and . . . the Dreyfus case and anti-Semitism" (51). That Wilde and Dreyfus appear, so conspicuously not contemporary or war-related although historical references, in a context in which so much else is being incorporated into the terms of war, can only suggest ongoing conflict around Jewish and homosexual difference.

Although she admitted nothing of the reality of the Holocaust at the time she was writing *Wars*, the reference to Dreyfus is only one of her references to Jews and anti-Semitism. But neither Jewishness nor anti-Semitism are personalized until the end of the text, when, in conjunction with her first reference to actual "persecutions against the Jews," she produces an anomalous anonymous narrative. "There is this about a Jewish woman, a Parisienne, well known in the Paris world," Stein begins:

She and her family took refuge in Chambéry when the persecutions against the Jews began in Paris. And then later, when there was no southern zone, all the Jews were supposed to have the fact put on their *carte d'identité* and their food card, she went to the prefecture to do so and the official whom she saw looked at her severely Madame he said, have you any proof with you that you are a Jewess, why no she said, well he said if you have no actual proof that you are a Jewess, why do you come and bother me, why she said I beg your pardon, no he said I am not interested unless you can prove you are a Jewess, good day he said and she left. It was she who told the story. Most of the French officials were like that really like that. (243–244)

This story, told just before she describes the American army's arrival in "their" village and her and Toklas's personal liberation, seems intended as an exoneration of the French (although French anti-Semitism has not even been mentioned earlier). But it is also perhaps an attempt to explain her own and Toklas's situation, as "It was she who told the story."

Stein did not return to Wilde, nor indicate the subject of the "public opinion" that she identifies with his case. But she explains that she became interested in Wilde,

> largely because of the poem he wrote about his imprisonment, [because] up to that time I had never conceived the possibility of anybody being in prison, anybody whose business it was not naturally because of natural or accidental crime to be in prison, and in California in those days even natural or accidental crime did not mean prison. And now in 1943 the large part of the men of a whole nation are in prison. . . . Anybody can be a prisoner now. (54)

Wilde's fate is identified with wartime, when there is both arbitrary and universal imprisonment. "Oscar Wilde and the Ballad of Reading Goal was the first thing that made me realise that it could happen, being in prison," she emphasizes (55). Yet also implicitly what Wilde the writer made her "realise" about "being in prison" is "that it could happen" to her, particularly given the possibility of unexplained "natural" as well as "accidental crime." Could lesbianism be natural, and Jewishness be accidental crime? Dreyfus, of course, also went to prison. War threatens imprisonment. But in this text, in which the whole of life is represented through war, is the whole of life also represented as shadowed by fear of punishment for natural or accidental crimes?[58]

That *Wars I Have Seen* was even understood by Stein as a completion of her literary uses of history is suggested by its epilogue. Here a discussion of literary difference is framed by war/history as a discussion of the American GIs who "know" her. She characterizes them in terms of the differences between their use of language and that of the doughboys of World War I. The GIs, she concludes, had achieved a distinctly American language. Her comments on their speech, however, apply equally well to her own achievement. "The American language instead of changing remained English," she observed:

> long after the Americans in their nature their habits their feelings their pleasures and their pains had nothing to do with England.
> So the only way the Americans could change their language was by choosing words which they liked better than other words, by putting words next to each other in a different way than the English way, by shoving the language around until at last now the job is done, we use the

same words as the English do but the words say an entirely different thing. (259)

In *Narration* Stein asked rhetorically, "What do you tell and how do you tell it" (31), and in *Four in America*, "How can you state what you wish to say. That is the question. What you wish. That is the question. To say. That is the question" (142). The connection between wishes (desire) and saying runs throughout Stein's work. One area of desire that might be spoken was, obviously, the lesbian: "He never felt awkward as married but he should recite only really who could or did recite or not quite. . . ./ The thing to wonder is did he not have to say what he did not have to say./ That can happen to any general who is regularly a general. Any general" (*Four*, 145). Stein "did not have to say." But at the same time, "did [she] not have to say what [she] did not have to say," like "any general who is regularly a general," which is to say, like any writer who is regularly a writer? We cannot forget Stein as a Civil War general or as Caesar. Nor can we ignore her observation, as she begins the *Geographical History of America*, "In the month of February were born Washington Lincoln and I."

Stein also expressed a desire for history. "I always wanted to be historical, from almost a baby on, I felt that way about it," she wrote at the end of her career.[59] To be historical, by the final narrative phase of Stein's career, was also to say the lesbian. "The history of establishment," Stein insisted, "is a history of bliss" ("Didn't Nelly," 232). The bliss of her lesbian love and the bliss of being historical are both fulfilled through the history she created of her establishment with Alice B. Toklas. This history is also necessary to secure her love, in a world of "prejudices" against her "way of loving." She achieves a "last touch of being," the validation that history, that is, representation, confers to oppose to those prejudices. And she wants her love recognized as a part of history:

Those who make history=Cannot be overtaken=As they will make=History which they do=Because it is necessary=That every one will=Begin to know that=They must know that=History is what it is.

# 4

# Djuna Barnes,
# Memory, and Forgetting

## I. "Looking at Her"

"Looking at her," Djuna Barnes began her description of *Nightwood*'s Nora Flood, "foreigners remembered stories they had heard of covered wagons."[1] Of the salon Nora presided over before the action of the novel has begun, Barnes wrote,

> At these incredible meetings one felt that early American history was being re-enacted. The Drummer Boy, Fort Sumter, Lincoln, Booth, all somehow came to mind; Whigs and Tories were in the air; bunting and its stripes and stars, the swarm increasing slowly and accurately on the hive of blue; Boston tea tragedies, carbines, and the sound of a boy's wild calling; Puritan feet, long upright in the grave, striking the earth again, walking up and out of their custom; the calk of prayers thrust in the heart. And in the midst of this, Nora. (51)

Barnes's work is dense with such references to history, from the narrator's proposition in the *Ladies Almanack* (1928) "that Priscilla herself was prone to a Distaff, and garbled her John for her Jenny," via the hallways of the Viennese home of *Nightwood*'s Guido and Hedvig Volkbein, "peopled with Roman fragments, white and disassociated" (5), to Augusta's declaration, in *The Antiphon* (1958), "I would be Helen/ Forgotten, day by day, for ever and for ever!"[2] These allusions to historical epochs, events, and characters are accompanied by a stream of comments about "history," made by Barnes as narrator or by her characters.

The evocations of historical detail and the discussions of "history" as such are however only part of a complex historical presence in Barnes's writing. Her characters are frequently as concerned about their relation to history as they are about their responses to each other. History is also the source of an additional cast (Helen of Troy, Catherine the Great, Dante, Sappho) who move in and out of her work, as well as a smaller group of more contemporary public figures (Dreyfus, Oscar Wilde, Radclyffe Hall) who are present only by implication, but whose individual histories shape Barnes's own.[3] Dreyfus, Wilde, and Hall represent the historical context in which standard fictional conventions could not accommodate Barnes's stories; Helen of Troy, Catherine the Great, Dante, and Sappho provide her textual world with its own alternative location and resonances. Barnes used history as a framework for her texts, within which she could situate both her practice as a writer and her anxieties about that practice. At the same time, implicit throughout her work is the sense that her texts are themselves additions to history, recording characters, experiences, and perspectives that history has preferred to ignore.

As a lesbian writer, for whom "looking at her" was potentially a prelude to sexual desire and emotional vulnerability, Djuna Barnes inverted history to record what was at the time often referred to as inversion, "the part about Heaven that has never been told," as she describes the genesis of the first "Woman born with a Difference" in the *Ladies Almanack* (25–26).[4] The first three of the "great moments of history" are recounted by Dr. O'Connor to one of Wendell Ryder's bastard children in *Ryder* (1928).[5] But the fourth, final, and lesbian moment, the story of Jezebel and the Queen of Sheba which rebukes the authority of biblical history itself, is told by one of a pair of women lovers to the other, Doll Furious to Dame Musset, in the *Ladies Almanack* (41). Barnes's interest in history, prefigured in *Ryder* and in such early stories as "Cassation," was fully developed in the *Ladies Almanack* as well as in Barnes's two major works, *Nightwood* and *The Antiphon*. The gesture of turning toward "women in history" is repeated by one of the women in each of these works: Bounding Bess in the *Almanack* (32); Robin Vote in *Nightwood* (47); and Augusta in *The Antiphon* (198–199). Of all the women whose memories they invoke (including Catherine of Russia, Sappho, Louise de la Valliere, Madame de Maintenon, Cleopatra, and Lily Langtry) only one, Sappho, offers an obviously applicable lesson. However, although her characters might look uncritically to these inappropriate models, the tenor of Barnes's own overall turning to history was more accurately represented by the critical spirit of the *Almanack's* narrator, who asks, "Was there a whisper of Ellen or Mary, of Rachel or Gretchen . . . or of Wives whispering a thing to a Wife? What's in a name before Christ? Were all Giants' doings a Man's. . . . No Time without God, no end without Christ!" (70).

\* \* \*

Stein divided "history" into the histories of "events" and "daily life." For Djuna Barnes history always had at least a double meaning. History was fixed, exact, monumental, and the source of power. It was also chaotic, fragmentary, and constantly under construction. History was the story of the Christians and the story of the Jews, the source of innocence and the source of depravity, a false lesson about male authority and an only superficially fantastic account of the lives of lesbian women "with a Difference" (*LA* 26). This multiplicity was possible because Barnes's sense of "history" incorporated both the official record and the stories of those who were either marginal to or completely excluded from that record.

Throughout her work, Barnes maintained a distinction between what might be recorded if historians told "the story of the world to the world" (161), as the Doctor advocates at the conclusion of *Nightwood*, and what actually is set down, history as a "commodity," as she refers to that Jewish history recognized by a Christian-dominated society (10). But she was not consistent in her labelling of the terms of this opposition. Sometimes she would define the official record as "history," in opposition to the stories of those who are politically powerless. Dr. O'Connor is in the process of drawing such a distinction as he is introduced into *Nightwood*:

> "We may all be nature's noblemen," he was saying . . . "but think of the stories that do not amount to much! That is, that are forgotten in spite of all man remembers (unless he remembers himself) merely because they befell him without distinction of office or title—that's what we call legend and it's the best a poor man may do with his fate; the other . . . we call history, the best the high and mighty can do with theirs. Legend is unexpurgated, but history, because of its actors, is deflowered." (15)

Later in the same novel, the Doctor reverses his terms, describing all that is excluded from the record as "history" and the record itself as "faulty." He tells Felix that "Man is born as he dies, rebuking cleanliness," and identifies "cleanliness" with "neatness" and "conformity" as well as with the history of the official record: "So the reason for our cleanliness becomes apparent; cleanliness is a form of apprehension; our faulty racial memory is fathered by fear. Destiny and history are untidy; we fear memory of that disorder" (118).

Barnes could not be consistent about which of these aspects of history she identified as the true history, because her project was founded on a challenge to the idea of a limited "history proper." She did not need to be consistent in this respect, because both were necessary parts of her own stories, each requiring the other. The history of those marginalized or excluded by the official record is shaped by their relation to that record, as Felix Volkbein in *Nightwood* and Augusta in *The Antiphon* are obsessively concerned with their relations to history. At the same time the official record, "our faulty racial memory," the Doctor has explained, is only comprehensible in conjunction with what it fears and therefore marginalizes or excludes.

But this understanding of the official record was only a secondary effect of Barnes's stories. The idea of a definitive history figures so significantly, and at the same time there had to be at least two "histories" contending (whichever is defined as "history" at any given moment), so that she could establish the negative relation of those excluded to the official record. Barnes's understanding of the effect of exclusion from the record, despite the fact that the effect itself is negative, provided her with a means of gaining access to the position of recorder herself. She was concerned with the stories of those whose lives were not usually recorded; those stories included the experience of that exclusion. By taking on the possibility of writing about that experience of exclusion, Barnes was able to situate her own work relative to the official record, circumventing the initial fact of her subjects' historical and, by extension, literary disqualification.

Within this framework, she traced the overlapping social divisions between genders, classes, races, and sexual persuasions that mark the limits of the history of the official record. She identified those for whose benefit that history is written: the aristocracy, the military, Christians, fathers, heterosexuals. But her account of the "high and mighty" is strictly contingent. She focuses on those who are outside the circle of power that the official history bestows and legitimates: Jews, wives, daughters, gay men, and lesbians.

## II. "Impermissible Blood"

The story of Felix Volkbein functions as a paradigm of Barnes's understanding of the relation of the powerless to the record of the "high and mighty." From the first sentence of *Nightwood*, she establishes both the Jewishness of the child about to be born, and the fact of the historical persecution of the Jews. In the succeeding pages, the child's father, Guido Volkbein, is described as "an outcast" even in the arms of his Christian wife (3). His outcast status is only emphasized by his concern for his place in history, his manufactured genealogy and title, and his ancestral portraits that are really studies of a forgotten actor and actress. Felix inherits his father's place and his preoccupation: his race and his relation to history will be his two most important characteristics. Around the stories of Guido and Felix Volkbein Barnes constructs an account of the relation of Jews and Christians; she describes a subject people as historically marginalized by the social order that scorns them. To the extent that they enter the history of the official record it is as victims, for the entertainment of the dominant group. Guido remembers,

the ordinance of 1468, issued by one Pietro Barbo, demanding that, with a rope about its neck, Guido's race should run in the Corso for the amusement of the Christian populace, while ladies of noble birth, sitting upon spines too refined for rest, arose from their seats, and, with the red-gowned cardinals and the *Monsignori*, applauded with that cold yet hysterical abandon of a people that is at once unjust and happy, the very Pope himself shaken down from his hold on heaven with the laughter of a man who forgoes his angels that he may recapture the beast. (2)

Even "four centuries later," this history identifies Guido and his son as outsiders. It also contains a threat that is not confined to the past; the victims of this history have to be aware that "history" is never ended. So, although Felix appears to be committed to a definition of history that is tied to the past, the history of *anciens régimes*, his own continuing sense of disqualification, as a Jew, and his attempts to remedy that, reflect his functional sense of an ongoing history. Acting on that understanding, Felix devotes his life to the hope that he can overcome his "outcast" status through reverence for the history, Christian and aristocratic, that excludes him. Barnes describes such submission as necessary and even inevitable: she refers to "the degradation by which his people had survived," and "the genuflexion the hunted body makes from muscular contraction, going down before the impending and inaccessible, as before a great heat" (2–3). Felix is "heavy with impermissible blood" (3).

Barnes's invocation of this history of social marginality and its accompaniment of persecution at the beginning of *Nightwood* provides a framework within which the social positions of all of the characters in the novel are circumscribed: Frau Mann and the other circus performers; Matthew O'Connor, transvestite homosexual and doctor of dubious credentials; and the lesbians, Nora Flood, Robin Vote, and Jenny Petherbridge. Felix's position as a member of a group which appears in the history of the official record, even though only to be recorded as marginal and persecuted, offers a clarifying pattern. This pattern provides Barnes with a means of elaborating her account of the parallel but more complex disqualification of her lesbian and gay characters from that record, and at the same time connecting them to its history. With the bridge provided by the paradigm of Felix's story, their part of the "story of the world" can also be recorded.

She uses Jewish history and the relation of Jews to the dominant Christian culture to suggest something for which there was then almost no trace of a record, the history of lesbians and homosexual men. Such a connection between the experience of Jews and that of homosexuals was not without its historical precedents. *Nightwood* indicates that Barnes was aware of the parallel between anti-Semitism and hostility toward gays in the European social context in which she was living and writing.[6] Proust's work provides a literary precedent for *Nightwood*. J.E. Rivers has argued that *A la recherche du temps perdu* (1913–1929) is structured around a parallel between Jewish and homosexual experience within a society dominated by Christianity and heterosexuality and hostile to both minorities.[7] Proust explicitly compared the social and historical experiences of Jews and gays in the first part of *Sodome et Gomorrhe* (1921), using Jewish stereotypes and history as analogies to illustrate his account of homosexuality.[8] Cather and Stein both drew on these connections. Barnes was familiar with Proust's work, and was particularly interested in his writing about homosexuality.[9] In *Nightwood*, her account of the relation of Jews to the dominant culture, expressed through their relation to the history of that culture, is completely interwoven with her account of her lesbian and gay characters. When Guido Volkbein is described as "an outcast," when she refers to Felix's "impermissible blood" (3), these terms must also be credited to Barnes's history of the Doctor, Robin Vote, and Nora Flood. The story of Guido and Felix Volkbein and their obsession with history is thus integral to *Nightwood*, not in real or false competition with, but as a contribution to the central concern with Robin and Nora.[10]

Both women are explicitly located outside the history of the official record. Barnes concludes her only extended description of Nora with the observation that "the world and its history were to Nora like a ship in a bottle; she herself was outside and unidentified" (53). Felix observes Robin after their marriage: "He felt that her attention, somehow in spite of him, had already been taken by something not yet in history. Always she seemed to be listening to the echo of some foray in the blood that had no known setting" (44). The explanation of a "foray in the blood" to which Robin is listening recalls Felix's "impermissible blood," the cargo of the "hunted body," and is also implicitly a sexual suggestion. The official record has "no . . . setting" for these women because they are lesbians.

At the same time they are both framed by historical trappings, from Nora's salon, where "early American history was being re-enacted" (51), to the antique cloth from which Robin initially has her dresses made. This is in part Barnes's acknowledgment of the fundamental paradox of their relation to history, as outsiders whose stories are nevertheless being recorded. It is also an indication within the text of her consciousness of dependence on the official history that these trappings all invoke, the necessity of establishing some relation to that record in order to be recorded. She makes this point overtly as part of her explanation of Felix, arguing that Jews only exist in a Christian-dominated society as outcasts from, and at the same time dependents on, the religion and therefore the history that denies them:

> A Jew's undoing is never his own, it is God's; his rehabilitation is never his own, it is a Christian's. The Christian traffic in retribution has made the Jew's history a commodity; it is the medium through which he receives, at the necessary moment, the serum of his own past that he may offer it again as his blood. In this manner the Jew participates in the two conditions; and in like manner Felix took the breast of this wet nurse whose milk was his being but which could never be his birthright. (10)

Christian control of Jewish history is a function of the politics of cultural domination. But given this, Felix's relation to history, even though it is negative, is the necessary basis for his existence within the dominant culture, and by extension, the only means through which his story can be told within that culture. Similarly, the fact that Robin and Nora's story can be told at all is contingent on a relation to the official record, in this case the relation that Barnes establishes within her own text, superficially with historical trappings, but critically through the framework of Jewish history.

Felix's relation to history is also a focus for the inevitable tensions within this project. As Nora and Robin can only be brought into the record by analogy with those who are officially recognized as marginal and potentially persecuted, they will also be locked into that role. The contradiction within this marginal position is acted out to its conclusion within the novel by Felix. His gestures of reverence toward "history," toward those individuals and institutions legitimized by the official record, become the definitive sign of his own disqualification from that history.

Barnes was also aware of the implications of the actions she recorded for her own practice. The glimpse of Jewish history that we are given at the beginning of the novel—Guido's memory of the fifteenth century—indicates more than the persecution of the Jews which is, paradoxically, the means by which they enter the dominant history. As a graphic image of the fate of those outcasts whose stories are partially recorded (objects of ridicule whose pain is entertaining to those whom history routinely secures), it also serves as an expression of the anxiety about the result of her own record that pervades Barnes's text.

At the beginning of *Nightwood*, she says of Felix, "He felt that the great past might mend a little if he bowed low enough, if he succumbed and gave homage" (9). The original title for the whole of *Nightwood* had been "Bow Down."[11] That became, instead, the title of the opening chapter, which is predominantly Felix's story. It is an explicit reference to Felix's abasement before the history of the official record. It also recalls the experience of the "hunted body" that made such abasement inevitable. That Barnes was willing to consider a description of abasement as representative of the novel is indicative of the anxiety at the center of *Nightwood*. Barnes's fundamental defiance of "history" is accompanied by her own consciousness of the "hunted body." Felix Volkbein, with his "impermissible blood," provides a paradigm for the relation of the author, as well as her characters, to the official record. Barnes's apprehension of the meanings, the effects, and history's interpretation of her own insistence on the place of these stories in the record can be seen behind her clear account of the abasement that Felix accepts in order to establish his own relation to history and thus his existence. This is an apprehension that echoes also in *The Antiphon*, where Dudley describes Miranda as a child:

> You had her so convinced she was the devil,
> At seven, she was cutting down the hedges,
> To furnish brier to beat her to your favour;
> All time since, been hunting for her crime. (164)

Augusta responds later in the play with the charge against her daughter, "She gives her weapons to the enemy" (162).

These images of humiliation, these charges and countercharges, are the expression of an anxiety based on history in the most concrete sense. If you announce your "impermissible blood," your "disqualification," to the world, perhaps especially in the process of asserting your right to a record, to history, then you are telling those whose power history always confirms where to find you. Such a consciousness would hardly have been excessive in the Europe of the 1930s. Given that Barnes was recording experience that was historically condemned, it is not possible to separate the conditions of her writing from history. But she was also faced with specifically literary difficulties: the narrative disenfranchisement of the lesbian writer, the absence of literary conventions for writing about lesbianism as other than deviance, as well as the fundamental prohibition against the subject that that absence represented. By choosing to locate her writing explicitly within the framework of history, she was then able to deal with those literary difficulties as well as the political situation they reflect, by translating them from literary into historical problems, and shifting the burden from her own shoulders onto her characters. The marginality of the Jews within the history of a Christian-dominated society, and the conflict that could generate in people required to humiliate themselves in order to survive, was more accessible as a subject to writer and readers than the exclusion of homosexuals from a heterosexist history, the social and political humiliation exacted from lesbians if they are to survive. Also, the exclusions, persecutions, and humiliations of political and social history were easier to map than the exclusions, persecutions, and humiliations reflected in or required by literary history and conventions: the difficulties of political/historical survival are easier to record than the difficulties of writing. But the anxiety within Barnes's text reflects the difficulty of her literary as well as her historical situation.

The pervasive connection between literature and history operating within *Nightwood* appears on the most superficial level in the number of historical references that are also literary references: Helen of Troy and Catherine of Russia are touchstones of equal value. But the actual link is forged through Barnes's interchangeable use of "history" and "stories," which leads into a refrain of statements about "telling" and its conditions. The Doctor's initial discussion of history in *Nightwood* is about stories, "stories that do not amount to much" because they befall people who may be "nature's noblemen" but who are not history's aristocrats. In the Doctor's final speeches, when he seems to be making a narrator's apology despite the fact that he is not the narrator, he defends the alternative histories Barnes has recorded before an imaginary "normal" audience who, he assumes, would scorn and ridicule his friends: "Only the scorned and the ridiculous make good stories . . . so you can imagine when you'll get told!" (159). He denies that his record is a betrayal in the same terms: "Nora, beating her head against her heart . . . rotten to the bone for love of Robin. . . . And that old sandpiper, Jenny! Oh, it's a grand bad story, and who says I'm a betrayer? I say, tell the story of the world to the world!" (161). On the one hand, the insistent references to telling implicitly deny the fact that the story is being written. They also make the Doctor's self-defense possible: "I wouldn't be telling you about it if I weren't talking to myself" (162). The implied refusal to acknowledge the permanence of the record that is being made is inextricable from the anxiety also expressed in the references to scorn, ridicule, and betrayal. This apprehension is produced by the telling of the story itself, as well as the real pain that is the subject of the story. It is this anxiety that ultimately underscores the fact that the record is irreversible, the story is being told "to the world," that is, being written.

Anxiety about the stories being told, about her own challenging of history, especially as expressed through the Doctor's framing statements, is more than a self-conscious context within the text for the production of its alternative record. This conflict about whether these stories should be told is part of the story Barnes records, in *Nightwood* and also in *The Antiphon*. The question of history, the record, incorporating both history and writing, is in both works a framework and also a central concern of the texts.

Toward the conclusion of *Nightwood*, Dr. O'Connor argues with Nora's grief: "If you, who are blood-thirsty with love, had left her alone, what? Would a lost girl in Dante's time have been a lost girl still, and he had turned his eyes on her? She would have been remembered, and the remembered put on the dress of immunity. Do you think that Robin had no right to fight you with her only weapon? She saw in you that fearful eye that would make her a target forever" (148). Barnes is referring to history, Dante's time, by means of a literary figure. As Dante was a writer, the implied connection between his having seen the lost girl and her being remembered is that he would have written about her. The conclusion is that to have been recorded by Dante, and so to become part of the official literature and history he represents, would be to become immune, safe. But safe from what? The fact that immunity is described as a dress is indicative. The lost girl, Robin, described elsewhere as a "girl with the body of a boy" (46), would have been certified as heterosexual, as the object of a male poet's gaze. The shift in the center of the passage, to the negative fate that Nora's love for Robin implies, is the shift from the safety of being recorded as a heterosexual love object to the prospect of being loved, and recorded, by a woman, being made a "target forever" by a woman's gaze.

There is an underlying ambiguity: the distinction between the possibility of being remembered/recorded by Dante and by Nora/Barnes is not clear-cut.

Dante is the poet of heterosexual love, the *Vita Nuova*, but also the poet of religious and social judgment, the *Divina Commedia*. As such, he represents a literature and a history that are strictly ordered, and are based throughout on an elaborate system of reward and damnation, of which one of the subjects is sexual behavior. Dante, seeing a lost *girl*, might have made her Beatrice, the object of his love poetry, forever narrowly and safely defined. Or, seeing a *lost* girl, he might have remembered her only to record her as a lesbian, a sinner, making her a "target forever" in the appropriate circle of Hell. The question of which gaze, which record, would damn or save a woman, remains unanswered. But it is clear that being made part of a lesbian record is "fearful." The Doctor is pointing to a struggle between Nora and Robin over the question of whether or not there would be a record, and is indicating that that struggle was fundamental to the destruction of their relationship and so to the story Barnes is recording.

Yet the question of a record is only presented indirectly in this passage, through the reference to a writer. And instead of saying explicitly that Dante would have desired and then written about the lost girl, and in his writing secured her reputation, Barnes uses the term "remembered" to indicate both the desire and the record. Throughout this passage Barnes equates the gaze, "looking at her," with memory, memory with love, and love and memory with writing, being remembered with being both loved and recorded.

"Memory" subsumes both history and literature, becoming the material of history and the means of writing. Barnes's anxiety about writing is worked out within her stories through the values of remembering and forgetting, and the conflicts between them. The Doctor does not say that the stories of the common people will not be written into history, he says they will be forgotten. The stories of the "high and mighty" will also not explicitly be written, they will be remembered. He tells us that we fear "memory" of the "disorder" of "destiny and history" (118). The history of the official record becomes "our faulty racial memory" (118). Doctor O'Connor initially declares that the only effort that can be made against exclusion from history is individual, to remember oneself.

Memory is the basis of Djuna Barnes's attempt to challenge the history of the official record, the source of the alternative stories she is recording. Memory is the fundamental mode of her texts themselves: *Nightwood* and *The Antiphon* are in part Barnes's personal acts of memory. She was writing against the absorption of her own history into the simple negatives that are used to define a woman without a man—the voice of the son and brother in *The Antiphon* who decries his sister Miranda as a "Manless, childless, safeless document" (179). Memory is also an action taken by characters within the text, especially Nora in *Nightwood* and Miranda in *The Antiphon*.

As Barnes's history has little relation to the conventional distinctions between past and present, Barnes's memory has no usual relation to forgetting. Augusta declares in *The Antiphon*, "I would be Helen/ Forgotten, day by day, for ever and for ever!" (207). In *Nightwood* the Doctor explains to Nora, "because you forget Robin the best, it's to you she turns. She comes trembling, and defiant, and belligerent, all right—that you may give her back to herself again as you have forgotten her" (152–153). But Helen is manifestly not forgotten. And Nora has just been telling the Doctor that her love means she cannot forget Robin: "Robin can go anywhere, do anything . . . because she forgets, and I nowhere because I remember" (152). Memory encompasses forgetting, because a person or story has to come within the frame of memory before they/it can be forgotten. To remember is the definitive gesture, because memory, identified with both history and writing, shares attributes of both. It functions like the history of the official record to the extent that whatever is outside the range of memory might as well not exist. It is necessary to come within the range of memory, as it is necessary to come or be brought into the range of history. At the same time, memory is synonymous with writing. Because of the potential historical seriousness of any record, Barnes is very aware that what has been written cannot be unwritten, as what is remembered cannot be forgotten in the sense that it could be beyond recall or consequence.

Memory is a source of conflict, between Robin and Nora in *Nightwood*, and between Augusta and Miranda in *The Antiphon*. Nora remembered Robin, which meant remembering her drunkenness and nighttime world as well as their love. After Robin has gone, Nora tells the Doctor, "She turned bitter because I made her fate colossal. She wanted darkness in her mind—to throw a shadow over what she was powerless to alter—her dissolute life, her life at night; and I, I dashed it down" (156). In *The Antiphon*, the ostensible source of the conflict between Augusta and Miranda is the daughter's denial of the mother's false version of history in general and family history in particular. When the facts of Miranda's childhood are revealed, Augusta curses: "Wolves! Mountebanks! Historians!" (186).

Memory is such a source of conflict because it bears the weight of writing, of history as record. It is the connection between the events within the text and the construction of the text. So when Robin fights Nora or Augusta resists Miranda, it is in part because of the written record that is pending, that Nora and Miranda represent, couched in terms of memory. But memory is, as writing, a source of conflict chiefly because of what would be remembered/written, which is the other attribute of memory, love. Robin might not want her drunkenness recorded. Augusta has reason to want the story of her husband's cruelty to her daughter suppressed. But it is not Robin's alcoholism which, recorded, will make her a "target forever." Augusta, struggling against Miranda's knowledge of family history and Miranda's warnings about the murderous intentions of the sons her mother prefers to her daughter, is also struggling against her daughter's love. "Who's Miranda?" she asks: "I can't afford her/ She's only me" (162). This echoes Nora's explanation of love between women in the previous work: "A man is another person—a woman is yourself, caught as you turn in panic" (143). Nora is explicitly talking about love and sexuality: "a woman is yourself, caught as you turn in panic; on her mouth you kiss your own. If she is taken you cry that you have been robbed of yourself. God laughs at me, but his laughter is my love" (143). Memory is fought because it is the memory, the record of a love that can be described as God's laughter, that could make the lovers "scorned and . . . ridiculous" (159).

Memory, as an act of love, is a sexual act. Felix, talking of Robin's sexual attractiveness, comments, "The Baronin had an undefinable disorder, a sort of 'odour of memory,' like a person who has come from some place that we have forgotten and would give our life to recall" (118). Nora remembers and describes to the Doctor a specific scene: "and I knew in that bed Robin should have put me down. In that bed we would have forgotten our lives in the extremity of memory, moulted our parts, as figures in the waxworks are moulted down to their story, so we would have broken down to our love" (158). Memory becomes sex. The story becomes love. But the lovers are represented as figures in waxworks, that is, figures from history, historical characters. Memory is a sexual act, and the story that would have been remembered is a story of love that is identified with history.

## III.  "How Do We Thaw from History"

As a lesbian, Barnes had every reason to see a connection between sex and history. In the *Ladies Almanack*, she records in comic terms very real historical changes in social attitudes and sexual possibility for lesbians. She recounts how, in the 1920s, Dame Musset had almost to fight off women whom, in the 1880s, she would have had to coax and cajole into her embrace. The narrator laments that what was once a matter of secrecy and trembling is now talked abroad at every slightest opportunity. Although only part of any full account of the times, these observations indicate that the *Almanack* was grounded in an accurate historical understanding of lesbian experience. Decades later *The Antiphon*, with its account of the rape of the daughter ordered by the father and attended by the complicitous silence of the mother, suggests a very specific sexual secret at the heart of its history of the family.

The difference between the lesbian sexual assumption of the *Almanack* and the domination of heterosexuality in *The Antiphon* produced very different accounts of history and uses of history in each work. In the *Almanack*, the chronology of many years is inverted into the chronology of one year, the passage of time from the 1880s to the 1920s and from birth to death in Dame Musset's ninety-nine-year lifetime is recorded between January and the next December. Barnes then scatters through her text a lesbian genesis story that takes place after the fall of Satan, as well as references to such diverse historical locations as the Old Testament and colonial America. She also records changing attitudes toward lesbianism between the 1880s and the 1920s, while failing to mention World War I. But such disruptions of any official record of history are very distant from *The Antiphon*. Although Barnes was writing the latter in the late 1940s and early 1950s, it is very clearly located in the history of the official record by its setting at the beginning of World War II. This wartime setting is emphasized by the presence of passing refugees who are frequently referred to and occasionally directed to appear. The play begins when Miranda and Jack arrive as refugees themselves from the Nazi invasion of Paris. The house to which they have come, the immediate setting of the play, is described in detail as the historic family residence. Although the play is full of other references to history, it is the history of the official record: Tudors, Nazis, courtesans, and warriors.

In both the *Ladies Almanack* and *Nightwood*, Barnes had already identified the history of the official record as male. As already noted, the narrator of the *Almanack*, looking for a lesbian history, protests, "Were all Giants' doings a Man's. . . . No time without God, no end without Christ!" (70). At the beginning of *Nightwood*, the institutions of the official record—the aristocracy, the military, and Christianity—are temporarily embodied in the female figure of Hedvig Volkbein. But this has the effect of masculinizing the woman: "When she danced, a little heady with wine, the dance floor had become a tactical manoeuvre; her heels had come down staccato and trained, her shoulders as conscious at the tips as those which carry the braid and tassels of promotion; the turn of her head had held the cold vigilance of a sentry whose rounds are not without apprehension" (4). Her Jewish husband, Guido, sees that Hedvig "had the same bearing" as "a general in creaking leather," and "looking at the two he had become confused as if he were about to receive a reprimand, not the officer's, but his wife's" (4).

The oppositional relation of both the *Almanack* and *Nightwood* to the history of the official record, as well as such statements as the Doctor's that "history, because of its actors, is deflowered" (15), imply that that history is also heterosexual. By the time she wrote *The Antiphon*, Barnes was willing to identify heterosexuality and masculinity overtly with the history of the aristocracy, Christianity, and the military—the Nazis who had driven Miranda from Paris. Jack/Jeremy describes the war at the beginning of the play in terms of an attack on the histories of Barnes's previous works:

> I expect to see myopic conquerors
> With pebbled monocles and rowel'd heels,
> In a damned and horrid clutch of gluttony
> Dredging the Seine of our inheritance.
> Or dragging from the Tiber and the Thames
> Cruppers, bridles, bits and casket handles,

> Rocking-horses, sabres from the fair.
> Trawling the Hellespont for log and legend
> And all things whatsoever out of grasp. (91)

"Legend" is one of the terms the Doctor uses in *Nightwood* to describe the stories of those who are excluded from the history of the "high and mighty." Carousel horses, "rocking-horses . . . from the fair," are part of the furnishings of the house that Nora and Robin create as a monument to their love (55).

In *The Antiphon*, this war is enacted within the family. Masculinity and heterosexuality are united with history in the person of the father. Augusta makes this identification explicit when she sees the image of Titus, her husband, reduced to a doll figure, and is able to indulge in a moment of temporary repudiation:

> How do we thaw from history. How many
> To this splinter have, like porcupines,
> Made careful love? What apes our eyes were
> Saw him great because he said so. (183)

The act of accepting this history is sexual. That is illustrated in the course of the play by Augusta. Her position relative to the history of the official record is parallel to that of Felix in *Nightwood*; like Felix, she is obsessed with her relation to history, and unable to recognize the humiliation this forces on her. She "would be Helen," "Empress Josephine," or "Lily Langtry . . . Waiting on the inert Prince of Somewhere" (199). Her sexual relation, real or fantasy, with the "Prince of Somewhere," is a heterosexual woman's claim on history. When her daughter remains obdurately skeptical, Augusta becomes only more frantic in her reconstructions:

> Never checked a victor's knobs and bosses
> On any field of any Marathon?
> Nor never, in great joy, kissed on the mouth
> By a mouth deposed between me and the kissing? (200)

Miranda comments on the futility of Augusta's history, summarizing all of the roles her mother imagines, and uniting them with the domestic service that is their corollary: "O unhappy wanderer—/ I've seen you dig for Antony/ With a kitchen spoon" (200).

In *The Antiphon*, the opposition to that history of the official record finally vested in the father and his sexual authority (to which the mother's sexual submission is tribute) is carried on by the dissident daughter.[12] The fact that the father is dead only reinforces the lesson of his power, as the authority he embodied and the patterns of male power and female submission it created are replicated, even in his absence, in the relations of his wife and sons, and their joint rejection of the daughter. The absence of the father also makes it clear that the mother is the ground of the daughter's struggle. In this context, the lesson at the center of history becomes the first lesson the daughter learns, and it is a sexual lesson, that of her father's favored access to her mother, and her own female inferiority. Her own existence is proof of the first part of this lesson. The proof of its corollary is that the mother will never be for her. Unlike the Freudian daughter, this girl-child does not agree to transfer her desire from her mother to her father. Unlike the Freudian son, waiting until adulthood will not change her situation, will not provide her with a wife/mother of her own. "History" begins with the heterosexual "facts of life." So history, whether explicitly identified with the father or not, is the first and ultimate antagonist, and the battle—to love, to remember, to write—is inescapably within history, and always in part a sexual contest.

## IV. "From Where, Say You, Come Such Women?"

When Bounding Bess in the *Ladies Almanack* and Robin Vote in *Nightwood* look to the women of history, even women they have "come to connect with women" (*Nightwood*, 47), as Barnes explains the quality that attracts Robin's attention, most of the women they look to are renowned as heterosexual lovers. That Sappho, "singing over the limp Bodies of Girls" (*Ladies Almanack*, 32), is the only obviously appropriate model recalled, seems to predicate Barnes's own defeat, to lead directly to Augusta's "kitchen spoon" and the lesson of the father's sexual authority in *The Antiphon*.

Barnes was not, however, defeated by the limits of the official record. As her presentation of both Sappho and Catherine of Russia, "twittering over a Man at ten" (32), as models for Bounding Bess suggests, she did not maintain a distinction between female sexuality and specifically lesbian sexuality. Despite the fact that the ladies of the *Ladies Almanack* are indirectly referred to as women "born with a Difference" (26), one such explains:

> "from where, say you, come such Women? Up from the Cellar, down from the Bed of Matrimony, under Sleep and over come. Past watching Eye and seeking Hand and well over Hedge. From Pantry and Bride's-sleep, in Mid-conception and in old Age, from Bank and Culvert, from Bog's Dutch and Fen's marrow, from all walks and all paths, from round Doors and drop Lofts, from Hayricks and Cabbage-patch, from King's Thrones and Clerks' Stools, from high Life and from low. . . . Indeed, some of all sorts, to swarm in that wide Acre where, beside some brawling March, the first of shes turned up a Hem with the Hand of Combat."

"Too true for you, perchance," admitted her Love. "But nevertheless, did not some and several return to their Posts?" "Indeed, and a few . . . but *how*!" (53–54)

Because such women can come "from the Bed of Matrimony," the mother retains a powerful promise. In *Nightwood*, Robin chooses the apartment she and Nora will live in in Paris, it is implied, because, "Looking from the long windows one saw a fountain figure, a tall granite woman bending forward with lifted head; one hand was held over the pelvic round as if to warn a child who goes incautiously" (55). Perhaps to redeem the mother would be to redeem all of the women of history, Helen, Cleopatra, and Catherine. So Miranda struggles with her mother even as Barnes illustrates, through Augusta's continuing hostility to her daughter, the strength of her father's power.

Barnes's writing is predicated on such contradictions. She records for history what she acknowledges is not part of history, insists on remembering what she defines as the forgotten. She incorporates the potential denial of her texts into the texts themselves. She subverts her own recognition of the limits and conditions of history and literature. Dr. O'Connor confronts Nora with the contrast between the security that Dante's heterosexual gaze would convey, and the fearful fate that her own lesbian gaze implies, for the lost girl, Robin. But this lesson is undercut finally because the Doctor, Matthew-Mighty-grain-of-salt-Dante-O'-Connor, is also Dante himself, and this Dante does assume the role of narrator within the text. As in H.D.'s *HERmione*, the debate has been decided in that the story is being recorded. Such contradictions are necessary because contradiction is fundamental to Barnes's work. As she acknowledged in the *Ladies Almanack*, she was writing stories that "could be printed nowhere and in no Country" (34). In *Nightwood* the Doctor insists, "Life is not to be told, call it as loud as you like, it will not tell itself" (129). Yet her stories were told and were printed.[13]

The author herself is finally in a contradictory relationship to such work. Barnes made a gesture toward anonymity: the title page of the *Ladies Almanack* bears the legend, "By a Lady of Fashion." But as she began her alternative history of the love between Nora Flood and Robin Vote, she wrote of Robin, "Two spirits were working in her, love and anonymity" (55). The logic and the tension of this pairing—"love and anonymity"—depend on history, the prohibition against lesbianism. They also depend on Barnes's own identification of love, by means of memory, with writing. If love must be written, the writer is faced with the difficulties of writing this love, and at the same time with the danger of losing the beloved, a beloved "fearful" of being made a "target forever" within history. If love and anonymity are set in opposition, for the beloved—by the connections between love, memory, and writing—they are also opposed for the lover/writer. Loving and therefore remembering and writing love inevitably bring the lover/writer back to telling the self. There is the fear that the only response will be scorn and ridicule, or alternatively that history will respond. As the Doctor, brought to bay, declares, "And what am I? I'm damned, and carefully public!" (163).

As Barnes's connection of writing and loving may cost the writer her beloved, the difficulties of writing, behind the tension between love and anonymity, are also the difficulties of loving. So, in *Nightwood*, memory is an attempt to hold love. Nora's last message to Robin is, as she advises the Doctor, "Tell her, if you ever see her, that it is always with her in my arms—forever it will be that way until we die. Tell her to do what she must, but not to forget" (150). From the beginning of their love, Barnes records, "Robin . . . kept repeating . . . her wish for a home, as if she were afraid she would be lost again, as if she were aware, without conscious knowledge, that she belonged to Nora, and that if Nora did not make it permanent by her own strength, she would forget" (55). This need is reemphasized by the Doctor's delivery of Robin's last message: "She says, . . . 'Remember me.' Probably because she has difficulty in remembering herself" (121). Barnes records this history to make it easier for the lesbian Robin to remember herself.

\* \* \*

The connection between sexuality and history that Barnes eventually elaborated was starkly presented in an early story, "Cassation":

> A great war painting hung over the bed; the painting and the bed ran together in encounter, the huge rumps of the stallions reined into the pillows. The generals, with foreign helmets and dripping swords, raging through rolling smoke and the bleeding ranks of the dying, seemed to be charging the bed, so large, so rumpled, so devastated. The sheets were trailing, the counterpane hung torn, and the feathers shivered along the floor, trembling in the slight wind from the open window.[14]

By the beginning of *Nightwood*, the bed has itself become a battlefield, on which Hedvig Volkbein, exhausted by struggling against the unspoken alienation of her "outcast" Jewish husband, gives birth to the son who will carry on his father's struggle with history:

> a canopied bed of a rich spectacular crimson, the valance stamped with the bifurcated wings of the House of Hapsburg, the feather coverlet an envelope of satin on which, in massive and tarnished gold threads, stood the Volkbein arms. . . . Turning upon this field, which shook to the clatter of morning horses in the street beyond, with the gross splendour of a general saluting the flag, she named [the child] Felix, thrust him from her, and died. (1)

In Barnes's last major work, *The Antiphon*, Miranda is given a bed made from a carousel car and shaped like a mythical animal, a gryphon. Her mother—

refusing to deny the father, denying instead Miranda's account of history—will neither let her sleep there, nor make love to her. Across that bed the women, struggling, die.

Earlier in the play Barnes had drawn on an echo of *King Lear*:

Augusta:   You won't even tell me how you are, or what.
Miranda:   Trappist—sprung—and of an hard-won silence.
Augusta:   Nothing else about your history?
Miranda:   Nothing.
Augusta:   Nothing at all?
Miranda:   Nothing at all. (202–203)

Lear asked his daughter for a protestation of her love for him, which she refused to make. Augusta, asking for Miranda's history, is also asking for an avowal of her love, as her "history" is her love for women, the lesbian memory never spoken in this play. What the mother expects is a statement of love for the father. What she cannot hear is a statement of love for herself. In their final struggle, Augusta accuses her daughter: "I know you. You are the one would lay/ Me ticking down, ten cities deep!" (222). To be laid "ticking" down, to be buried alive, is the fate of Antigone. Ten cities deep is the site of the history of Helen of Troy. To be buried alive beneath a myth is the fate of women within the history of the official record, the history of the father. Miranda denies that history, offering instead an alternative sexual fate as an alternative history. "Nay, sparrow," she protests, "I'd lay you in the journey of your bed,/ And unbed you, and I could, in paradise" (222).

# 5

# Virginia Woolf and the Sexual Histories of Literature

## I. "The Retreat from Moscow" / "The Charm of a Woman"

Gertrude Stein invokes Napoleon's retreat from Moscow in her anecdotes about cannon, history, and representation. Virginia Woolf invokes "the retreat from Moscow" at a paradigmatic moment in *Mrs. Dalloway* (1925), when this history is offered as an alternative to heterosexuality.[1] After Clarissa Dalloway returns from her June morning walk through London's West End, observing the city, ordering the flowers for her party that evening, "Like a nun withdrawing, or a child exploring a tower, she went upstairs" to "the heart of life; an attic room" where "The sheets were clean, tight stretched in a broad white band from side to side. Narrower and narrower would her bed be. The candle was half burnt down and she had read deep in Baron Marbot's *Memoirs*. She had read late at night of the retreat from Moscow."[2] Clarissa would rather read about the retreat from Moscow than have sex with her husband: "really she preferred to read of the retreat from Moscow. He knew it" (35–36). Their sexual relationship has never been consequential: "a virginity preserved through childbirth ... clung to her like a sheet" (36). Some critics—Jane Marcus, Sandra Gilbert, and Susan Gubar—have claimed this "virginity" as the sign of a valuable independence.[3] But Woolf presents it as a matter of failure: "Lovely in girlhood, suddenly there came a moment—for example on the river beneath the woods at Clieveden—when, through some contraction of this cold spirit, she had failed him. And then at Constantinople, and again and again" (36).[4] Moreover, this "virginity" is—as most understandings of virginity are—strictly heterosexual.

Clarissa articulates her disinterest in heterosexuality as a preference for history. But Woolf goes on to suggest that lesbianism is either another alternative to both heterosexuality and history, or the true content of this "history." "[C]ontrasted" with "the bed and Baron Marbot and the candle half-burnt" (37), are Clarissa's sexual responses to other women: "she could not resist sometimes yielding to the charm of a woman, not a girl, of a woman confessing, as to her they often did, some scrape, some folly. And whether it was pity, or their beauty, or that she was older, or some accident—like a faint scent, or a violin next door . . . she did undoubtedly then feel what men felt" (36). Woolf draws on the structure of the lesbian novel by having Clarissa feel "what men felt," momentarily framing her within the heterosexual plot to confirm the sexual nature of her responses. This framing is reinforced when Clarissa, however unwillingly, contrasts her understanding of the "cold contact of man and woman, . . . [and] women together. For *that* she could dimly perceive. She resented it, had a scruple picked up Heaven knows where, or, as she felt, sent by Nature (who is invariably wise); yet she could not resist" (36). And despite her "scruple" she moves immediately on from sex to "this question of love . . . this falling in love with women," and an account of the passion for Sally Seton that, after three decades, still remains her most vivid memory: "Had not that, after all, been love?" (37).

Although Woolf uses the history represented by Baron Marbot's *Memoirs* to mediate between her representations of Clarissa's heterosexual failure and lesbian desire, Clarissa's sexual responses to women, like her passion for Sally Seton, are not "history." Critics who acknowledge the possibility of lesbianism in *Mrs. Dalloway* almost invariably limit Clarissa's response to women to Sally Seton, to the past. Clarissa does disavow her own experience in Woolf's brilliant portrait of a woman unable to accept and therefore to interpret her own desire. But this novel echoes the lesbian novels of its period (and gay novels such as Woolf's friend E. M. Forster's *Maurice*); not only is Clarissa's response to women figured, however briefly, as masculinizing her, but her sexuality is represented as an impulse independent of her social self. She might "resent" but cannot "resist." She still "sometimes yield[s]" to the "charm" of other women. Napoleon's "retreat from Moscow" has been read here, by Elizabeth Abel, as a metaphor for what can then be understood as Clarissa's icy withdrawal from heterosexuality.[5] But why identify Clarissa with Napoleon? The "retreat from Moscow" was a long-drawn-out and bitter defeat for the great man, suggesting the vulnerability of great men and the authoritative narratives they represent—a vulnerability demonstrated when they can be pressed into the service of accounts of lesbian desire.

Napoleon appears repeatedly in Woolf's accounts of "the public and the private worlds . . . inseparably connected; . . . the tyrannies and servilities of the one . . . the tyrannies and servilities of the other."[6] In *A Room of One's Own* (1929), after arguing that "Women have served all these centuries as looking-glasses possessing the magic and delicious power of reflecting the figure of man at twice its natural size," she moves immediately from the individual to the state, by way of "Napoleon and Mussolini [who] both insist so emphatically upon the inferiority of women."[7] "What was the great Napoleon like?" is the kind of question Mr. Ramsay and his friends, authoritative "old gentlemen," Oxford and Cambridge men, can answer in *To the Lighthouse* (1927).[8] In *The Years* (1937), completing this pattern, it is their inability to understand "the psychology of great men" such as Napoleon that is the sign of Nicholas's and Eleanor's social marginality as, respectively, a gay "foreigner," and an aging, unmarried, upper-middle-class Englishwoman.[9] But Nicholas continues to assert, and Eleanor to agree, that this question—"What Napoleon was like," "the psychology of great men"—is important, that it is somehow related to the possibility of "know[ing] ourselves," and so to reshaping public and private lives, to "mak[ing] religions, laws, that . . . fit, that fit" (281). The history Napoleon represents is an inescapable source of social, psychological, and narrative authority. But Woolf's use of the "retreat from Moscow" in *Mrs. Dalloway* reflects her ability to exploit this history that her more vulnerable characters find intractable.

After more than two decades of feminist literary criticism, within which Woolf has served as a central—even an iconic—figure, narrative, history, and lesbianism have all been the focus of discussions of her writing. Rachel DuPlessis has plotted Woolf's rejection of the heterosexual plot. More recently, Pamela Caughie, in the cause of postmodernism, has reemphasised her ongoing commitment to narrative.[10] Others have expanded on Jane Marcus's description of Woolf as "a writer whose first impulse was to be an historian."[11] In *Virginia Woolf and the Real World*, Alex Zwerdling offers a detailed account of Woolf's use of historical detail, in an attempt to rescue her from a feminist criticism he posits as ahistorical. Feminist critics Sandra Gilbert and Susan Gubar have more recently argued for a division in Woolf's account of history, between "masculine" public and "feminine" private realms.[12] Woolf's representations of lesbianism have been read as responses to the problem of the heterosexual plot, or responses to specific biographical events that resulted in specific texts.[13] Elizabeth Abel has brought together a number of these critical developments, offering the most extensive account of narrative, history, and sexuality in Woolf's writing to date, in her *Virginia Woolf and the Fictions of Psychoanalysis*. She assimilates Woolf's narratives to "the Oedipal story . . . Freud's preeminent fiction of engendering" (4–5). Although she reads Woolf as rewriting Freud, as "pluralizing history," she reads this plural history as merely double and strictly gendered, as a fictional version of "Freud['s] radically gendered developmental narrative, decisively split between a maternal prehistory and a paternal history" (8). Lesbianism becomes a stage in a plot of female development that turns out to look just like the heterosexual plot.[14]

Woolf has still not been read broadly as a lesbian writer. As noted in my introduction, it was she who rejected the literary repetition of "Tom and Judith, Judith and Tom." She proposed Chloe's liking for Olivia as a new subject for women's fiction, but "Are girls necessary?" was also, after all, her question. Her discussion of Chloe and Olivia in *A Room of One's Own* reflects the difficulty of separating public and private when representing a "personal" that is not heterosexual. For this reason, neither Woolf's narratives most broadly nor her uses of history more specifically can be easily assimilated to a story of personal and/or gendered development. If lesbianism is treated as a factor in its own right, and if the crucial relation of Woolf's histories to her representations of lesbians and gay men is taken into account, her histories cannot be read as simply double, as they are not simply gendered. The point of connection between Woolf's narratives, histories, and lesbianism, as is increasingly foregrounded in her fiction in the later 1920s and the 1930s, is "writing"—representation itself. It is not possible to offer full readings of Woolf's complex novels here. I will however consider her representation of "history," and the relations among her use of this history, her representations of lesbians and gay men, and "writing" as a subject of her fiction, discussing *Mrs. Dalloway* (and Abel's account of that novel) in some detail. This chapter will conclude with a reading of Woolf's last novel, *Between the Acts* (1941), in which all of these aspects of her writing, and all of the terms of this study, come together.

## II. "Men in Clubs and Cabinets" / Middle-Class Women Who Write

As for Cather, Renault, and Stein, history becomes crucial in Woolf's writing as she abandons the heterosexual plot, in her case in her third novel, her first extensively experimental work, *Jacob's Room* (1922).[15] In the pattern that Cather was employing at the same time in *One of Ours*, the history of World War I provides a structural and interpretive frame for an individual story.[16] Woolf's "hero" Jacob Flanders's fate on a Great War battlefield and the potential meanings of his life are both already marked in his name.[17] In this novel, Woolf represents the history to which she has turned for narrative structure as compounded of authority and violence. It is the work of "the men in clubs and Cabinets," and in particular "sixteen gentlemen, lifting their pens or turning perhaps rather wearily in their chairs, [who] decreed that the course of history should shape itself this way or that." This history is identified with order: they are "manfully determined . . . to impose some coherency . . . to control the course of events."[18] Their desire for control encompasses the British empire and World War I, "Rajahs and Kaisers." It produces:

> battleships ray[ed] out over the North Sea, keeping their stations accurately apart. . . . guns . . . trained on a target which . . . flames into splinters. With equal nonchalance a dozen young men in the prime of life descend with composed faces into the depths of the sea; and there

impassively (though with perfect mastery of machinery) suffocate un-
complainingly together. (147–148)

When these descendants of "Pitt and Chatham, Burke and Gladstone" (164)
are not "manfully" sending young men to their deaths, they are dismissing literature, "character drawing," in gendered terms, as "a frivolous fireside art, a
matter of pins and needles, exquisite outlines enclosing vacancy, flourishes,
and mere scrawls" (147); "we live, they say, driven by an unseizable force. They
say that the novelists never catch it; that it goes hurtling through their nets and
leaves them torn to ribbons" (148).

The "unseizable force" of these men could be neatly contrasted with
Woolf's modest proposal, in *A Room of One's Own*, for a "supplement to history . . . call[ed] . . . of course, by some inconspicuous name so that women
might figure there without impropriety" (78).[19] But Woolf undoes any easy
opposition between masculine and feminine, public and private histories, with
her alternative, far-from-modest proposal, also in *A Room*, for rewriting English history to the advantage of women and novelists, to give proper weight to
"a change" in the late eighteenth century "which . . . I should describe more
fully and think of greater importance than the Crusades or the Wars of the
Roses. The middle-class woman began to write" (112). Woolf would repay the
scorn of "the men in clubs and Cabinets" for literature and women by replac-
ing them in the history of events with literary women.[20]

For Woolf—as indicated by her interest, in *Jacob's Room*, in what the "men
in clubs and Cabinets" have to say about novelists—"history" is always as
much literature as battlefields, as much women as men. As for Stein, for Woolf
"history" had also became a lens through which to "explain" the literary. She
put literature into history in *A Room of One's Own*, not only by proposing to
rewrite history, but by offering a material analysis of English literature based
on English history, the distribution of money, class distinctions, and gender
politics. She went on to develop her identification of literature and history in
*Orlando* and *Between the Acts*, in both of which narrative structure is supplied
by a history of England represented as a history of English literature, and both
of which are focused on ambiguously gendered "women" writers. This development indicates the extent to which her interrelation of literature and history
is related to lesbian representation. That her putting literature into history val-
idates women writing is clear enough: a woman did not write the plays of
Shakespeare, she demonstrates famously in *A Room*, not because women lack
literary genius, but because of history. But it is also crucial for the lesbian
writer that literature and history be interrelated, as she will demonstrate in
*Between the Acts*.

In the meantime, the emphasis on history as written in *A Room* produced
two other accounts of history to compete with the threat and the terror of the
"unseizable force." There is that history as a discourse, a narrative of events,

that she draws on in *Orlando*, *The Years*, and *Between the Acts*, but that is represented dramatically in *The Waves* (1931). In *The Waves*, history's value as a source of narrative order is foregrounded through a questioning of history. The novel's six characters meet for a final dinner at Hampton Court, the royal residence become public park. " 'Listen,' said Louis, 'to the world moving through abysses of infinite space. It roars; the lighted strip of history is past and our Kings and Queens; we are gone. . . . lost in the abysses of time, in the darkness.' "[21] They wish to believe in this "lighted strip":

> "It is true, and I know for a fact," said Bernard, "as we walk down this avenue, that a King, riding, fell over a molehill here. But how strange it seems to set against the whirling abysses of infinite space a little figure with a golden teapot on his head. Soon one recovers belief in figures; but not at once in what they put on their heads. Our English past—one inch of light. Then people put teapots on their heads and say, 'I am a King!' . . . It is a trick of the mind—to put Kings on their thrones, one following another, with crowns on their heads." (194)

The little strip of light and the men with golden teapots on their heads might be "a trick of the mind," but this history is, after all, "light" in "darkness." "What has permanence?" Bernard asks. "Our lives too stream away, down the unlighted avenues, past the strip of time, unidentified" (195). This sense of the darkness is why they journey to Hampton Court, yet find history frail defense when they arrive.

Elsewhere Woolf emphasizes that this "strip of light," of "time," is constructed not only out of the doings of kings. She offers as alternative to the discourse of "teapots," "that record of the public life which is history. . . . convey[ing] through the mouths of Parliaments and Senates the considered opinions of bodies of educated men" (*Three Guineas*, 26). She writes less ironically in *A Room*, "the common life . . . is the real life and not . . . the little separate lives which we live as individuals" (198). This sense of history is also reflected in her memoir, "A Sketch of the Past" (1940), where she invokes

> The invisible presences. . . . other groups impinging upon ourselves; public opinion; what other people say and think; all those magnets which attract us this way to be like that, or repel us the other and make us different from that. . . . Consider what immense forces society brings to play upon each of us, how that society changes from decade to decade; and also from class to class.[22]

She writes, "I see myself as a fish in a stream; deflected; held in place; but cannot describe the stream." Yet her fiction relies structurally and for its subjects on this "stream," as much as on "the lighted strip" of kings.

Woolf's fiction depends for its narrative upon a history at once "unseizable force" and "strip of light," public record and common life. This history is as inseparable from the literary as from her needs as a lesbian writer. It cannot be divided by gender, because of the ways in which it is entangled with her representations of lesbians and gay men, who themselves, though often destructively, are repetitively identified through and with historical events and discourses. Woolf was conscious of her own position as both outsider and inheritor. Throughout most of her writings, "history" does not have *a* value—except instrumentally—as a literary/narrative resource.

*Jacob's Room*, for example, both the most structurally radical and historically grounded of the early works, is also the first of Woolf's novels with a gay character, reflecting connections not only between literary experiment and history but between literary experiment, history, and representations of homosexuality.[23] This emergence of the gay character out of history echoes Cather's and Renault's writings. Not surprisingly, in the context of their work, Woolf's first gay character is a man—Jacob's devoted friend Bonamy, "who couldn't love a woman and never read a foolish book" (132).[24] This analogy between women and "foolish books" reflects Woolf's distinct ambivalence about the privileged positions gay men retain as men.[25] But by creating in Jacob Flanders a "hero" who is always going to his death, and who therefore does not have to choose between the various respectable and unrespectable women who admire him and whom he admires, or between the women and the men who love him, Woolf herself can avoid dramatizing such a choice. Yet when, as the novel ends, Jacob's death is marked by a final repetition of the calling of his name ("Jacob! Jacob!" [168]) that has echoed through the novel, it is Bonamy who is calling. Bonamy's loss of Jacob becomes the definitive loss. Woolf affirms a male pair at the moment that they are divided by the war, by history. They are even placed in the space in the text where the heterosexual couple would conventionally have been affirmed; a heterosexual conclusion is then simultaneously displaced by history and homosexuality, at the moment that homosexuality is denied by history. The moment is equally complex in terms of its representations of gender. Cather immolates her male couple together on the battlefields of history at the conclusion of *One of Ours*. But Woolf refuses to show Jacob on his battlefield. Moreover she divides her male pair across the line between home front and battlefield. The two realms are linked through Bonamy's devotion to Jacob, while any easy feminine/masculine distinction is disrupted when the devotion that links home front and battlefield is male.

### III. "Had Not That, After All, Been Love?": *Mrs. Dalloway*

*Mrs. Dalloway* has to be central to any reading of Woolf as a lesbian writer because of the ways in which narrative, history, and representations of lesbianism are brought together in this novel. Woolf's formal experimentation and her uses of history enable her to exploit the structures out of which lesbian novels are made, but not to produce a lesbian novel. Yet the proximity of *Mrs. Dal-loway* to the lesbian novel in its underlying structure, and even in its potential framing of lesbianism as a problem, must be accounted for. Elizabeth Abel's well-regarded reading of this novel, which I will consider in some detail here, demonstrates the degree to which even astute and well-intentioned critics collaborate in containing the literary effects of lesbianism. While Abel laments the social repression of lesbianism, her account of narrative, history, and sexuality depends on the same heterosexual assumptions that mystify Clarissa Dalloway's interpretation of her own experience.

In *Mrs. Dalloway*, Woolf represents Clarissa Dalloway's lesbianism by invoking but subordinating the heterosexual plot through her use of "history." As Abel notes, the question of who Clarissa should marry is fundamental to the structure of this novel. Should it be Peter Walsh, or Richard Dalloway? And the marriage is made, the heterosexual plot completed. But the fact that the marriage has been made does not conclude the story, as Woolf "writes beyond the ending," in Rachel DuPlessis's terms, embedding the marriage in the past. Moreover World War I plays a crucial structural role in *Mrs. Dalloway*. The war marks the separation between the novel's two locations—its present, London in the 1920s, and the past, its own history, Clarissa's family's country house, Bourton in the 1890s. Dividing present and past, the war separates and links the drama of Clarissa's courtship and its consequences. The war is at the same time central to the story of Septimus Smith, which serves as a crucial interpretive template for Clarissa Dalloway's story. And the novel's identification of Clarissa and Septimus links Clarissa back to the war.

At Bourton in the 1890s, in the novel's historical past, all Clarissa's recollections indicate, it was love she felt for Sally Seton.[26] Sally's "was an extraordinary beauty of the kind she most admired, dark, large-eyed, with that quality which, since she hadn't got it herself, she always envied—a sort of abandonment, as if she could say anything, do anything" (37). Sally's

> charm was overpowering, to her at least, so that she could remember standing in her bedroom at the top of the house holding the hot-water can in her hands and saying aloud, "She is beneath this roof. . . . She is beneath this roof!" [. . .] and feeling as she crossed the hall "if it were now to die, 'twere now to be most happy." That was her feeling—Othello's feeling, and she felt it, she was convinced, as strongly as Shakespeare meant Othello to feel it, all because she was coming down to dinner in a white frock to meet Sally Seton! (39)

Abel argues that "Sally replaces Clarissa's dead mother and sister" (31), and so "this adolescent love assumes the place of the early female bond" (32). She can then read Clarissa's feeling for Sally as a pre-Oedipal mother/daughter interaction. But Clarissa's reference to *Othello*, repeated throughout the novel, is an invocation of adulthood as well as sexuality. And with this allusion to the interracial pairing of Othello and Desdemona, Woolf connects her female couple to another doomed, because socially transgressive, relationship, in what might be seen as a pointed mirroring of the social place and fate of the female couple.

Abel posits a gendered contrast between the novel's past and present. Bourton, she writes, "is a pastoral female world spatially and temporally disjunct from marriage and the sociopolitical world of (Richard's) London" (31). But Clarissa chooses between Sally, Peter, and Richard at Bourton, and chooses marriage there. "Clarissa's recollected history proceeds from a female-centered natural world to the heterosexual and androcentric social world," Abel writes (31). But Woolf emphasizes the social implications of Clarissa's response to Sally. The relation between the two women is liberating for Clarissa: "Sally it was who made her feel, for the first time, how sheltered the life at Bourton was. She knew nothing about sex—nothing about social problems." Just as "sex" and "social problems" are paired, Clarissa's liberation is political as well as emotional: "There they sat, hour after hour, talking in her bedroom at the top of the house, talking about life, how they were to reform the world. They meant to found a society to abolish private property. . . . read Plato in bed before breakfast; read Morris; read Shelley by the hour" (38). In contrast, while in the 1920s her husband is a member of Parliament, and the Prime Minister comes to her parties, Clarissa is relegated to the category of wives, distant from all political questions—she cannot even remember which causes her husband works on.

If Abel can establish the past as female and the present as male, and identify Sally with "the female-centered world anterior to heterosexual bonds" (34), then the passage of time itself requires and naturalizes Clarissa's "development" towards a heterosexuality identified with adulthood. Lesbianism can be the history, but is always only the history, of heterosexuality. Clarissa and Sally do see marriage as inevitable: "they spoke of marriage always as a catastrophe," but it was "bound to part them" (39). But their fatalism reflects the social absence of any visible future for their own relationship, an absence mirrored in Clarissa's sense of the "completely disinterested" nature "of her feeling for Sally" (39). Woolf also describes the female couple as a target of male hostility, particularly at the moment it is marked as sexual:

> they all went out on to the terrace and walked up and down. . . . She and Sally fell a little behind. Then came the most exquisite moment of her whole life passing a stone urn with flowers in it. Sally stopped; picked a flower; kissed her on the lips. The whole world might have turned upside down! The others disappeared; there she was alone with Sally. And she felt that she had been given a present, wrapped up, and

told just to keep it, not to look at it—a diamond, something infinitely precious, wrapped up, which, as they walked (up and down, up and down), she uncovered, or the radiance burnt through, the revelation, the religious feeling!—when old Joseph and Peter faced them:

"Star-gazing?" said Peter.

It was like running one's face against a granite wall in the darkness! It was shocking; it was horrible!

Not for herself. She felt only how Sally was being mauled already, maltreated; she felt his hostility; his jealousy; his determination to break into their companionship. All this she saw as one sees a landscape in a flash of lightning—and Sally (never had she admired her so much!) gallantly taking her way unvanquished. (40–41)

Abel reads this moment as "a revised Oedipal configuration: the jealous male attempting to rupture the exclusive female bond, insisting on the transfer of attachment to the man, demanding heterosexuality. For women this configuration institutes a break as decisive and unyielding as a granite wall" (32–33). This account naturalizes male hostility to lesbianism and the success of this disruption. But the hysteria of Clarissa's response—"Oh this horror!"— does not mitigate the brutality of Woolf's image of opposition—"It was like running one's face against a granite wall in the darkness!" The disruption is even more dramatic coming from Peter Walsh, who is usually in league with Sally's challenges to convention, except, apparently, in the competition of their mutual interest in Clarissa.[27] Clarissa's hysteria, coupled with her disavowal— "Not for herself. She felt only how Sally was being mauled already"—can be read as the signs of a prior anxiety about her relationship to Sally, and particularly about how vulnerable to "hostility" that could make her. Finally, this scene literalizes Woolf's narrative setting of Clarissa and Sally within heterosexual plot frames: explicitly opposing Clarissa and Sally to Clarissa and Peter, and by implication Clarissa and Richard, and thereby establishing the female couple as on a par with the heterosexual.

Clarissa's vulnerablity, reflected in this passage, might explain why she accepts Peter Walsh's arbitration:

Yet how much she owed Peter Walsh later. Always when she thought of him she thought of their quarrels for some reason—because she wanted his good opinion so much, perhaps. She owed him words: "sentimental," "civilized"; they started up every day of her life as if he guarded her. A book was sentimental; an attitude to life sentimental. "Sentimental," perhaps she was to be thinking of the past. (41)

Peter's concern is expressed through "quarrels." He continues to "guard . . . her." In the present, her memory of his comments cuts short her thoughts of

Sally, as "sentimental." Her love for Sally freed Clarissa into a world beyond the domestic confines of her own upbringing. But she defaulted, withdrew, became instead a female companion to "the men in clubs and Cabinets."

Compelled to marry by every assumption of her social context, however, Clarissa rejected Walsh's intrusiveness in this relation. Committed to conventional assumptions about women, he observes her with decision but completely without understanding: "But women, he thought, shutting his pocket-knife, don't know what passion is. They don't know the meaning of it to men. Clarissa was as cold as an icicle" (89–90). Abel argues that Clarissa refuses to marry Peter out of "revenge" for his challenging her relationship with Sally, and that Richard instead provides her with a "space that can incorporate the memory of Sally" (33). "For in marriage a little licence, a little independence there must be. . . . which Richard gave her, and she him," Clarissa thinks. "But with Peter everything had to be shared; everything gone into. And it was intolerable" (10).[28] But Sally does not need to be so quickly relegated to memory, nor as noted does Clarissa's lesbianism have to be so simply confined to Sally. Her choice of the more conventional and distant Richard Dalloway over Peter Walsh could be read more forcefully as ensuring space in a relation Clarissa is not suited for. Woolf indicates that Clarissa has still chosen against her own sexuality, when the young Richard Dalloway observes magisterially, "no decent man ought to read Shakespeare's sonnets because it was like listening at keyholes (besides, the relationship was not one that he approved)" (84).

"The relationship" that Dalloway does not approve of in Shakespeare's sonnets is experienced in Woolf's novel by Septimus Smith. His story mirrors Clarissa's, forces the issue of homosexuality in the novel's present, and provides the basis for her final affirmation of her lesbianism. Abel argues that, in this novel, the war, "symbolic[ally] associat[ed] . . . with the developmental turn from feminine to masculine dispensations," is represented "as a vast historical counterpart to male intervention in women's lives" (41). But Clarissa's identification with Septimus places her in as complicated a relation to the war as his.

The meaning of "the Great War" for Septimus is, as for Cather's men and boys, entirely contradictory. It is the location of his homosexuality—his relationship with his officer Evans:

> he drew the attention, indeed the affection of his officer, Evans by name. It was a case of two dogs playing on a hearth-rug; one worrying a paper screw, snarling, snapping, giving a pinch, now and then, at the old dog's ear; the other lying somnolent, blinking at the fire, raising a paw, turning and growling good-temperedly. They had to be together, share with each other, fight with each other, quarrel with each other. (96)[29]

It also destroys their relationship—Evans is "killed, just before the Armistice, in Italy" (96). Moreover his wartime experience initiates Septimus into "masculine" emotional repression: "The War had taught him. It was sublime. He had gone through the whole show, friendship, European war, death, had won promotion, was still under thirty and was bound to survive" (96). But what he must in particular repress is his love for Evans, that is, then, his grief over Evans's death: "Septimus, far from showing any emotion or recognizing that here was the end of a friendship, congratulated himself upon feeling very little and very reasonably" (96). But this repression in turn generates fear: "He started up in terror. What did he see? . . . That was it: to be alone for ever. That was the doom" (160). Afraid that he would "be alone for ever," he marries an Italian girl, Rezia, immediately after Evan's death, and brings her back to London. If marriage is a protection from isolation, it is also popularly supposed to be a guarantee of heterosexuality.

But marriage does not defeat this terror, which becomes the cause of his eventual breakdown in the novel's present, produced by "the panic . . . that he could not feel" (96). The source of Septimus's breakdown is the repression of feeling that war and masculinity require, but that is required particularly when it is homosexual love that might be acknowledged. His collapse is marked by hysterical horror of (hetero)sexuality: "Love between man and woman was repulsive to Shakespeare. The business of copulation was filth to him before the end. But, Rezia said, she must have children. They had been married five years" (99). He has visions of Evans himself returning: "the branches parted. A man in grey was actually walking towards them. It was Evans! But no mud was on him; no wounds; he was not changed" (78). In this state his revelation is, "there is no crime; next, love, universal love" (75). Sexual activity between men was of course criminal at this period in Britain (and since the Wilde trials most publicly associated with prosecution). Hence the connection between Septimus's rejection of crime and the validation of "universal love."[30]

The war also provides a socially acceptable explanation of his breakdown and even his suicide: the psychiatrist Bradshaw can declare that he is simply a victim of shell shock. It has provided that same explanation for readers not willing to deal with the homosexual element of the novel.[31] The war—especially when identified as simply "masculine"—and the explanation of Septimus it provides can also seem to signify an irrevocable distance between Septimus Smith and Clarissa Dalloway. Despite the fact that it is conventional, following a comment of Woolf's, to read these two as paired, critics have only recently begun to acknowledge the homosexuality that links them.[32] Even then, it seems that it is hard to regard homosexuality as a sufficient connection: Abel describes Septimus as "opposing the 'insane' truth to the 'sane' and the desire for death to the choice of life, while mirroring [Clarissa's] unresolved homoerotic bond" (38). But Septimus' "desire" is not for death. He "would wait till the very last moment. He did not want to die" (165).

When she hears the news of Septimus's death, Clarissa identifies with him, and acknowledges her own withdrawal from the battle which has defeated him:

> She had escaped. But that young man had killed himself.
>
> Somehow it was her disaster—her disgrace. It was her punishment to see sink and disappear here a man, there a woman, in this profound darkness, and she forced to stand here in her evening dress. She had schemed; she had pilfered. She was never wholly admirable. She had wanted success. . . . And once she had walked on the terrace at Bourton. (204–205)

Septimus's suicide—his final refusal to be a victim either of history or the "human nature" ("human nature was upon him") manufactured by the doctors of his historical moment—is an affirmation of his love for Evans. Clarissa affirms his gesture:

> A thing there was that mattered; a thing, wreathed about with chatter, defaced, obscured in her own life, let drop every day in corruption, lies, chatter. This he had preserved. Death was defiance. Death was an attempt to communicate, people feeling the impossibility of reaching the centre which, mystically, evaded them; closeness drew apart; rapture faded; one was alone. There was an embrace in death.
>
> But this young man who had killed himself—had he plunged holding his treasure? "If it were now to die, 'twere now to be most happy," she had said to herself once, coming down, in white. (204)

Abel notes the ways in which these passages echo Woolf's earlier accounts of Clarissa's desire (39). When Clarissa "walked on the terrace at Bourton" Sally kissed her, and it was "the happiest moment of my life?" Her "treasure"—"If it were now to die, 'twere now to be most happy," she had felt, while "coming down, in white,"—had been her love for Sally. "She felt somehow very like him—the young man who had killed himself. She felt glad that he had done it" (206), because their treasure is the same. Woolf's narrative placement of Clarissa's affirmation of Septimus's suicide as the novel's climactic moment underlines Clarissa's lesbianism as central to the novel.

Abel, however, sees Clarissa's final return to the party, after this moment of identification with Septimus, as a sign of her ultimate "embrace [of] the imperfect pleasures of adulthood" (40), which is to say, heterosexuality. As she notes, "Woolf abruptly terminates" Clarissa's thoughts of Septimus and her "recollection" of Sally, "replaying with a brilliant stroke Peter Walsh's interruption, the sudden imposition of the granite wall. This time, however, the masculine intervention is enacted not by Peter but by Richard, and not as external imposition but as choice" (40). Clarissa switches from "once she had walked on the terrace at Bourton" to "It was due to Richard; she had never been so happy."[33] But as Abel has just discussed Septimus's fate as "demonstrat[ing] . . . Clarissa's alternatives: to preserve the intensity of passion through death or to accept the changing offerings of life" (40), it is hard to see why Clarissa's abrupt turn to an insistence on the happiness of her marriage represents much of a "choice." The very abruptness of the switch and the excessiveness of her declaration of happiness with Richard could be read as signs of Clarissa's still-inescapable anxiety about her feelings for women. If she no longer needs Peter or Richard to do the work of interrupting, surely this reflects her own complete internalization of the heterosexual plot, that the process already in motion at Bourton will never be undone. Clarissa returns to her party, and into the perpetually controlling field of Peter Walsh's voice. Where else can she go? Abel wants development and resolution, assuming lesbianism is a state of stasis but never a conclusion, but that heterosexuality would signify both change and closure. But *Mrs. Dalloway* is not a lesbian novel, and not just because, given the absence of a narrative account of Clarissa and Sally, the book has not been read as such. However Woolf plays with narrative conventions in her modernist text, she has refused to produce a text in which lesbianism itself is a problem requiring thematic resolution, and has evaded the formal necessity of having to produce a conclusion. Woolf offers a woman who "had the oddest sense of being herself invisible; unseen; unknown; . . . this being Mrs. Dalloway; not even Clarissa anymore; this being Mrs. Richard Dalloway" (13). She is "invisible . . . unknown" as "Mrs. Richard Dalloway." The irony of the novel is that Clarissa is made "visible" to readers, but remains "unknown" to herself, unable to interpret her own history.

According to Abel, in *Mrs. Dalloway*, not only is Clarissa's personal history of progress from pre-Oedipal female bonds to adult heterosexuality encouraged by a masculine public history which actively imposes, in the form of the war, the transition from feminine to masculine, but the masculine history of the war produces male domination in the postwar world to reinforce Clarissa's heterosexual adulthood: "the progress of society precludes any personal or cultural return to the pastoral pre-Oedipal world" (41). But the novel opens linking Bourton and London, and is all about linking past and present: Peter and Sally at Bourton; Peter and Sally in London; it begins and ends with Peter commenting, in the past and the present. Through her identification with Septimus, Clarissa is linked to the war-history, as a source of possibility as well as repression.

Moreover, beside her pairing with Septimus, Clarissa is also matched with the novel's third gay character, Doris Kilman, who not coincidentally is a historian. Miss Kilman teaches modern European history; she has, according to Richard Dalloway, "a really historical mind" (14). She is paired with Septimus in that her life has also been shaped by the war; she lost her teaching job because of her refusal to go along with popular anti-German feeling, that is, to conform to the popular interpretation of historical events. In the stories of both Septimus and Miss Kilman, "history" is enabling of homosexuality as well as destructive. In the novel's present, Miss Kilman emerges from the economic and social margins to tutor Clarissa's daughter, Elizabeth, in "history." Clarissa is not so mystified as not to understand the relation between Elizabeth and Miss Kilman: "It might be only a phase, as Richard said, such as all girls go through," but "It might be falling in love" (14).[34] "Richard would say, What nonsense!" (193), she thinks, but Clarissa's jealousy of Doris Kilman suggests the recognition of a fellow creature, and for all Miss Kilman's inferior class status, something Clarissa cannot have: "Kilman her enemy. That was satisfying; that was real. Ah, how she hated her—hot, hypocritical, corrupt; with all that power; Elizabeth's seducer; the woman who had crept in to steal and defile" (193).[35] The lesbian historian is ugly and grasping. Her experience of desire for Clarissa's Elizabeth echoes and parodies Clarissa's feeling for Sally Seton: "If she could grasp her, if she could clasp her, if she could make her hers absolutely and forever and then die; that was all she wanted" (146). But Clarissa identifies: "She hated her: she loved her. It was enemies one wanted, not friends" (193).

## IV. "Living Differently"?

Both of the history teachers in Woolf's fiction are lesbians. Woolf's other story of a young woman in love with her female history teacher can be found at the beginning of *The Years*. Kitty Lasswade, the daughter of the master of an Oxford college, gets her lessons from poor but independent Lucy Craddock, who lives in the "cheap red villas" of a less august part of town (63). But "Kitty saw them haloed with romance. Her heart beat faster as she . . . saw the steep steps of the house where Miss Craddock actually lived" (63). Lucy Craddock is drawn to her student: "How lovely she is, Miss Craddock thought; for she was sentimental about Kitty. But I will not be sentimental, she told herself" (65). Miss Craddock here echoes Clarissa's decision to stop thinking about Sally, because that would be "sentimental." But while Doris Kilman, who dissents from popular interpretations of historical events, posed a real threat to Clarissa Dalloway if not to Elizabeth, Lucy Craddock still admires the university historians who have kept her outside their ordered and richly rewarded ranks. While "Old Chuffy," Dr. Andrews, the famous historian who wrote *The Constitutional History of England* that Lucy is teaching from, only responds to Kitty herself by placing "a heavy hand on her knee" (66).[36] So Miss Craddock disappears from the novel, and Kitty learns her place in history; she goes on to marry a future governor of India.

Woolf's continuing use of history in her narrative experiments of the 1920s and 1930s made it possible for her to represent gay men more successfully than lesbians, echoing the work of Cather and Renault. But the relation of these

men to history is as contradictory as the effect of history on the lives of gay
men in *Jacob's Room* and *Mrs. Dalloway*. Neville in *The Waves* and Nicholas in
*The Years* are contrasting portraits, even though they both fare better than the
potential lesbians in either text.

In *The Waves*, Neville is represented directly through reference to history, as
in the work of Cather and Renault, but also as Woolf has already done herself in
*Mrs. Dalloway*. "Let us read writers of Roman severity and virtue," Neville thinks:

> let us seek perfection through the sand. Yes, but I love to slip the virtue
> and severity of the noble Romans under the grey light of your eyes, and
> dancing grasses and summer breezes and the laughter and shouts of boys
> at play—of naked cabin-boys squirting each other with hose-pipes on
> the decks of ships. . . . And the poem, I think, is only your voice speak-
> ing. Alcibiades, Ajax, Hector and Percival are also you. (154–155)

Neville is both devoted to ancient history and enthusiastic about modern political authority because of his love for Percival. Percival, the cricketing schoolboy who grows up to be an imperial administrator, can be the focal point of
*The Waves*, always beyond the consciousnesses of the other six characters, because he is "always already" in the ordered public world of the history of "clubs
and Cabinets." He is posed as a magnetic figure: "His magnificence is that of
some medieval commander. A wake of light seems to lie on the grass behind
him. Look at us trooping after him, his faithful servants, to be shot like sheep,
for he will certainly attempt some forlorn enterprise and die in battle" (31).
But he is also, on the same terms, identified with the "boys in brakes," "the
boasting boys" (56):

> They are the volunteers; they are the cricketers; they are the officers of
> the Natural History Society. They are always forming into fours and
> marching in troops with badges on their caps; they salute simultaneously
> passing the figure of their general. . . . they also leave butterflies trem-
> bling with their wings pinched off. . . . They make little boys sob in
> dark passages. (39)

Yet Neville still believes that Percival "would have done justice for fifty years,
and sat in Court and ridden alone at the head of troops and denounced some
monstrous tyranny" (129).

In contrast, in *The Years*, Nicholas, who is significantly introduced during
World War I, is skeptical of the existing social order.[37] He is also after all introduced, by Sara, as someone "who ought to be in prison. . . . Because he
loves. . . . the other sex, the other sex, you see" (297). But Nicholas and the
war together create, for Woolf's protagonist Eleanor, a space for new perceptions: "A little blur had come round the edges of things. It was the wine; it was

the war," Eleanor thinks. "Things seemed to have lost their skins; to be freed from some surface hardness" (287). In particular, "He seemed to have released something in her; she felt not only a new space of time, but new powers, something unknown within her" (297). From these shifts, during wartime, come expressions of hope: Eleanor wants to ask Nicholas, "When will this new world come? When shall we be free? When shall we live adventurously, wholly, not like cripples in a cave? . . . We shall be free, we shall be free" (297).

When, in the novel's final section, "living differently" becomes the form of this hope, the possibility of "living differently" is represented by the unconventional pair made by Nicholas and Sara: " 'Nicholas?' she exclaimed. 'I love him!' " (324). "Living differently" is about the meaning of "love" as well as social structures. Nicholas and Sara are the focus one of the few discussions of love in this novel:

> This is their lovemaking, Eleanor thought, half listening to their laughter, to their bickering. Another inch of the pattern, she thought. . . . And if this lovemaking differs from the old, still it has its charm. . . . they are aware of each other; they live in each other; what else is love? she asked, listening to their laughter. (370)[38]

But despite the gay sign Nicholas represents in this vision, the couple he makes with Sara looks "hetero," if not sexual. In this way, despite the hope of living differently he represents, he can, like Neville, "fit" into existing social structures.

The capacity of Neville and even Nicholas to fit in *The Waves* and *The Years* can be contrasted with the potentially lesbian characters Woolf describes. In *The Waves*, Rhoda as a girl is drawn to other girls:

> I attach myself only to names and faces; and hoard them like amulets against disaster. I choose out across the hall some unknown face and can hardly drink my tea when she whose name I do not know sits opposite. I choke. I am rocked from side to side by the violence of my emotion. I imagine these nameless, these immaculate people, watching me from behind bushes. I leap high to excite their admiration. At night, in bed, I excite their complete wonder. I often die pierced with arrows to win their tears. (36)

Woolf's reference here to the gay icon, St. Sebastian, underlines the possibility of a reading of Rhoda as matched with Neville.[39] However, despite the vision of "golden glory where some girl whose name I forget stood on the pavement," Rhoda makes no contact with these girls, "it was the name only" (175). Later she will be Louis's lover, but "I left Louis; I feared embraces" (175). Are these Louis's embraces that she fears, or the embraces of men? For

Rhoda history is "an immense pressure. . . . I cannot move without dislodging the weight of centuries" (90). Not only is Rhoda the only one of the novel's six characters who does not survive to the end of the novel, but she kills herself.

In *The Years*, it is Peggy who introduces the ideal of "living differently," but her own position is left unclear. She is a doctor, one of the professional women whose lives have been made possible by the social changes that have occurred in the course of the historical span the novel records, from 1880 to the 1930s. As an adult in the 1930s, she is acutely conscious of her historical context: "But how can one be 'happy'? she asked herself, in a world bursting with misery. On every placard at every street corner was Death; or worse—tyranny; brutality; torture; the fall of civilization; the end of freedom" (388). She is challenged by her uncle: "But you . . . your generation I mean—you miss a great deal. . . . Loving only your own sex." But " 'I'm not that generation,' she said" (356). There are only ambiguous suggestions: she thinks of her brother, contrasting their lives, "He'll tie himself up with a red-lipped girl, and become a drudge. He must, and I can't, she thought. No, I've a sense of guilt always. I shall pay for it, I shall pay for it" (396).[40] Peggy's conviction of guilt is either a response to this moment of public crisis, when she thinks she should not turn to a personal solution, or a response to the possibility of turning to "a red-lipped girl."

## V. The Language of Lovers

Nevertheless, by the later 1920s, Woolf was invoking a "language such as lovers use" as her model for literary form and the relation between an author and her subject. In *Orlando*, Orlando muses:

> What has praise and fame to do with poetry? . . . Was not writing poetry a secret transaction, a voice answering a voice? So that all this chatter and praise and blame . . . was as ill suited as could be to the thing itself—a voice answering a voice. What could have been more secret, she thought, more slow, and like the intercourse of lovers, than the stammering answer she had made all these years to the old crooning song of the woods, and the farms . . . and the gardens. (229)

This "voice answering a voice . . . like the intercourse of lovers" is both "the thing itself," and the author's mode of addressing her subject. At the conclusion of *The Waves*, Bernard, like Orlando a writer, asks, "What is the phrase for the moon? And the phrase for love? By what name are we to call death? I do not know. I need a little language such as lovers use, words of one syllable such as children speak when they come into the room and find their mother sewing and pick up some scrap of bright wool, a feather, or a shred of chintz" (254). In both passages, the language of lovers is directed toward some object other than a beloved, or some relation other than that of lovers—woods and fields, or child and mother. This reinforces the implication that these lovers are central to Woolf's general understanding of language. That these lovers are female is suggested by the traces in these passages of her discussion of Chloe and Olivia in *A Room of One's Own*, where she writes that the "shortest of short-hand, . . . words that are hardly syllabled yet," are necessary to convey "those unrecorded gestures, those unsaid or half-said words, which form themselves, no more palpably than the shadows of moths on the ceiling, when women are alone" together (147).

For Woolf, in a way that echoes the role of the writer-protagonist as a solution to the limits of the lesbian novel, the relationship between lesbianism and history is resolved by art/writing, as in *To the Lighthouse*. In *To the Lighthouse*, as in *Mrs. Dalloway*, World War I divides past and present, and events on the battlefields of Europe continue to be connected by significant parallels to the home front. In the central "Time Passes" section of the novel, it is while the war progresses over Flander's fields that Mrs. Ramsay dies in London. Her son Andrew dies in battle—"A shell exploded. Twenty or thirty young men were blown up in France, among them Andrew Ramsay, whose death, mercifully, was instantaneous"—and her daughter, Prue, after being "given in marriage that May," "died that summer in some illness connected with childbirth" (152, 150, 151). By creating a parallel in these sacrifices of the Ramsay children, one to war and one to marriage, Woolf connects Mrs. Ramsay's death at a world historical moment with her preference for male authority:

> Indeed, she had the whole of the other sex under her protection; for reasons she could not explain, for their chivalry and valour, for the fact that they negotiated treaties, ruled India, controlled finance; finally for an attitude towards herself which no woman could fail to feel or to find agreeable . . . and woe betide the girl—pray Heaven it was none of her daughters!—who did not feel the worth of it. (8)[41]

Men are granted emotional priority partly because of their roles in history, and take precedence even over Mrs. Ramsay's own daughters.

But in *To the Lighthouse*, Woolf also continues to use reference to the heterosexual plot to represent lesbianism. Mrs. Ramsay has been explicitly lost, during the wartime interlude, to her husband: "he stretched his arms out. They remained empty" (147). But she has also been lost by Lily Briscoe, whose attempt to continue painting her portrait after Mrs. Ramsay's death "sent all up her body a hardness, a hollowness, a strain. And then to want and not to have—to want and want—how that wrung the heart, and wrung it again and again!" (203). Elizabeth Abel, with many other critics, reads Lily Briscoe's re-

lationship to Mrs. Ramsay as a mother-daughter interaction. But even before
Woolf sets up this parallel between Mr. Ramsay and Lily's relation to Mrs.
Ramsay through their shared experiences of loss, Lily's feeling for Mrs. Ramsay is established, in the first half of the novel, around the older woman's insistence that the younger "must marry."

Woolf represents Lily's love for Mrs. Ramsay through Lily's laughter at this
suggestion and at the complete lack of understanding Mrs. Ramsay reveals.
Lily "had laid her head on Mrs. Ramsay's lap and laughed and laughed and
laughed, laughed almost hysterically at the thought of Mrs. Ramsay presiding
with immutable calm over destinies which she completely failed to understand. . . . had looked up at last, and there was Mrs. Ramsay, unwitting entirely what had caused her laughter, still presiding" (59). The language of Lily's
desires combines the sexual and the historical:

> Sitting on the floor with her arms round Mrs. Ramsay's knees, close as
> she could get, smiling to think that Mrs. Ramsay would never know the
> reason of that pressure, [Lily] imagined how in the chambers of the
> mind and heart of the woman who was, physically, touching her, were
> stood, like the treasures in the tombs of kings, tablets bearing sacred in-
> scriptions, which if one could spell them out would teach one every-
> thing, but they would never be offered openly, never made public.
> What art was there, known to love or cunning, by which one pressed
> through into those secret chambers? What device for becoming, like
> waters poured into one jar, inextricably the same, one with the object
> one adored? Could the body achieve it, or the mind, subtly mingling
> in the intricate passages of the brain? or the heart? Could loving, as peo-
> ple called it, make her and Mrs. Ramsay one? for it was not knowledge
> but unity she desired, not inscriptions on tablets, nothing that could be
> written in any language known to men, but intimacy itself, which is
> knowledge, she had thought, leaning her head on Mrs. Ramsay's knee.
> (59–60)[42]

Even before the possibility of a sexual relationship is posed as a question—
"Could loving, as people called it, make her and Mrs. Ramsay one?"—Woolf
evokes the sexual with her references to the "art . . . by which one pressed
through into . . . secret chambers," and the lesbian by reference to "what
would never be offered openly, never made public," "nothing that could be
written in any language known to men." This sexual question is presaged by allusions to a historical search, the goal of love identified with "treasures in the
tombs of kings, tablets bearing sacred inscriptions."

Woolf pursues alternative understandings of "love" in *To the Lighthouse.*
There are the "unclassified affections" of William Bankes: "Mrs. Ramsay sometimes thought that he cared, since his wife's death, perhaps for her. He was not

'in love' of course; it was one of those unclassified affections of which there are so many" (120). And there is the "love" that is creativity, when Woolf echoes H. D.'s statements about love that is writing/art. As she approaches her final vision, Lily concludes,

> Love had a thousand shapes. There might be lovers whose gift it was to choose out the elements of things and place them together and so, giving them a wholeness not theirs in life, make of some scene, or meeting of people (all now gone and separate), one of those globed compacted things over which thought lingers, and love plays. (218–219)

At the conclusion of *To The Lighthouse*, Woolf relents, and Mrs. Ramsay returns not to her husband, but to Lily. As Lily tries again to paint the scene that Mrs. Ramsay had once occupied,

> Some wave of white went over the window-pane. The air must have stirred some flounce in the room. Her heart leapt at her and seized her and tortured her.
> "Mrs. Ramsay! Mrs. Ramsay!" she cried, feeling the old horror come back—to want and want and not to have. Could she inflict that still? And then, quietly, as if she refrained, that too became part of ordinary experience, was on a level with the chair, with the table. Mrs. Ramsay— it was part of her perfect goodness to Lily—sat there quite simply, in the chair, flicked her needles to and fro, knitted her reddish-brown stockings, cast her shadow on the step. There she sat. (229–230)

Woolf has established Lily's love for Mrs. Ramsay through the negative terms of the heterosexual plot, but her love is resolved in the positive terms of painting, producing an affirmation of the value of artistic work that is at the same time an affirmation of her love. Despite her loss of Mrs. Ramsay to the history of the war, because of Mrs. Ramsay's return to her, the no-longer-young woman, Lily, can become the artist:

> There it was—her picture. . . . It would be hung in the attics, she thought; it would be destroyed. But what did that matter? she asked herself, taking up her brush again. She looked at the steps; they were empty; she looked at her canvas; it was blurred. With a sudden intensity, as if she saw it clear for a second, she drew a line there, in the centre. It was done; it was finished. Yes, she thought, laying down her brush in extreme fatigue, I have had my vision. (237)

Painting is identified with writing throughout *To the Lighthouse* by Charles Tansley's mocking, "Women can't paint, can't write" (181). And Lily presides over the novel's conclusion paired with Mr. Carmichael, who loved and lost Andrew Ramsay and is now holding that sign of sex in literature, a French novel, in his hand.[43] Art, especially "writing," becomes a way of negotiating between passion and history.

## VI.  "Did the Plot Matter?": *Between the Acts*

As noted earlier, Woolf made narrative out of literary history around the figures of writers in *Orlando* and *Between the Acts*. While *Orlando* has been much discussed as a lesbian text, more or less as a version of a lesbian novel, *Between the Acts* has not been considered as the work of a lesbian writer. But the status of a "lesbian writer," the narrative disenfranchisement imposed by the heterosexual plot, and the limits of "history" were all articulated by Woolf in her final novel. In *Between the Acts* Isa, who would in a more conventional text have been the heroine, instead observes one of the multiple sets of heroines and heroes in another text, the play within Woolf's novel:

> Who came? Isa looked. . . . Love embodied.
>   All arms were raised; all faces stared.
>   "*Hail, sweet Carinthia!*" said the Prince, sweeping his hat off. And she to him, raising her eyes:
>   "*My love! My lord!*"[44]

Isa asks, "Did the plot matter? . . . The plot was only there to beget emotion. There are only two emotions: love, and hate. There was no need to puzzle out the plot" (67). Later she would add: "Peace was the third emotion. Love. Hate. Peace. Three emotions made the ply of human life" (68). However, despite her earlier conclusion—"Don't bother about the plot: the plot's nothing" (67)— by the end of the novel she is protesting, "Love and hate—how they tore her asunder! Surely it was time someone invented a new plot, or that the author came out from the bushes" (150). Rather than love, hate, and peace, the novel ends with love, hate, and war. Although *Between the Acts* does not include the invention of a new plot, it does contain a parodic critique of the old, which has become the subject rather than the structuring principle of the text. And at the end of the play, the text within the text, after the audience and the actors have dispersed, an author does come out from the bushes: she is the lesbian writer, Miss La Trobe.[45]

Not at all paradoxically, given the dependence of representations of lesbianism on the heterosexual plot—within the novel of Woolf's most concerned with the heterosexual plot—Miss La Trobe is the most conventionally marked of her lesbian characters. This author's coming out from the bushes is also tied to the occasion of her "coming out" within the text. Although there are earlier references to a certain lack of femininity—"perhaps, then, she wasn't altogether a lady?" (45)—as well as to the cottage in which she lived with another woman, it is not until the end of the play that Woolf refers to "the actress who had shared [Miss La Trobe's] bed and her purse" (146). Woolf goes on to illustrate the social implications of this personal history: Miss La Trobe is isolated within the village in which she lives; the women from the neighboring cottages who may themselves be widows, but have the dignity of visiting their husbands' graves to sustain them, "cut" her when they pass. Woolf concludes her account of Miss La Trobe's sexuality with a direct statement: "She was an outcast. Nature had somehow set her apart from her kind" (147).

Woolf specifically sets this ostracism, this sexuality described in terms of separation and difference, in relation to Miss La Trobe's art, her writing: "She was an outcast. Nature had somehow set her apart from her kind. Yet she had scribbled in the margin of her manuscript: 'I am the slave of my audience'" (147). With that "yet," Woolf connects Miss La Trobe's lesbianism and her writing by posing the two as contradictory. This contradictory connection is at the center of *Between the Acts*. It is not, however, a contradiction between her sexuality and the fact of her writing, but a contradiction between her sexuality and the content of that writing. That content is determined by the demands of her audience, because, as Woolf had observed twenty years before, in "Mr. Bennett and Mrs. Brown," the possibility of communication, of representation, depends on shared assumptions and conventions.[46] Through Miss La Trobe, Woolf illustrates the situation of the lesbian writer confined to literally reflecting her audience back to themselves, as in the final scene of her pageant, when she has the actors face the audience with mirrors they have carried on to the stage. *Between the Acts* is a novel by a lesbian writer dealing with the heterosexual plot in literature and history, about a lesbian writer dealing with the heterosexual plot in the context of history.[47]

*Between the Acts* was for Woolf a backward-looking work. She restates with extraordinary clarity the paradigmatic problem the heterosexual plot represents for lesbian writers; but she could not weigh her own efforts toward resolution, throughout all of her previous writings, against the threat of "history" represented by World War II. Written between 1938 and 1941, *Between the Acts* is very much a work that reflects the present danger of its own historical moment, when the problem seemed so obviously to have more than literary dimensions and consequences, and to require more than literary solutions.[48]

Miss La Trobe's work, her pageant, consists of a history of England transposed into literary terms, told through a series of versions, a literary history, of the heterosexual plot. It begins with England, female child and then "grown a girl," her speeches accompanied by the song of the "valiant Rhoderick/ Armed and valiant/ Bold and blatant" (59). "Merry England" is represented by the villagers' chorus, a collective voice which sings of kissing girls and tumbling them "in the straw and in the hay" (61). Queen Elizabeth presides over the story of the Prince and "sweet Carinthia"; Queen Anne introduces the successful romance of Flavinda and Valentine, and the more tortuous relations of Sir Spaniel Lilyliver and Lady Harpy Harraden. During the picnic of the Victorian Age, Edgar and Eleanor become engaged to be married and convert the African heathen, while Mrs. Hardcastle, an anxious mother of four unmarried daughters, initiates a crucial chorus of enquiry about the new clergyman: "O has Mr. Sibthorp a wife?" (118).

These patterns in the performance are repeated among the audience, which is itself dominated by the heterosexual plot. Before the pageant begins, William Dodge and Mrs. Swithin, looking from an upper story on the people arriving for the performance below, observe: "cars were assembling . . . here old ladies gingerly advanced black legs with silver-buckled shoes; old men stripped trousers. Young men in shorts leapt out on one side; girls with skin-coloured legs on the other" (54–55). All of the characters in the novel are placed in some relation to the plot—Mrs. Swithin in her widowhood; Bart with his son and daughter-in-law and grandchildren; the nurses walking on the terrace saying something about a "feller"; even William Dodge, married despite his homosexuality, and trailing in the wake of Mrs. Manresa—not to mention the absolutely conventional pattern of love and hate enacted between Isa and Giles, Isa and Haines, Giles and Mrs. Manresa.

The continuity between the patterns of relations among the members of the audience and the plot repeated through the various acts of the play, is emphasized by the audience's acceptance of literary conventions: the narrator observes of Mrs. Manresa, "Somehow she was the Queen; and he (Giles) was the surly hero" (69); Isa constantly invokes cliché in order to generate in herself the appropriate feelings for Giles: "He is my husband . . . The father of my children" (38). While her initial question about plot ("Did the plot matter?") was prompted by her observation of the play, Isa's first response was to turn in her seat, to look behind her for the farmer Haines, whom she desires; when at the conclusion of the novel she demands a new plot, she is again prompted by the patterns of her own life—in this case, her relation to her husband.

*Between the Acts*, a work which appears to consist of two texts or a "double" text—the pageant (formally a pastiche of various modes in literary history) embedded within a (formally) modernist context—must also be seen as continuous. The pageant's "context" of country house and village, luncheon at the manor and drinking in the evening at the local pub, is an extended account of the "Present Time" Miss La Trobe promises to represent in the pageant's last act, and then delivers via the mirrors she has the actors carry on-stage. These mirrors, reflecting the audience back to themselves, indicate the relation between the novel's "two" texts, as well as its author/director's relation to her audience.

Woolf's critique of the heterosexual plot through the pageant and its context is marked most obviously by the self-conscious references to the question of plot within the novel (Isa's "Someone should invent a new plot"), and also the range of commentary on the subject of the plot. A voice in the audience comments, in response to Flavinda's anxiety about Valentine during the "Age of Reason," " 'All that fuss about nothing!' . . . People laughed. The voice stopped. But the voice had seen; the voice had heard. For a moment Miss La Trobe behind her tree glowed with glory" (98). Cobbet of Cobb's Corner observes, "the little game of the woman following the man to the table in the West as in the East" (80). The lyrics of one of the tunes Miss La Trobe chose to draw the audiences' attention back to the play describe "The lamp of love burn[ing] high," and declare, "lady, I love till I die" (84–85). Someone—the narrator or perhaps old Oliver—complains: "the tune with its feet always on the same spot, became sugared, insipid; bored a hole with its perpetual invocation to perpetual adoration" (85).

The second aspect of both Woolf's critique of the heterosexual plot and her formal solution to the problem it presents is her use of history. The critique is founded in the connections she makes between the heterosexual plot and particular aspects of "history," particularly the British Empire and World War II. That connection is itself established in the pageant, where she offers a series of versions of the heterosexual plot as the basis of her history of England. The critique is most bluntly stated, within the pageant, during the nineteenth-century scenes, when a policeman-narrator describes the union of "prosperity and respectability" under the rule of the "White Queen Victoria":

> It's a Christian country, our Empire; under the White Queen Victoria. Over thought and religion; drink; dress, manners; marriage too, I wield my truncheon. Prosperity and respectability always go, as we know, 'and in 'and. The ruler of an Empire must keep his eye on the cot; spy too in the kitchen; drawing-room; library; wherever one or two, me and you, come together. Purity our watchword; prosperity and respectability. If not, why let 'em fester in . . . Cripplegate; St. Giles's; Whitechapel; the Minories. Let 'em sweat at the mines; cough at the looms; rightly endure their lot. That's the price of Empire; that's the white man's burden. (114)

However, the most dramatic connection Woolf makes between the heterosexual plot and history is part of the pageant's context, at the conclusion of the novel, when its final scenes of Isa and Giles's struggle, love and hate, are equated with the immediate, dangerous, and horrifying history of the novel's present, the coming world war.[49] That the novel builds structurally as well as thematically to this final connection between the heterosexual plot and history also illustrates the extent to which history as a source of critique is still simultaneously history as a source of structure, a crucial element of Woolf's final, formal solution to the problem of the heterosexual plot.

\* \* \*

In *Between the Acts*, the heterosexual plot of the pageant and the pageant's version of "history" are located within a multileveled account of the public world, perhaps Woolf's most complex "history." Beyond the pageant itself, this history has three other levels: the June afternoon in 1939 on which the play is described as taking place; the political and social history of England and Europe in which June 1939 takes its place; and finally, what might be called "natural history," which incorporates all of the other histories in the novel.

The history of 1939 is inevitably present in the novel, given Woolf's choice of the date, but it is also emphasized by recurring references—scraps of conversation, for example, about refugees, persecutions, the imminence of war, and the fate of the Jews. Giles, the normative, young, upper-class, heterosexual male, is obsessed with the impending violence (as a challenge to his masculinity). Isa, his wife, is herself thirty-nine years old, explicitly "the age of the century" (18). As the play ends, warplanes flying in formation overhead interrupt the clergyman's attempt to sum up Miss La Trobe's work with a comforting formula.

The year 1939 itself is contextualized by references to a history that contains Roman roads and Napoleonic wars, the manor house, and the villagers whose ancestors have lived in the surrounding countryside for centuries and lie buried intertwined in the local churchyards. The sense of continuity such references evoke is also contradicted. Although Oliver, when he dozes, remembers his past as a dutiful servant of the nation, fighting savages in a sunburnt outpost of empire, the portraits that line his walls are as likely to be simply views as ancestors; his family has only lived in Pointz Hall for 120 years. The ghost who is said to wander on the terrace is admittedly manufactured from a fiction, of course the story of a lady who drowned herself for love. However, certain social and sexual fictions, as well as class mobility (upwards, or alternatively down—the obliteration of ancient titles in "trashy" new names) become a part of this social and political history. Within this history, references to wars are still pervasive.

The immediate frame of imminent war and the larger frame of conventional political and social history are both in turn contextualized within the natural history represented by the *Outline of History* Mrs. Swithin is reading at the beginning and end of *Between the Acts's* fictional day.[50] That history begins and is identified with the primeval:

> rhododendron forests in Piccadilly; when the entire continent, not then,
> [Mrs. Swithin] understood, divided by a channel, was all one; populated,
> she understood, by elephant-bodied, seal-necked, heaving, surging,
> slowly writhing, and, she supposed, barking monsters; the iguanodon,
> the mammoth, and the mastodon; from whom presumably, she thought
> . . . we descend. (10)

The presence of this "primeval" in Woolf's writing can be traced through her fiction from her first novel, *The Voyage Out* (1915), where Rachel Vinrace is "haunted by absurd jumbled ideas—how, if one went back far enough, everything perhaps was intelligible; . . . for the mammoths who pastured in the fields of Richmond High Street had turned into paving stones and boxes full of ribbon, and her aunts."[51] This "primeval" is tied to the question of explanation, which becomes by *Between the Acts* a question of our "descent."

* * *

The complexity and flexibility of the revisionary "history" Woolf had been fashioning since *Jacob's Room*, twenty years before, gave her a context alternative to that of conventional domestic realism, and also both serious and capacious enough to contain and put into perspective the assumptions of that domestic realism. In *Between the Acts*, history also provides a context that can contain both literary convention and the writer-critic—can contain in tension both the heterosexual plot and the lesbian writer.

Miss La Trobe is the third focus of dissent from the heterosexual plot in *Between the Acts*, and her presence centers all of the other parodies, comments, and connections. She enters the novel within a frame of "historical" reference—described as a "commander" and then an "admiral" pacing a quarterdeck, about to direct her pageant, described as an "engagement," which might as easily be a military as a theatrical event (48).

Woolf has already, in this novel, given us a gay man, William Dodge, whose sexuality is represented through negatives. Dodge wants to explain to Lucy Swithin, who is also, as an old woman, a sexually and socially marginal character: "At school they held me under a bucket of dirty water, Mrs. Swithin; when I looked up, the world was dirty, Mrs. Swithin; so I married; but my child's not my child, Mrs. Swithin. I'm a half-man, Mrs. Swithin; a flickering, mind-divided little snake in the grass, Mrs. Swithin; as Giles saw" (55). Giles Oliver excludes Dodge from the community: " '*We?*' said Giles. '*We?*' He looked, once, at William. . . . It was a bit of luck—that he could despise him, not himself" (80). But although Dodge desires Giles—"the muscular, the hirsute, the virile plunged him into emotions in which the mind had no share" (77)—he has married, he follows Mrs. Manresa, Mrs. Swithin, and Isa. He remains silent. But Miss La Trobe writes.

That the writer of this play should be a lesbian who creates even as she critiques or parodies heterosexual plots, illustrates the authority of literary convention (the authority of the audience).[52] Yet that Woolf has created her author a lesbian calls that plot into question in a way she had never done before, challenging the sense of inevitability that it rests on and produces, the universality it boasts. At the same time, that the lesbian should be the writer marks the fact that there is no space for her within the pageant, within the plot, and perhaps within history; so her outcast status is underlined.

Miss La Trobe is shown without her lover; no attempt is made to construct an alternative story for her beyond an indication of this separation. The absent lover (who was an actress) further signals the absence of the writer-director from her own play, and connects that absence with her sexuality. At the same time, the range of lesbian relation to the plot is thus encompassed by a pair—the actress, always performing someone else's lines, and the writer, ostensibly producing those lines, though their form must still fit the expectations of an alien audience. Both of these options tie the lesbian to the idea of a script, the question of representation, and to the text itself, in a relation to the text different from that of the other characters contained within the novel: stockbroker, clerk, wife and mother, retired Indian civil servant, or widow. Lacking the context or place that might be provided by family, profession, or history, the lesbian depends on representation for her social existence. This is why the heterosexual plot—as "love embodied," the source only of denying texts—is such an acute problem.

Woolf shows Miss La Trobe, the lesbian writer—as the "slave" of her audience—confined, by a convention that can claim the authority of history, to literally reflecting that audience back to themselves. But the implications of this relation between lesbian writer and audience are double and deeply ironic: the writer need not, and does not, reflect her audience in a flattering light (her project is satirical); at the same time, despite her fantasy of a play without an audience, the writer depends on that audience for her own existence as a writer—it is through her willingness to repeat the heterosexual plot that she gains access to the possibility of representation at all. From her overarching authorial perspective, Woolf holds Miss La Trobe and her audience/subject in tension, via the structuring possibility of a revisionary history—deepening the pageant's critique of the heterosexual plot by extending its analysis into accounts of the lives of the audience, and eventually into history itself, but also, it appears, finally acquiescing in the lesson of constraint Miss La Trobe represents, attempting to write both herself and her writer-character out of a history that ends and begins with the heterosexual couple.

\* \* \*

Finally, Woolf suggests that "the lesbian's" problematic relation to the plot, narrative, and history is unavoidable. Despite the critical debate about the extent to which this novel is concerned with ideals of community, it is impossible to deny the fact that Miss La Trobe, the "outcast," is part of no community offered.[53] As such, Miss La Trobe is also evidence of Woolf's own problematic relation to the plot, whatever the source of the plot's authority.

That remains the fundamental question of the novel. Woolf finally explains Miss La Trobe's outcast status in terms of "nature." This recalls Clarissa Dalloway's pause: "she could not resist sometimes yielding to the charm of a woman," but "She resented it, had a scruple picked up Heaven knows where, or, as she felt, sent by Nature (who is invariably wise)" (36). "Nature" is also, in *Mrs. Dalloway*, the force that drives Septimus to "embrace" his homosexual love in death: "Human nature, in short, was on him—the repulsive brute, with the blood-red nostrils" (102). Woolf's invocation of "nature" again in *Between the Acts* points to a subterranean fault line running from the earlier work but especially through that final novel, beneath the patterns of the lesbian writer's relation to the heterosexual plot and the plot's connection to history.

The heterosexual plot figures heterosexuality itself, and the question that underlies *Between the Acts* is whether heterosexuality can be considered a product of "culture" or "nature," whether it is a function of literature and an aspect of "history," or the cause of "history" (the primeval as the source or the unconscious) and hence literature.[54] Should Woolf's despair at the advent of World War II be present despair at that manifestation of history, or permanent despair at history itself? Gillian Beer argues that Woolf was drawn to the idea of prehistory (which I have described as the primeval) because "prehistory implies a pre-narrative domain which will not buckle to plot . . . prehistory tells no story. It is time without narrative."[55] But in *Between the Acts* prehistory represents not simply the primeval mammoths and mastodons, but the continuing presence and power of "nature," not a realm without narrative but—Woolf's fear is—the source of narrative, as the source of heterosexuality.

What is most significant about the conclusion of *Between the Acts* is, then, not Woolf's equation of heterosexuality and history as war. This was an equation she had been proposing in various forms since at least *A Room of One's Own*.[56] The crucial factor is the equation of heterosexuality, history as war, and nature, the primeval: "night before roads were made, or houses. . . . the night that dwellers in caves had watched from some high place among rocks" (152). But the subterranean tension in the novel is even then not finally resolved, despite this apparent verdict in favor of nature, because the final vision of the novel belongs to Miss La Trobe.

After the pageant is ended, as she sits drinking alone, just before she herself will disappear from the text, Miss La Trobe has a vision of her next play: "There was the high ground at midnight; there the rock; and two scarcely perceptible figures. Suddenly the tree was pelted with starlings. She set down her glass. She heard the first words" (147). This becomes the scene with which Woolf ends her novel:

Isa let her sewing drop. The great hooded chairs had become enormous. And Giles too. And Isa too against the window. The window was all sky without colour. The house had lost its shelter. It was night before roads were made, or houses. It was the night that dwellers in caves had watched from some high place among rocks.

Then the curtain rose. They spoke.

If heterosexuality is a force of nature, and so no critique will have any effect on the plot and its historical conclusion in the violence of war, nature is also responsible for Miss La Trobe. The reader does not hear what Isa and Giles say— the last words of this work, the first words of the next. But even though it seems that this scene writes Miss La Trobe out of history, she hears what is said, she hears "the first words," her vision then encompassing both heterosexuality and war, perhaps history itself. Assuming the lesbian writer's vision, even while the lesbian is writing herself out of history, Woolf identifies herself with the lesbian writer, the lesbian with writing.

# Afterword

# "Reading and the Experiences of Everyday Life"

I have written here about the relations among a series of subjects: lesbian novels and lesbian writing, lesbianism and the literary, lesbian and gay studies and literary criticism. The fulcrum of my discussion of these relations—and often I would argue the fulcrum of these relations—is narrative: the uses, the limits, and the possibilities of narrative. For the purpose of my discussion, I have concentrated on two narrative patterns. On the one hand, the heterosexual plot: "Reader, I married him," of which "it would be Carol, in a thousand cities," is a significant variant, but nevertheless still a variant. On the other hand, history: "Great Alexander lov'd Hephaistion" as well as "the House of Commons . . . the Hundred Years' War . . . The Wars of the Roses . . . The Renaissance Scholars," and "the retreat from Moscow." These different narrative structures might seem to exemplify distinctions between the private and the public, the domestic and the social, the "feminine" and the "masculine." But these are not distinctions that ever sheltered the lesbian writers I have considered here, disenfranchised as lesbians by the heterosexual plot and as women by history.

Lesbian novels and lesbian writing are overlapping, interpretively interdependent bodies of work, both of which can be read from the perspective of lesbian narrative disenfranchisement by the heterosexual plot. Twentieth-century lesbian writing—I am arguing more broadly—bears subtle but discernible traces of its writers' literary position, as well as their social and sexual situations. My argument, that some lesbian writers made a narrative turn to history in the first half of this century, is one possible way of tracing the dimensions of lesbian writing. These dimensions can also be traced, in the lesbian writing of this period, in the work of those writers who avoided fiction altogether, those writers whose relation to fiction was always conflicted, or in those writers whose nonfiction—Alice Dunbar-Nelson's journals, Janet Flanner's journalism—could be read under the rubric of the expansive version of history developed by Stein, Barnes, and Woolf, as alternative forms of the turn to history. That the writers I discuss keep returning to writing as a subject reflects not only their positions as modernists, or within the modern, but also the problem of writing for lesbian writers whatever their formal choices, the constitutive force of "writing" for lesbian writers.

Writing is no less constitutive of lesbianism for readers. In Ann Bannon's *I Am a Woman* (1959), women who love other women meet in New York's Greenwich Village in a bar called The Colophon. Bars were the locus of lesbian public life in the first half of the twentieth century. That Bannon's fictional bar should be The Colophon is an acknowledgment of the printed word as the locus of lesbian representation in the post-Wilde, pre-Stonewall decades. This is hardly surprising, given the feminist accounts I discuss in my introduction of the role of the literary in the social construction of gender and sexuality. "Reading" has been promoted in modern and postmodern accounts of sexuality, social organization, and lesbian-gay cultures. Krafft-Ebing argues in *Psychopathia Sexualis* (1886–1903) that "The development of sexual life has its beginning in the organic sensations which arise from the maturing reproductive glands," but it is "Reading and the experiences of everyday life . . . [that] convert these notions into clear ideas."[1] "Reading" takes priority over "everyday life" as an element of a sexuality represented as simultaneously "organic" and inseparable from "ideas." Krafft-Ebing's "reading" becomes specifically "the literary" in Erving Goffman's classic early 1960s study of social marginalization, *Stigma*, where he argues that "Americans who are stigmatized tend to live in a literarily-defined world, however uncultured they might be." Goffman's justification of this view is that

in America at least, no matter how small and how badly off a particular stigmatized category is, the viewpoint of its members is likely to be given public presentation of some kind. . . . If they don't read books on the situation of persons like themselves, they at least read magazines and see movies; and where they don't do these, then they listen to local, vocal associates. An intellectually worked-up version of their point of view is thus available to most stigmatized persons.[2]

Goffman merges "public presentation," "books . . . magazines . . . movies," and "intellectually worked-up" accounts to produce the literary. By the time Cindy Patton announces, in a recent essay on postmodern politics, that "queers are nothing if not good readers," and goes on to argue that queer "subject[s], [are] constructed both through reading and as a rhetorical effect of reading," her statements seem self-evident.[3]

Nonetheless, there is anxiety about the literary in lesbian/gay studies these days. Eve Sedgwick apologized, in the introduction to *Epistemology of the Closet*, for "the book's limitation to what may sound, in the current climate of exciting interstitial explorations among literature, social history, and 'cultural studies,' like unreconstructedly literary readings of essentially canonical texts" (13).[4] Patton criticizes "The near hegemony in gay studies of deconstructive and psychoanalytic techniques" that she identifies with "the (in reality quite narrow) arena of literary criticism" (164). The question of canons remains a problem. There are some rubrics—although they are not the ones Sedgwick is invoking—under which Willa Cather, Gertrude Stein, Djuna Barnes, and Virginia Woolf could all be read as canonical. But the criticisms of "literary criticism" in gay and lesbian studies are less about canons than about identifying "literary criticism" with a "theory" that is in turn identified with deconstruction or psychoanalysis. This "theory" is then implicitly defined as that which is not "activist"; Patton explains that what she represents as the hegemony of literary criticism "has upset both newer activists who want ways of thinking about what to do *now* and more tenured scholar-activists whose work . . . seems to have been forgotten" (164). But theory/activism distinctions are generally inaccurate representations of more complex circumstances. A theory/activism distinction based on literary criticism will not hold because literary criticism cannot simply be identified with "theory" (deconstruction/psychoanalysis), productive as these approaches have been for literary study and lesbian/gay studies. And a theory/activism distinction based on literature cannot be sustained, because what the "queers" Patton describes as "nothing if not good readers" read are literary texts.

Lesbians in particular read literary texts, as is reflected in a history of lesbian literary studies in the 1970s and 1980s by scholars not "in" literature (but rather "in" anthropology, history, and so on, such as Gayle Rubin, Esther Newton, Blanche Wiesen Cook), as well as by writers working outside of the university, who identify as activitists as often as critics (Barbara Grier, Barbara Smith, Jewelle Gomez, and so on). When philosopher Judith Butler suddenly begins writing about Willa Cather and Nella Larsen, it is surely clear that the literary retains its particular value for lesbian scholarship, even in the new world of queer theory. Dismissals of literary criticism, and dismissals of the literary, from within lesbian/gay studies are then particularly problematic in relation to lesbian studies.

While there is anxiety about the literary in lesbian and gay studies, literary critics are not always happy to welcome lesbian and gay analyses into the fold. Alan Sinfield's description of the construction of the proper critic as heterosexual in his analyses of British "Englit" is easily replicated on this side of the Atlantic.[5] If feminist criticism can still be marginalized, lesbian and gay literary analyses—and particularly ones that focus on women, that make no claim on the "real" canon—are still vulnerable to being dismissed as lesbian/gay rather than critical projects. For the purposes of this book, the distinction between lesbian/gay and literary critical studies is a distinction without a difference. *Are Girls Necessary?* is neither a lesbian study of the literary nor a literary study of lesbianism, but both/and. As the history of lesbian writing tells us, the lesbian and the novel were made for each other—except, of course, when they were not.

# Notes

After an initial note giving bibliographical details, subsequent references to works cited are incorporated into the text.

## Notes to Preface

1. Virginia Woolf, *Orlando* (Harmondsworth: Penguin, 1975), p. 188.
2. Vita Sackville-West, *Collected Poems* (New York: Doubleday and Doran, 1934), "The Land," p. 58.
3. Sherron E. Knopp, " 'If I Saw You Would You Kiss Me?': Sapphism and the Subversiveness of Virginia Woolf's *Orlando*," *PMLA*, 103, 1 (January 1988), pp. 24–34.
4. Because this is a study of effects rather than causes, I am not going to specify the aspects of power Woolf identifies simply as "the spirit of the age." Their contemporary manifestations can be traced in any daily newspaper.
5. Thomas Yingling, *Hart Crane and the Homosexual Text: New Thresholds, New Anatomies* (Chicago: University of Chicago Press, 1990), p. 3.
6. See Terry Castle's introduction to her *The Apparitional Lesbian: Female Homosexuality in Modern Culture* (New York: Columbia University Press, 1993).
7. See, for example, Elizabeth Kennedy's and Madeline Davis's *Boots of Leather, Slippers of Gold: The History of a Lesbian Community* (New York: Routledge, 1993), for a discussion of definitions of lesbianism in a mid-twentieth-century, working-class, lesbian community.
8. See, for example, Biddy Martin's "Lesbian Identity and Autobiographical Difference[s]," in *Life-Lines: Theorizing Women's Autobiography*, eds. Bella Brodzki and Celeste Schenck (Ithaca: Cornell University Press, 1988), pp. 77–103, and Elizabeth Meese's *(Sem)erotics: Theorizing Lesbian : Writing* (New York: New York University Press, 1992).
9. Judith Butler, "Imitation and Gender Insubordination," in *The Lesbian and Gay Studies Reader*, eds. Henry Abelove, Michèle Aina Barale and David Halperin (New York: Routledge, 1993), pp. 307–20, 308, 309.

10. Similar questions are raised in the context of Marlon Rigg's last film, *Black Is . . . Black Ain't*, about the dimensions of African-American identities.

11. Michel Foucault, *The History of Sexuality, An Introduction: Volume 1* (New York: Vintage Books/Random House, 1990), p. 101.

12. Even Judith Butler is willing to talk about "lesbian sexuality," although she defines "lesbianism as a refracted sexuality, consituted in translation and displacement," in "Dangerous Crossing," *Bodies That Matter: On the Discursive Limits of "Sex"* (New York: Routledge, 1993), p. 145.

13. David Halperin and Carol Dinshaw, "From the Editors," GLQ Vol. 1, No. 1 (1993), pp. iii–iv.

14. Judith Roof seems to want to downplay the sexual. While she does not want "to deny the material existence and desire of lesbian women, nor to suggest that the category is not meaningful. . . . [a] sexuality, though important, does not constitute an identity. . . . And lesbian does not constitute a monolithic category" (p. 251). But the inability of sex to produce identity becomes a statement about the inadequacy of lesbianism as a social category only if sex is assumed as the sole basis for "lesbian" as a social category. History and culture have disappeared. And when Roof finally proposes that we "Adopt . . . a desire for desire instead of a desire for identity or stability" (p. 254), sex is revalued as desire; it turns out that the prior limits on sex had been the limits of its object. *A Lure of Knowledge: Lesbian Sexuality and Theory* (New York: Columbia University Press, 1991).

15. Teresa de Lauretis, "Queer Theory: Lesbian and Gay Sexualities, An Introduction," *differences*, 3, 2 (Summer 1991), pp. iii–xviii, iii.

16. Diana Fuss, "Inside/Out," *Inside/Out: Lesbian Theories, Gay Theories* (New York: Routledge, 1991), pp. 1–10, 1.

17. Eve Kosofsky Sedgwick, *Epistemology of the Closet* (Berkeley: University of California Press, 1990), p. 53.

18. Sandra Gilbert and Susan Gubar, for example, pronounce firmly, "Although . . . the issue of heterosexual desire was a central concern for many modernists, a number of their contemporaries were influenced by the new discourse of sexology, which led them to analyze alternate modes of eroticism. During the same period in which, for example, Edward Carpenter and Havelock Ellis defined what they called 'the intermediate sex' or 'the invert,' such writers as Radclyffe Hall, H. D., Gertrude Stein, and Virginia Woolf explored lesbianism, bisexuality, transvestism, and transsexuality in a quest for sex-role metamorphosis." Lesbianism is, then, "an alternate mode of eroticism," produced out of sexology, and for the purpose of "sex-role metamorphosis." *No Man's Land: The Place of the Woman Writer in the Twentieth Century*, Vol. 3, *Letters From the Front* (New Haven: Yale University Press, 1994), p. 364. Elizabeth Meese makes a more promising move when she writes, " 'Lesbian' is applied to me in a system I do not control, that cannot control itself. Yet it is a word I want to embrace, re-write and re-claim, not to install it but to explode its meaning" (p. 14). However her "lesbian writer" is highly romanticized: "The words of love multiply, acquire color and form, powerful descriptions, yes even determinants, of what we are doing in our lesbian silence. . . . the lesbian-writer (re)writes us as 'ourselves' " [*Sem*]*erotics*, p. 20). For an example of the lesbian writer as biographical spectacle, see Diane Souhami's *Gertrude and Alice* (London: Pandora, 1991).

19. Nancy K. Miller, *Subject to Change: Reading Feminist Writing* (New York: Columbia University Press, 1988), pp. 28–29.

20. Teresa de Lauretis, "Film and the Visible," *How Do I Look: Queer Film and Video* (Seattle: Bay Press, 1991), pp. 223–264, 264.

21. Gloria T. Hull discusses Grimké in her *Color, Sex, and Poetry: Three Women Writers of the Harlem Renaissance* (Bloomington: University of Indiana Press, 1987). See also Ann duCille's *The Coupling Convention: Sex, Text, and Tradition in Black Women's Fiction* (New York: Oxford University Press, 1993), for a discussion of the roles of heterosexual plot conventions in the development of African-American women's fiction; and Carolyn Steedman's *Landscape for a Good Woman: A Story of Two Lives* (New Brunswick, NJ: Rutgers University Press, 1987), for her account of the narratives of white working-class British women's experience.

22. See Lambda Literary Awards, press release, March 1, 1993; *Lambda Rising News* (Spring 1993), p. 1; *Lambda Book Report* 3, 10 (May/June 1993), pp. 13, 35; *Lambda Book Report* 3, 11 (July/August 1993), pp. 4, 9. Allison's novel did win the 1992 Ferro-Grumley Award for Best Lesbian Fiction of the year, presented annually by the Ferro-Grumley Foundation in honor of the late authors and lovers Robert Ferro and Michael Grumley.

23. "First Person Singular—II: Dorothy Allison, Crossover Blues," Blanche McCrary Boyd, *The Nation*, "A Queer Nation" special issue, ed. Andrew Kopkind, 257, 1 (July 5, 1993), pp. 20–21.

24. The first comment comes from "Defining Our Literature: Jim Marks Interviews Dorothy Allison," *Lambda Book Report* 3, 11 (July/August 1993), p. 9.

25. Gertrude Stein, "A Conversation" with John Hyde Preston. *Atlantic Monthly* LVI (August 1935), pp. 187–194, 193.

## Notes to Introduction

1. Teresa de Lauretis, *Alice Doesn't: Feminism, Semiotics, Cinema* (Bloomington: Indiana University Press, 1984), p. 106.

2. Peter Brooks, *Reading for the Plot: Design and Intention in Narrative* (New York: Vintage, 1985), p. 10.

3. Joanna Russ, "What Can a Heroine Do? Or Why Women Can't Write," *Images of Women in Fiction: Feminist Perspectives*, ed. Susan Köppelman Cornillon (Bowling Green, OH: Bowling Green University Popular Press, 1972), pp. 3–20, 9.

4. Nancy K. Miller, *Subject to Change: Reading Feminist Writing* (New York: Columbia University Press, 1988), p. 44. See also Joseph Allen Boone, *Tradition Counter Tradition: Love and the Form of Fiction* (Chicago: University of Chicago Press, 1987).

5. Rachel Blau DuPlessis, *Writing Beyond the Ending: Narrative Strategies of Twentieth Century Women Writers* (Bloomington: Indiana University Press, 1985), p. 5. Lesbian novelist Jane Rule comments, "Morality for the novelist is expressed not so much in the choice of subject matter as in the plot of the narrative. . . . Resisting judgement in plot is not simply a matter of squeamishness, uncertainty, or lack of responsibility. It is, in my case, resisting mistakes and lies, particularly in the

realm of sexual experience." "Sexuality in Literature," in Jane Rule, *Outlander: Stories and Essays* (Tallahassee, FL: Naiad Press, 1982), pp. 149–155, 151–152.

6. Djuna Barnes, *Nightwood* (New York: New Directions, 1937), p. 97.
7. Lesbian writing has developed one narrative convention since Stonewall, the "coming out story," discussed by Biddy Martin in "Lesbian Identity and Autobiographical Difference[s]," *Life/Lines*, eds. Bella Brodzki and Celeste Schenck (Ithaca: Cornell University Press, 1988), pp. 77–103. But "coming out stories" are still concerned with lesbianism as a problem.
8. Also see Judith Butler's analysis of the construction of sex and gender in conjunction with the construction of heterosexuality in *Gender Trouble: Feminism and the Subversion of Identity* (New York: Routledge, 1990).
9. Butler, *Gender Trouble*, p. 151.
10. See Vera Brittain, *Radclyffe Hall: A Case of Obscenity?* (London: Femina, 1968), and Michael Baker, *Our Three Selves: The Life of Radclyffe Hall* (New York: Morrow, 1985).
11. Suzanna Danuta Walters argues, in "As Her Hand Crept Slowly Up Her Thigh: Ann Bannon and the Politics of Pulp," *Social Text* 23 (Fall/Winter, 1989), pp. 83–101, that the "popularly written pulps reached a different class of lesbians than . . . *The Well of Loneliness* (p. 85)." This argument is contradicted by publishers' use of references to Hall's work, by *The Well*'s publication history, and by such studies of its readership as Rebecca O'Rourke's *Reflecting on The Well of Loneliness* (London: Routledge, 1989).
12. Terry Castle argues that the relationship between the two women requires the elimination of male homosocial possibilities. But the two women are brought together through the heterosexual plot, around the figure of Frederick, whose rejection when they bond signifies the seriousness of their relationship. "Sylvia Townsend Warner and the Counterplot of Lesbian Fiction," in *Sexual Sameness: Textual Differences in Lesbian and Gay Writing*, ed. Joseph Bristow (New York: Routledge, 1993), pp. 128–147.
13. Because lesbian and heterosexual relationships are opposed, there is particular scope for critiques of heterosexuality. In *The Friendly Young Ladies*, Mary Renault satirizes a young male doctor who sees himself as the savior of every woman he meets. Anticipating Betty Friedan's *Feminine Mystique*, Ann Bannon's *Journey to a Woman* begins with a very persuasive account of Beth's dissatisfaction with her choice of suburban marriage and children over her college romance with Laura.
14. Both methods for using the heterosexual plot, triangulation and overlay, can appear in the same novel, as in *The Well*, where Hall creates a masculine/feminine couple, and then sets Stephen's relation to Mary against Martin Hallam's offer to marry Mary. The construction of the lesbian story around the heterosexual plot and its completion by a movement of repression can also pivot on each other, as in *The Well*: Stephen's lesbianism is confirmed by her repulsion at Hallam's declaration of his love for her; Stephen's punishment is completed when Hallam returns to marry her lover.

    The lesbian minor character, the lesbian episode, and the lesbian in a short story are constructed out of the same terms as the lesbian novel, via some contrast with the heterosexual plot, and punishment. See, for example, the 1930s novels of

Kate O'Brien, Lillian Smith's *Strange Fruit* (1944), and Henry Handel Richardson's "Two Hanged Women" (1934).

15. There are at least two subgenres among "lesbian novels": schoolgirl fictions and "autobiographies." In the schoolgirl fictions, for example Henry Handel Richardson's *The Getting of Wisdom* (1910), Christa Winsloe's *The Child Manuela* (1933), and Rosemary Manning's *The Chinese Garden* (1962), the protagonist is a student at an all-female boarding school, where the beloved is either another student or a teacher. The sexuality becomes more explicit when the "schoolgirl stories" shift during the 1950s from the European public school to the U.S. university campus sorority house, as in Vin Packer's *Spring Fire* (1952) and Ann Bannon's *Odd Girl Out* (1957). A number of individual lesbian authors (for example Maureen Duffy, Rosemary Manning, and Radclyffe Hall herself), moved from producing a schoolgirl fiction to an adult lesbian novel. For a discussion of "autobiographical" fictions, see my introduction to Diana Frederics's *Diana* (New York: New York University Press, 1995).

16. H. D., *HERmione* (New York: New Directions, 1981), p. 12.

17. The only working women in the novel are Mandy, the Gart family's African-American maid, and the white working-class girl who nurses Hermione during her breakdown. Susan Stanford Friedman has considered race in the context of H. D.'s work as a whole in her essay "Modernism of the 'Scattered Remnant': Race and Politics in H. D.'s Development," *Feminist Issues in Literary Scholarship*, ed. Shari Benstock (Bloomington: Indiana University Press, 1987), pp. 208–232.

18. In " 'I Had Two Loves Separate': The Sexualities of H. D.'s *Her*," *Montemora* 8 (1981), pp. 7–31, Susan Stanford Friedman and Rachel Blau DuPlessis record H. D.'s autobiographical identification of the novel's characters, of which the most important are George Lowndes as Ezra Pound and Fayne Rabb as Frances Josepha Gregg, while warning that the novel "is not reliable as factual biography" (pp. 10, 26). Too much attention to biography obscures the formal questions the novel raises.

19. In " 'I Had Two Loves Separate'," Friedman and DuPlessis argue that the structure of *HERmione* is a "double love plot," "heterosexual and homosexual," overlooking the inequality between the lesbian and heterosexual narratives' relations to the authority of literary convention (p. 11). To focus, as DuPlessis does in *Writing Beyond the Ending*, on the novel's critique of the romance narrative, is to privilege the heterosexual plot while still simplifying the lesbian writer's relation to that plot. Without denying H. D.'s heterosexual experience, it is necessary to acknowledge that no use of the heterosexual plot is simply the result of an autobiographical impulse.

20. Patricia Highsmith (Claire Morgan), *The Price of Salt* (Tallahassee, FL: Naiad Press, 1984), p. 275. This was the only work Highsmith published as Morgan. The psychological thrillers for which she became known, such as *Strangers on a Train* (1951) and *The Talented Mr. Ripley* (1955), often focus on the interactions between a central male pair.

21. Butler, *Gender Trouble*, p. 31.

22. Ibid.

23. See Highsmith, *The Price of Salt*, "Afterword."

24. Kate Adams, in "Making the World Safe for the Missionary Position," discusses the "normality" of the lovers in *The Price of Salt*, in contrast to the sensationalism of other novels of the period. She argues that the comparative blandness of High-

smith's novel rendered her lesbians invisible, but this claim has to be reconciled with the novel's multiple editions and extensive sales. *Lesbian Texts and Contexts: Radical Revisions*, eds. Karla Jay and Joanne Glasgow (New York: New York University Press, 1991), pp. 255–274.

25. This is a quotation from a cover blurb for Ann Aldrich, ed., *Carol in a Thousand Cities* (New York: Fawcett, 1960).

26. Michele Barale discusses Jack's first sighting of Beebo Brinker in "When Jack Blinks: Si(gh)ting Gay Desire in Ann Bannon's *Beebo Brinker*," in *The Lesbian and Gay Studies Reader*, eds. Henry Abelove, Michele Aina Barale, and David M. Halperin (New York: Routledge, 1993), pp. 604–615.

27. The circulation of women within a system of heterosexual plots can also be disrupted by triangulations through mother/daughter relationships. In *The Price of Salt*, Carol's daughter is the focus of the divorce proceedings and so of the narrative structure, and she is the "price" Carol will pay for her lesbianism. The daughter ties the two women to the heterosexual plot through her father. But she also distances them from the plot. Carol finally chooses not between her husband/heterosexuality and her lover/lesbianism, but between motherhood and lesbianism. Highsmith also pushes the limits of the lesbian novel in *Price* by linking lesbianism and motherhood: Carol's struggle to keep her child establishes her fitness as a mother; the separation of parents and children is represented as an aspect of the persecution gays and lesbians face, and as a hardship also for the children of gay and lesbian parents.

28. Therese's job also takes her and Carol beyond the conventional settings of lesbian novels—girls' schools, sororities, women's prisons, and gay bars. While these settings were exotic to the majority of women, department stores were not: the urban department store was a primary setting for women's employment in the first half of the twentieth century.

29. Maureen Duffy, *The Microcosm* (New York: Simon and Schuster, 1966), p. 298.

30. These lesbian writer protagonists are supported by a range of other lesbian "artist" figures—Woolf's Lily Briscoe, a painter in *To The Lighthouse*; Gale Wilhelm's Jan Morales, a sculptor in *We Too Are Drifting*; Highsmith's Therese, a stage set designer, in *The Price of Salt*, and so on—and other writers whose sexuality is more ambiguous, such as Woolf's eponymous Orlando.

31. Sandra Gilbert and Susan Gubar, *No Man's Land: The Place of the Woman Writer in the Twentieth Century*, Volume I, *The War of the Words* (New Haven: Yale University Press, 1988).

32. See also H. D.'s discussion of "vision" in "Notes on Thought and Vision," written in 1919, at the beginning of her relationship with Bryher. She insists that "There is no great art period without great lovers" (p. 21), and her lovers include the homosexual: "We must be 'in love' before we can understand the mysteries of vision. A lover must choose one of the same type of mind as himself, a musician, a musician, a scientist, a scientist, a general, a young man also interested in the theory and practice of arms and armies" (p. 22). *"Notes on Thought and Vision" and "The Wise Sappho"* (San Francisco: City Lights Books, 1982).

33. DuPlessis argues, in relation to *HERmione* and *Bid Me to Live*, that for H. D., " 'Writer' is a third term, mediating between the polarized sexes. This accommodating solution of drawing on the two sides of human personality, the psychic and

intellectual androgyny that Woolf explored in *A Room of One's Own* and in *Orlando*, was also H. D.'s way of transcending the antinomies of sexual polarization. Status as an artist is a way of resisting women's definitional dependence on heterosexual ties, in which one is judged by access to men." *Writing Beyond the Ending*, p. 74. But status as an artist does not mean, in these texts, being androgynous.

34. Love is writing in the literal sense that images of this love can be found only in books, rather than the social world—in the Greek books and in the German books about people who "loved . . . differently" that H. D. self-consciously invokes as her intertexts (p. 203). Loving differently, Hermione has to realize the limits of conventional language, as used by her mother to describe her competing loves: " 'normal, unwholesome, their vocabulary gets more meagre' " (p. 177).

35. The play is identified in the text as the work of George Bernard Shaw, but Shaw's *Pygmalion* obviously contains no Greek garb or sea coasts. See Collecott, "Images at the Crossroads: The H. D. Scrapbook," for a more accurate identification and discussion of the play. *H. D.: Woman and Poet*, ed. Michael King (Orono, ME: National Poetry Foundation, 1986), pp. 319–367.

36. For surveys of lesbian criticism, see Bonnie Zimmerman, "What Has Never Been: An Overview of Lesbian Feminist Criticism," *The New Feminist Criticism: Literature and Theory*, ed. Elaine Showalter (New York: Pantheon, 1985), pp. 200–224; and my "History as Explanation: Writing About Lesbian Writing, or 'Are Girls Necessary?' " *Left Politics and the Literary Profession*, eds. Lennard J. Davis and M. Bella Mirabella (New York: Columbia University Press, 1991), pp. 254–283.

37. Foster recorded every reference she could find to emotional as well as sexual involvements between women in literature and in the lives of women writers, from Sappho to writers of the 1950s. Foster defines "variance" at once narrowly and broadly: "this study includes not only women who are conscious of passion for their own sex, with or without overt expression, but also those who are merely obsessively attached to other women over a longer period or at a more mature age than is commonly expected. If 'commonly expected' is another nebulous phrase, a species of pooled judgement is available to clarify it. During the past few decades—that is, since Freudian concepts have become a part of the common background—most works on sex guidance have taken some account of homosexuality. These agree in general that passionate attachments during puberty and early adolescence may lie within the norm, but if occurring later they constitute variance. Without here debating the absolute validity of this opinion, one may borrow it as a working criterion." Jeannette Foster, *Sex Variant Women in Literature* (Baltimore, MD: Diana Press, 1975), p. 12.

38. Gene Damon (Barbara Grier), Jan Watson, and Robin Jordan, eds., *The Lesbian in Literature: A Bibliography* (2nd ed.) (Reno, NV: The Ladder, 1975); Barbara Grier (ed.) *The Lesbian in Literature* (Naiad Press, 1981); J. R. Roberts, ed., *Black Lesbians: An Annotated Bibliography* (Naiad Press, 1981); Barbara Grier, *Lesbiana: Book Reviews From "The Ladder," 1966–1972* (Naiad Press, 1976).

39. This anonymous review is quoted in Jane Marcus, "Mousemeat: Contemporary Reviews of *Nightwood*," *Silence and Power: A Reevaluation of Djuna Barnes*, ed. Mary Lynn Broe (Carbondale: Southern Illinois University Press, 1991), pp. 195–204, 197–198.

40. Henry Reed, *New Statesman and Nation* (October 14, 1944).
41. Many of the novels reprinted as pulps were originally produced by "respectable" presses: Harcourt, Brace and Company; The Modern Library; Random House; Jonathan Cape, and so on.
42. Reproductions of these covers can be found in Roberta Yusba, "Odd Girls and Strange Sisters: Lesbian Pulp Novels of the '50s," *Out/Look* 12 (Spring, 1991), pp. 34–37.
43. Judith Roof, *A Lure of Knowledge: Lesbian Sexuality and Theory* (New York: Columbia University Press, 1991), p. 91.
44. Cassandra Laity, "Introduction," H. D., *Paint It Today* (New York: New York University Press, 1992), pp. xvii–xliii, xviii.
45. Bonnie Zimmerman, *The Safe Sea of Women: Lesbian Fiction 1969–1989* (Boston: Beacon Press, 1990), pp. 14–15.
46. Barbara Smith, "The Truth That Never Hurts: Black Lesbians in Fiction in the 1980s," in *Third World Women and the Politics of Feminism*, eds. Chandra Talpade Mohanty, Ann Russo, and Lourdes Torres (Bloomington: Indiana University Press, 1990), pp. 101–129, 111.
47. Castle, "Sylvia Townsend Warner," p. 213.
48. Dr. Arthur Guy Mathews, M.D., "Introduction," G. Sheila Donisthorpe, *Loveliest of Friends!* (New York: Arco, 1952), pp. 9–11, 10, 11. "Dr. Matthews" is identified as the "Director of Kings Bureau of Investigation and Psychotic Research, Author of *Take it Easy! The Art of Conquering Your Nerves*."
49. Aldrich continues with a repetition of Hall's linking of fiction and science: "We may know just as much about a subject as lesbianism by reading fiction about it, as we may learn by reading scientific works." *Carol in a Thousand Cities*, p. 11.
50. Arnold Bennett, "Is the Novel Decaying?" in *Virginia Woolf: The Critical Heritage*, eds. Robin Majumdar and Allen McLaurin (London: Routledge and Kegan Paul, 1975), pp. 112–114, 113.
51. Virginia Woolf, "Modern Fiction," *The Common Reader, First and Second Series* (New York: Harcourt, Brace and Company, 1948), pp. 207–218, 213.
52. Terry Castle argues that "lesbian fiction" is antirealist. But most of her examples are drawn from the post-Stonewall period, when there was a wider range of literary options available to the text that would be read as lesbian. Moreover, most of the "lesbian fictions" she cites were not lesbian novels: they were not initially read as lesbian, whether they were first published in the pre- or post-Stonewall periods. *The Apparitional Lesbian: Female Homosexuality and Modern Culture* (New York: Columbia University Press, 1993), p. 90.
53. Adrienne Rich, "It is the Lesbian in Us . . ." *On Lies, Secrets, and Silence: Selected Prose, 1966–1978* (Norton, 1979), pp. 199–202.
54. Barbara Smith, "Towards a Definition of Black Feminist Criticism," *The New Feminist Criticism: Women, Literature and Theory*, ed. Elaine Showalter (New York: Pantheon, 1985), pp. 168–185, 168.
55. Catharine R. Stimpson, "Zero Degree Deviancy: The Lesbian Novel in English," *Where the Meanings Are: Feminism and Cultural Spaces* (New York: Methuen, 1988), pp. 97–110, 99.

56. Teresa de Lauretis, "Sexual Indifference and Lesbian Representation," *Theatre Journal* 40, 2 (May, 1988), pp. 155–177, 155.

57. Elizabeth Meese, "Theorizing Lesbian : Writing—A Love Letter," *Lesbian Texts and Contexts*, eds. Jay and Glasgow, pp. 83–84. She repeats these arguments in *(Sem)erotics*.

58. Bonnie Zimmerman, "What Has Never Been: An Overview of Lesbian Feminist Criticism," *The New Feminist Criticism*, ed. Showalter, pp. 200–224, 207. Recent examples of the use of "coding" can be found in Cassandra Laity's introduction to H. D.'s *Paint It Today* (New York: New York University Press, 1992), and Suzanne Raitt's discussion of Woolf and Sackville-West's fictions in *Vita and Virginia: The Work and Friendship of Vita Sackville-West and Virginia Woolf* (Oxford: Oxford University Press, 1993).

59. D. H. Lawrence, for example, refers to the Greeks in his characterization of the (temporarily) lesbian Winifred Inger in *The Rainbow* (1915), and Compton Mackenzie quotes Sappho in his *Extraordinary Women* (1928). The Greeks also, of course, accompany many literary references to gay men.

60. On the back cover of the most recent American edition of *The Well* it is still described as "the thinly disguised story of Radclyffe Hall's own life," echoing Blanche McCrary Boyd's (1980) "Afterword," in which she declares that "Stephen Gordon is a thinly disguised version of the author": *The Well of Loneliness* (New York: Anchor, 1990), p. 441.

61. However, in accord with the actual workings of "the closet," even as writers worried about being identified as lesbian, reviewers, critics, and even biographers studiously overlooked potentially controversial details in the behavior of women writers who did not draw attention to themselves by producing lesbian novels. Sharon O'Brien notes, "E. K. Brown wondered about Cather's sexual identity; there is a card among his papers at Yale with the heading 'Homosexuality.' But as the official biographer, working closely with [Cather's partner] Edith Lewis, Brown could not make his private speculations public." *Willa Cather: The Emerging Voice* (New York: Oxford University Press, 1987), p. 142. There was such reluctance to label authors that it could encompass even a "lesbian novel." After the publication of Jane Rule's first novel, *The Desert of the Heart*, in 1964, "When my reappointment as a university lecturer was challenged because of the book, my more liberal colleagues defended me with the argument that writers of murder mysteries were not necessarily themselves murderers; therefore it followed that a writer of a lesbian novel was not necessarily a lesbian. I was reappointed." Jane Rule, *Lesbian Images* (New York: Doubleday, 1975), p. 1.

62. Gertrude Stein, *Everybody's Autobiography* (New York: Random House, 1973), p. 171.

63. Marianne Hirsch, *The Mother/Daughter Plot: Narrative, Psychoanalysis, Feminism* (Bloomington: Indiana University Press, 1989), p. 97.

64. Such limited acknowledgement of lesbianism is unfortunately not unusual. In Bonnie Kime Scott's anthology, *The Gender of Modernism* (Bloomington: Indiana University Press, 1991), lesbianism, indexed as "lesbian sexuality," gets seven references in a 718-page volume, although nine out of the twenty-one women included in the collection could be read as lesbian or bisexual.

65. Attention to lesbianism would complicate Hirsch's vision of the mother-daughter plot as *the* alternative to heterosexual plots, in terms of the larger argument she is making, and also in relation to her specific readings. For example, Hirsch discusses Lily Briscoe's "conception of her art" as founded on an intimacy between women: "In her new borderline language unknown to men, but in which men are also involved, intimacy redefines knowledge and constitutes art: not possession, it becomes a form of momentary contact, continually in need of being remade" (*Mother-Daughter Plot*, p. 116). But Lily Briscoe's intimacy with Mrs Ramsay is not simply a matter of mother-daughter dynamics.

66. Teresa de Lauretis, *Technologies of Gender: Essays on Theory, Film, and Fiction* (Bloomington: Indiana University Press, 1987), p. 113.

67. Virginia Woolf, "Mr. Bennett and Mrs. Brown," *The Captain's Death Bed and Other Essays*, (New York: Harcourt Brace Jovanovich, 1968), pp. 94–119, 110–111.

68. Virginia Woolf, "The Narrow Bridge of Art," *Granite and Rainbow* (New York: Harcourt Brace Jovanovich, 1975), pp. 11–23, 19.

69. Gertrude Stein, *Narration* (Chicago: The University of Chicago Press, 1935), p. 20.

70. Virginia Woolf, "Phases of Fiction" (1929) in *Granite and Rainbow*, pp. 93–145, 108.

71. Renault's example is Murasaki:

    It would have been impossible to Murasaki, for all her more than Proustian subtlety, to set *The Tale of the Genji* in the Imperial court of eleventh-century Kyoto where she was a bored lady-in-waiting known to everyone. Her masterpiece begins, "At the court of an Emperor—he lived it matters not when. . . ." No doubt the ceremonies, houses, temples, gardens, landscapes through which she leads the Shining Prince were all of them those she knew. (Mary Renault, "History in Fiction," *Times Literary Supplement* [March 23, 1973], pp. 315–316, 315).

72. Barbara Guest, *Herself Defined: The Poet H. D. and Her World* (New York: Morrow, 1984), pp. 105–110. They celebrated the date of their first meeting, July 17, 1918, "as an anniversary. If separated they would make certain that a special letter arrived. H. D.'s nearly always included the phrase 'Every year I thank you for saving me and Pup [her child]' " (p. 110).

73. Hayden White, "The Value of Narrativity in the Representation of Reality" *Critical Inquiry* 7, 1 (Autumn 1980), pp. 5–28, 10. See also White, *Tropics of Discourse: Essays in Cultural Criticism* (Baltimore: The Johns Hopkins University Press, 1978), p. 69.

74. Mary Renault, *The Charioteer* (1953; reprint New York: World Publishing Co., 1966), p. 178. Renault was aware of this history from the beginning of her career: in her first novel, *Purposes of Love* (1939), the lesbian Colonna Kimball alludes to *Edward II*.

75. Lesbians did claim "history." Karla Jay discusses Renée Vivien's and Natalie Barney's interest in recovering lesbian history and recreating Sappho's model in *The Amazon and the Page* (Bloomington: University of Indiana Press, 1988). Terry

Castle describes an early twentieth-century female couple's claims to have shared a vision of Marie Antionette in "Contagious Folly: *An Adventure* and Its Skeptics," *Critical Inquiry* 17, 4 (Summer 1991), pp. 741–772.

76. Woolf had identified history with masculinity as early as her first novel, *The Voyage Out*, where St. John Hirst, the consummate young male intellectual, attempting to discover if women are educable, advises Rachel Vinrace to read Gibbon, and sends her a volume of the *Decline and Fall*, which he happens to have brought with him to South America as one of the necessities of life, even when traveling.

77. Christina Crosby, *The Ends of History: Victorians and "The Woman Question"* (New York: Routledge, 1991), pp. 3, 1.

78. Marguerite Yourcenar, *Memoirs of Hadrian* (New York: Farrar Straus Giroux, 1981), pp. 327–328.

79. There are at least two "lesbian novels" that are also historical novels: Sylvia Townsend Warner's *Summer Will Show*, and Kate O'Brien's *As Music and Splendour* (1956). But they are "lesbian novels"; their historical settings provide distance as much as structure. (That these are the only "lesbian novels" by each of these writers suggests their anxiety about the form.) Both are set in the nineteenth century—*Summer Will Show* in England and Paris in 1848, *As Music and Splendour* in Paris and Rome in the 1880s—and neither deals with centers of orthodox political power. Townsend Warner combines the artist as a middle-aged woman with revolutionary politics; O'Brien takes additional refuge in the assumptions of the *Künstlerroman* for her story of a pair of young Irish opera singers (one lesbian and one heterosexual). The art and the politics provide the basis for working out the narratives of these relationships: Sophia and Minna revolt together; Clare and her lover Luisa sing.

80. Eve Kosofsky Sedgwick, "Across Gender, Across Sexuality: Willa Cather and Others," *South Atlantic Quarterly* 88, 1 (Winter 1989), pp. 53–72, 66.

81. Castle, "Sylvia Townsend Warner," n. 3, p. 244.

82. Gay men are notably absent from lesbian novels of the 1970s and eighties, returning only recently with, for example, Sarah Schulman's *People in Trouble* (1990). Lesbian characters rarely appear in novels about gay men until the 1980s, arriving, for example, in David Leavitt's *The Lost Language of Cranes* (1986) and Edmund White's *The Beautiful Room Is Empty* (1988).

83. This pattern in gay fiction can be traced from the flamboyant Risley in E. M. Forster's *Maurice* (1913/1971)—who is the first homosexual Maurice meets, and whom he mysteriously recognizes as kindred without understanding either Risley's or his own sexuality—to the equally extravagant Sutherland in Andrew Holleran's *Dancer From the Dance* (1978), who counterpoints the post-Stonewall gay identity of Holleran's hero Malone.

84. Jehlen suggests that "an impotent feminine sensibility is a basic structure of the novel" (p. 600), which requires "a definition of female characters that effectively precludes their becoming autonomous, so that indeed they would do so at the risk of the novel's artistic life" (p. 595), in "Archimedes and the Paradox of Feminist Criticism," *Signs* 6, 4 (Summer 1981), pp. 575–601.

85. Nancy K. Miller, " 'I's in Drag: The Sex of Recollection," *The Eighteenth Century* 22, 1 (1981), pp. 45–57, 49.

86. Mary Jacobus, "Is There a Woman in This Text?" *New Literary History* 14, 1 (Autumn 1982), pp. 117–142, 130.

87. Eve Kosofsky Sedgwick, *Between Men: English Literature and Male Homosocial Desire* (New York: Columbia University Press, 1985), pp. 25, 27.

88. Castle, "Sylvia Townsend Warner," p. 142.

89. Lesbians' identifications with masculinity and with gay men have both been described as useful strategies, although the effects can be strikingly divergent. Esther Newton, for example, argues that middle- and upper-class lesbians adopted masculine identifications in the first decades of this century to indicate their "difference," and that their relationships with other women were sexual. In contrast, Sue-Ellen Case argues that contemporary cross-gender identifications among lesbians and gay men produce a "queer" identity that is not gendered, as the basis of a queer theory that works "not at the site of gender, but at the site of ontology, to shift the ground of being itself." See Esther Newton, "The Mythic Mannish Lesbian: Radclyffe Hall and the New Woman," *Hidden From History: Reclaiming the Gay and Lesbian Past*, eds. Martin Duberman, Martha Vicinus and George Chauncey, Jr. (New York: Meridian, 1989), pp. 281–293. and also *Cherry Grove, Fire Island: America's First Lesbian and Gay Town* (Boston: Beacon, 1993), for a rare account of interactions among lesbians and gay men from the 1930s to the present, over the history of the resort community of Cherry Grove. Sue-Ellen Case, "Tracking the Vampire," *differences* 3, 2 (1991), pp. 1–20, 3.

90. Marianne DeKoven, "History as Suppressed Referent in Modernist Fiction," *ELH* 51, 1 (Spring 1984), pp. 137–152, 137.

91. These efforts include Rachel Blau DuPlessis's work on narrative strategies in *Writing Beyond the Ending*, Sandra Gilbert's and Susan Gubar's *No Man's Land*, Susan Stanford Friedman's *Penelope's Web: Gender, Modernism, H. D.'s Fiction* (New York: Oxford University Press, 1992), and DeKoven herself in *Rich and Strange: Gender, History, Modernism* (Princeton: Princeton University Press, 1992).

92. The most detailed discussion of history in the work of a modernist woman has been Friedman's account of H. D.'s prose in *Penelope's Web*.

93. Friedman and DuPlessis argue that H. D. was stylistically indebted to her reading of Dorothy Richardson and Virginia Woolf, her knowledge of psychoanalysis, and her interest in film techniques. See "I Had Two Loves Separate" and *H. D.: The Career of That Struggle* (Bloomington: Indiana University Press, 1986).

94. For a discussion of H. D.'s use of the Greek and what it meant to her see DuPlessis, *The Career of That Struggle*, chapter 1.

95. For another discussion of the Greek, with particular reference to Greek images and statues and the erotic in the work of H. D., see Diana Collecott, "Images at the Crossroads."

96. Many of the fictional representations of lesbianism in the 1920s and 1930s, for example most notably *The Well of Loneliness*, but also, for example, Rosamund Lehmann's *Dusty Answer*, Mary Renault's *The Friendly Young Ladies*, Christa Winsloe's *The Child Manuela*, Compton MacKenzie's *Extraordinary Women*, and Virginia Woolf's *Orlando* use the crossing of conventional gender boundaries as a sign of lesbianism.

97. White, "The Value of Narrativity," p. 18; and White, *Tropics of Discourse: Essays in Cultural Criticism* (Baltimore: The Johns Hopkins University Press, 1978), p. 69.

98. Fredric Jameson, *The Political Unconscious: Narrative as a Socially Symbolic Act* (Ithaca: Cornell University Press, 1981), p. 148.

## Notes to Chapter 1

1. Jane Rule began the discussion of Cather as a lesbian writer with a chapter in *Lesbian Images* (New York: Doubleday, 1975). Subsequent essays include Deborah Lambert's "The Defeat of a Hero: Autonomy and Sexuality in *My Ántonia*," *American Literature* 53, 4 (January 1982), pp. 676–690; Blanche Gelfant, "The Forgotten Reaping-Hook: Sex in *My Ántonia*," *Women Writing in America: Voices in Collage* (Hanover: University Press of New England, 1984), pp. 95–116; Judith Fetterly, "*My Ántonia*, Jim Burden, and the Dilemma of the Lesbian Writer," in *Lesbian Texts and Contexts: Radical Revisions*, eds. Karla Jay and Joanne Glasgow (New York: New York University Press, 1990), pp. 145–163. Sharon O'Brien has offered the most extensive analysis to date in her essay "'The Thing Not Named': Willa Cather as a Lesbian Writer," *Signs* 9, 4 (Summer, 1984), pp. 576–599, and in her critical biography *Willa Cather: The Emerging Voice* (New York: Oxford University Press, 1987). Eve Kosofsky Sedgwick has added "Across Gender, Across Sexuality: Willa Cather and Others," *South Atlantic Quarterly* 88, 1 (Winter 1989), pp. 53–71. Most recently, Judith Butler has responded to Sedgwick in "'Dangerous Crossing': Willa Cather's Masculine Names," *Bodies That Matter* (New York: Routledge, 1993), pp. 143–166.

   Cather is famous for her obsession with privacy. But even biographers who cannot admit that she was a "lesbian" have acknowledged Isabelle McClung (they met in 1899, lived together in the McClung family household from 1901 to 1906, and were still so close that Cather nursed her during her final illness in 1935) as "the romance" of Cather's life, and been unable to overlook the decades (1908 to 1947) she lived with Edith Lewis. Such biographers have been reduced to splitting the difference between emotional and sexual connections, arguing that while she may have indulged in "romantic friendships" she was much too attentive to social propriety to have had sexual relationships with the women she adored (Carl Woodress, *Willa Cather: A Literary Life*, [Lincoln: University of Nebraska Press, 1987], pp. 138–142); or that while it might apply, the term "lesbian" is simply too reductive (Hermione Lee, *Willa Cather: Double Lives* [New York: Vintage, 1991], pp. 10–11). Both of these approaches collapse questions of identification into questions of sexual practice, and reinforce while acceding to the narrowest possible understandings of lesbianism.

   Cather's novels have most often been recast as lesbian novels, with her heterosexual male characters identified as "really" lesbians because they are not sufficiently manly, and the male/female relationships she depicts read as "really" lesbian, because her insufficiently manly men do not pursue her women with sufficient vigor. More interestingly, Sharon O'Brien has taken up Cather's emphasis on "the thing not named" in her 1922 statement of fictional ideals, "The Novel

Demeuble." "Whatever is felt upon the page without being sufficiently named there—that, one might say, is created," Cather wrote. "It is the inexplicable presence of the thing not named, of the overtone divined by the ear but not heard by it, the verbal mood, the emotional aura of the fact or the thing or the deed, that gives high quality to the novel or the drama, as well as to poetry itself." (*Willa Cather on Writing: Critical Studies on Writing as an Art.* Foreword by Stephen Tennant (New York: Knopf, 1949): pp. 35–43, 42.) O'Brien argues that this is the credo of both Cather "the modernist writer endorsing allusive, suggestive art and inviting the reader's participation in the creation of literary meaning," and Cather "the lesbian writer forced to disguise or to conceal the unnameable emotional source of her fiction, reassuring herself that the reader fills the absence in the text by intuiting the unwritten subtext" (*Willa Cather*, p. 127). Unfortunately, this approach depends on "the unnameable," "absence," "the unwritten," "the subtext," a "source" which is wholly emotional, and all in the singular. It also ties lesbian writing to modernism, as if only a modernist could produce a fiction complex enough to encompass the lesbian, with her secrets, absences, subtexts and so on, and as if Cather must be read as a modernist in order to be read as a lesbian. But reading Cather might be more simply an exercise in naming the "named." For example, Cather herself frames "the thing not named" in *The Novel Démeublé* with discussions of Nathaniel Hawthorne's *The Scarlet Letter*, a famous novel of sexual transgression, and D. H. Lawrence's *The Rainbow*, the work of a writer famous for his transgressively explicit descriptions of sexual experience.

2. O'Brien, *Willa Cather*, p. 428.

3. O'Brien, *Willa Cather*, p. 443. Committed to an antihomophobic analysis, O'Brien needs to see Cather rejecting romantic love rather than heterosexuality, in an interpretive climate in which feminist critics such as Sandra Gilbert and Susan Gubar can read this narrative as part of what they call Cather's "extraordinary attack on heterosexuality." They go on to read this "attack on heterosexuality" as a motive power behind her fiction, "Whether . . . [the attack] was motivated by what Blanche Gelfant identifies as regressive anxieties or by what Sharon O'Brien and Judith Fetterley consider covert lesbian allegiances." That "covert lesbian allegiances" would produce an "attack on heterosexuality" is taken for granted. Sandra M. Gilbert and Susan Gubar, *No Man's Land: The Place of the Woman Writer in the Twentieth Century*, Volume 2, *Sexchanges* (New Haven: Yale University Press, 1989), p. 170.

4. Willa Cather, *O Pioneers!* (New York: Houghton Mifflin, 1941), p. 163.

5. Cather even raises the question of etiology to which lesbians and gay men are continually subjected. Emil looks for an explanation of his bad fortune, and even his conclusions are couched in terms of publicity and silence: "It was like that when Alexandra tested her seed corn in the spring. . . . From two ears that had grown side by side, the grains of one shot up joyfully into the light, projecting themselves into the future, and the grains from the other lay still in the earth and rotted; and nobody knew why" (pp. 163–164).

6. Gilbert and Gubar, following from Eudora Welty, argue that the absence of history is the basis of Cather's fascination with pioneer stories. But they are concerned with the history of gender:

> As Eudora Welty has shown, Cather was inspired by "the absence of his-
> tory as far as she could see around her," a blank that "only made her look
> further, gave her the clues to discover a deeper past." But in particular
> Cather can be said to be uncovering the 'universal history' of gender in
> those works that examine the primacy of the female in the context of the
> "historical enigma" of the development of patriarchy. For her, the west is
> a place in which women at least briefly experienced an exhilarating au-
> tonomy. (*Sexchanges*, p. 187)

Cather's histories can only be read as a story of female autonomy and its subjection if the focus is kept on her earlier work.

7. "Curiously enough," Niel finally realizes, "it was as Captain Forrester's wife that
   she most interested [him], and it was in her relation to her husband that he most
   admired her." This understanding of her value is dramatized after her husband's
   death. Without him she is no longer a lady: "All those years he had thought it was
   Mrs. Forrester who made that house so different from any other. But ever since the
   Captain's death it was a house . . . where common fellows behaved after their kind
   and knew a common woman when they saw her." Moreover, "what he most held
   against Mrs. Forrester; [was] that she was not willing to immolate herself, like the
   widow of all these great men, and die with the pioneer period to which she belonged; that she preferred life on any terms." Marian Forrester is admired for her
   admiration of the railroad-builder, but the railroad-builder himself is the representative of the passing era, the real source of value, and the proper focus of attention. Willa Cather, *A Lost Lady* (New York: Vintage, 1972), pp. 78, 170, 169.
8. The manuscript she was working on at her death was set in fourteenth-century
   Avignon, the main characters, two boys. Lee, *Willa Cather*, p. 371.
9. Willa Cather, *One of Ours* (New York: Vintage, 1971), p. 266.
10. That Claude and David should die places Cather's work within the endlessly fatal
    traditions of gay fiction, as well as within the tradition of war novels.
11. Sedgwick argues in "Across Gender" that "the male-homosocial romance represents
    at the same time the *inside* lining of the heterosexual bond (since the two segments
    of the domestic story flank their own history in the flashback interpolation of the
    mesa story) and equally its *exterior* landscape (since the Blue Mesa romance of Tom
    Outland . . . [offers the Professor] the empowering distance for his intellectual
    achievements and desires)" (pp. 68–69). In "Dangerous Crossing" Butler refers to
    *The Professor's House* as a novel "in which a homoerotic relationship between two
    men is quite literally contained within the narrative frame of a heterosexual family
    arrangement, arid almost to the point of death" (p. 144). She is able to simplify the
    novel because she focuses on that part, "Tom Outland's Story," that Cather pub-
    lished first and separately, before she incorporated it into the Professor's story.
12. Willa Cather, *The Professor's House* (New York: Vintage, 1973), pp. 22–23.
13. Their pairing is confirmed when Roddy reciprocates Tom's physical protection by
    nursing the boy through pneumonia, and finding jobs for them together where
    Tom could recuperate.
14. Proust was transposing Dreyfus and Wilde, Jews and homosexuals, in *A la
    recherche du temps perdu*, especially *Sodome et Gomorrhe* I and II, which appeared
    in 1921 and 1922: Cather began writing *The Professor's House* in 1923. All of her

biographers note Cather's reading of Proust's work. See ahead to chapter 4 for a discussion of Barnes's use of Proust's parallel between Jews and homosexuals, and the end of chapter 3, for reference to Stein's invocation of gay/Jewish parallels.

15. Marsellus's effeminacy links him to other Cather characters, such as Paul in "Paul's Case" (1905), Landry in *Song of the Lark* (1915), and Mockford in *Lucy Gayheart* (1935), all of whom can be read as "gay" partly through their effeminacy.

16. Cather also triangulates the Professor's relation to Tom through both of the Professor's daughters: Rosamund is engaged to him, and Kathleen is also in love with him.

17. At least one reader, Hermione Lee, notes this as "Cather's most direct reference to homosexual feeling in her fiction, as a 'natural' but sad deviation" although her conclusion—"and it is a melancholy remark"—probably says more about the reader than the text (Lee, *Willa Cather*, p. 250).

18. Willa Cather, *The Kingdom of Art: Willa Cather's First Principles and Critical Statements, 1893–1896*, ed. Bernice Slote (Lincoln: University of Nebraska Press, 1966), p. 323.

19. The final mother in the novel is Tom Outland's, who like "Mother Eve" has a brief narrative of female allegiance to the heterosexual plot. Her husband drowns, and the wife, seized by grief, only pauses to give birth to the child she is carrying before she hurries after him. The fatefully reappearing Father Duchene, who gives voice to misogyny between the "histories" of Virgil and World War I, is as much of a consistent family as Tom then has.

20. The other of these dummies—"a full-length female figure in a smart wire skirt with a trim metal waist line. It had no legs . . . no viscera behind its glistening ribs, and its bosom resembled a strong wire bird-cage" (p. 18)—suggests that women have no interiority.

21. "Mother Eve" still escapes the history of the Professor's boy. Discovered by a male couple, she will not be traded in male exchange. When she is bought as an artifact by a European collector, who attempts to transport her out of the mesa along with jars and tools, the crate in which she is packed goes crashing down a ravine.

22. It is possible to produce a biographical reading of the novel's implication of homosexual and heterosexual relationships and its focus on betrayal. Cather dedicated *The Professor's House* to Jan Hambourg, the man who, during World War I, married Isabelle McClung, now routinely identifed as the "romance" of Cather's life. Given the dedication, the Jewish Hambourg has often been identified with the figure of Louie Marsellus. In his own person, and as a figure for Tom Outland, Marsellus is the focus of heterosexual, homosexual, and self-betrayals in the novel. The Professor's wife turns from the Professor to Marsellus. As a figure for Tom Outland, he is also the man the Professor turns away from his wife toward. As a figure of Tom Outland in relation to the Professor, he is a sign of the homosexual threat to heterosexual relationships, and as a figure of Tom in relation to Roddy, a sign of self-betrayal within homosexual couples. To complicate matters even further, Sharon O'Brien suggests that Cather's only heterosexual relationship took place on her 1912 visit to Mesa Verde, the basis for the novel's Blue Mesa. Cather referred to the man in question as a "young Antinous of a singer," placing this

relation into a male homosexual and historical frame, as "Antinous" was the male beloved of the Emperor Hadrian. O'Brien, *Willa Cather,* p. 412.

23. According to Woodress, Cather sent "The Old Beauty" to "her old friend Gertrude Lane at the *Woman's Home Companion.* To her obvious surprise and dismay Lane didn't like the tale, thought it below her usual standard" (*Willa Cather,* p. 495). According to Edith Lewis, Cather "herself thought highly of 'The Old Beauty.' She had found it interesting to write, and she felt that she had carried through her idea successfully" (quoted by Woodress, *Willa Cather,* p. 475). The story finally appeared in a collection, *The Old Beauty and Others,* put together by Lewis and Alfred Knopf, Cather's publisher and friend, in 1948, the year after her death.

24. Gabrielle Longstreet is also presented within female pairings as a young woman: firstly in relation to her mother, who accompanies her to London; later with a spinster cousin of her husband, who stays by her and confers respectability when he divorces her, tired of a wife who overshadows him in public esteem.

25. Willa Cather, "The Old Beauty," *The Old Beauty and Others* (New York: Vintage, 1976), pp. 3–74, 40.

26. Chetty rescues Gabrielle, whom she discovers alone and ill in a Paris hotel after her second brief marriage has ended with her husband's death in battle.

27. Cather wrote "The Old Beauty" after the death of Isabelle McClung, the "beauty" in her life. Sharon O'Brien paraphrases an 1899 letter: "Here I am chez the goddess, she told [Dorothy] Canfield exultingly. Isabelle had met her at the train station, she explained in a tone of amazed delight, looking as if the frieze of the Parthenon ought to have been with her" (*Willa Cather,* p. 237). But although the two women lived together in McClung's family home in the prewar period, McClung never participated with Cather in a female couple that challenged heterosexual appearances. During the war, in 1916, seventeen years after she and Cather had met, McClung married. (O'Brien suggests in a note that the attacker interrupted while threatening Gabrielle Longstreet is an image of Jan Hambourg, the man Isabelle McClung married, his "foreignness" a reference to Hambourg's being Jewish [p. 244].) "The Old Beauty" could be read as a representation of Cather's loss of her beauty to the sexual shame which appears with the decline of the tacit acceptance of female friendship that envelopes the story's older couple.

28. "Tommy the Unsentimental" was first published in 1896. "Flavia and Her Artists" was included in Cather's first collection of short stories, *The Troll Garden* (1905). Both of these boyish figures are posed initially in a friendship with another woman, and then as observers of a heterosexual couple.

29. Cather's story recalls another account of different lesbian generations in the concluding scenes of Radclyffe Hall's *The Unlit Lamp* (1924), where Joan Ogden, who never escaped her mother's clutches to take up a life with the woman she loved, is contrasted sadly with a pair of lesbian bright young things "with bobbed hair and well-tailored clothes" who represent a new type: "Active, aggressively intelligent women, . . . women who did things well, important things; women who counted and who would go on counting; smart, neatly put together women, looking like well-bred young men." Radclyffe Hall, *The Unlit Lamp* (New York: Dial, 1981), p. 284.

## Notes to Chapter 2

1. See David Sweetman, *Mary Renault: A Biography* (New York: Harcourt Brace and Company, 1993).
2. See Renault's afterword to *The Friendly Young Ladies* (New York: Pantheon, 1984).
3. Renault, *The Friendly Young Ladies*, p. 43.
4. Eve Sedgwick discusses the coexistence of cross-sex and cross-gender understandings of homosexuality in modern Western culture, in the first chapter of *Epistemology of the Closet* (Berkeley: University of California Press, 1990).
5. Renault simultaneously denied and drew connections between her histories and contemporary events. "No one, after all, is compelled to write about the past," she insisted; "if what you are really talking about is Nazi Germany or Vietnam or Texas, why not say so instead of misleading your readers about Nero or Caesar or Troy?" But she also claimed that "the past is part of our environment, our internal ecology. . . . We are not mere sightseers, foreign tourists to the past, but a part of its continuum, and also its product. It still moves in our blood." "History in Fiction," *Times Literary Supplement* (March 23, 1973), pp. 315–316, 316. In a letter to a critic who had written to her, she was willing to admit, "I was not without thoughts of our local government when I was writing . . . [*The Last of the Wine*]; in the case of Anytos' views on Sokrates, I rather think the late unlamented McCarthy was uppermost in my mind" (Sweetman, *Mary Renault*, p. 187).
6. This statement was made, however, in the afterword to the 1984 edition of *The Friendly Young Ladies*, a novel that would have been consigned to literary oblivion long ago if not for "congregated homosexuals waving banners" (p. 283).
7. Mary Renault, *The Charioteer* (Cleveland: World Publishing Co., 1966), p. 319.
8. Such expressions of hostility to the gay world distance Renault's heroes from a straight reader's prejudices about the majority of gays. But they still contain contradiction, indicating, as they do, that there is a network, however tainted.
9. Mary Renault, *The Bull from the Sea* (New York: Vintage, 1972), p. 149.
10. In his biography, Sweetman quotes from the innumerable letters she received from heterosexual and gay readers thanking her for her portrayals of homosexuality (*Mary Renault*, pp. 148–149).
11. James Baldwin, *Giovanni's Room* (New York: Dell, 1988), p. 188.
12. Renault referred to the Amazons, created tangential female societies among the women of the Cretan bull-dancers court (in *The King Must Die*) and the harems (in *The Persian Boy*), and made late references to Sappho (in *The Praise Singer*). But as lesbian references, these notes cannot be sustained.
13. The inferiority of "queer books" was self-evident to many. *The Charioteer* itself was not published in the United States until 1959, six years after its English publication, because the American publisher of her previous books, William Morrow and Company, would not accept it. Renault subsequently took her work to Pantheon, but they waited until both *The Last of the Wine* and *The King Must Die* had first appeared successfully in the U.S. before they risked the earlier novel.

    Renault wrote in a climate of hostility, despite her success. Her historical novels garnered rave reviews, but this praise contained barbs: for example, "In *The Last of the Wine* . . . Miss Renault showed how certain personal relationships and the practice of infanticide which we find distasteful and abhorrent could be an integral element in the luminous period of the Peloponnesian War." Moses Hadas, New York *Herald Tribune Book Review*, July 13, 1958. Most of the little critical attention she achieved was homophobic, such as a 1965 essay insisting that the relationship between Alexias and Lysis in *The Last of the Wine* was only a deep friendship, but that nevertheless, "there are sections [of the novel] which appeal to the prurient." Landon C. Burns Jr, "Men Are Only Men: The Novels of Mary Renault," *Critique*, VI, 3 (Winter 1963), pp. 102–121, 120. The two books on Renault's work, in both of which the authors claim her help and support, Peter Wolfe's *Mary Renault* (New York: Twayne, 1969) and Bernard F. Dick's *The Hellenism of Mary Renault* (Carbondale: Southern Illinois University Press, 1972), are rabidly homophobic, while going to great lengths to both deny the gay element of her work and portray her as straightforwardly hostile to her own gay characters. Hugh Kenner, while calling *The King Must Die* a "magic book," dubs the rest the much inferior work of a "workmanlike and resourceful British fictionist" who is also "a male impersonator." "Mary Renault and her Various Personas," *The New York Times Book Review* (February 10, 1974), p. 15. On the contrary, in "The Masks of Mary Renault," *The New York Review of Books*, February 8, 1979, pp. 11–14, Peter Green claims that the Theseus novels were "her worst tactical error . . . in which her quirks and self-indulgences stood out with horrific clarity—not least in the warrior Moon Maiden Hippolyta, athletic, bisexual." He asks rhetorically, "Where is the borderline between art and self-therapy with an epidemic appeal?" although he refuses to specify the "clear symbiotic relationship between Miss Renault's life and her work." Even in Renault's obituary (December 14, 1983), the London *Times* noted that *The Charioteer* was "about a young soldier who tries to come to terms with his homosexuality. This theme, sympathetically and even aggressively treated—almost as a panacea for the world's ills—was seldom absent from her fiction thereafter," except of course in the Theseus novels, where they observe "her ideas about matriarchy—inspired perhaps by factors in her personality . . . anthropologically mistaken . . . represent a serious flaw in her work, and may have lost her many admirers among the educated." Finally, Kevin Kopelson's discussion of *The Persian Boy* in *Love's Litany* (Stanford University Press, 1994), offers a gay reading.

14. *Treasure Island* (1883) itself occupies such an ambiguous cultural position, produced by a respected writer, Stevenson, and praised by such major contemporary figures as Henry James, but written for boys and initially published in a boys magazine.

15. This beginning with death becomes almost routine in her historical fiction, where it is often the death of a parent: Theseus's father in *The Bull from the Sea*, Nikeratos's father in *The Mask of Apollo*, Alexander's father and Bagoas's entire family in *The Persian Boy* (also the King Horse in *The King Must Die* and Alexander himself in *Funeral Games*).

16. Apart from *The Friendly Young Ladies* and *The Charioteer*, the strikingly uneven half-dozen contemporary novels Renault wrote before she turned to historical fiction all turn on socially problematic heterosexual relationships and the need to dispel a threat of gender ambiguity.

17. In *The Charioteer*, Alec comments sardonically on "Greece," "Yes, well, we know under the social system the women were illiterates in semi-purdah, and most of the men were bisexual from choice" (p. 200).
18. Mary Renault, *Fire from Heaven* (New York: Pantheon, 1969), p. 292.
19. Mary Renault, *The Persian Boy* (New York: Bantam, 1982), p. 409.
20. It is interesting to contrast Renault's *The Persian Boy* with Marguerite Yourcenar's *Memoirs of Hadrian*. Both are centrally concerned with the "favorite" of a great ruler, but it is a measure of Renault's development that, in contrast to *Hadrian*, her novel is told from the perspective of the boy, not the emperor. Kopelson discusses the two novels together in his *Love's Litany*, chapter 4.
21. Mary Renault, *The Mask of Apollo*, (New York: Bantam, 1978), p. 4.
22. Mary Renault, *Funeral Games* (New York: Pinnacle Books, 1981), p. 212.
23. Epigraph, Renault, *The Mask of Apollo*, reprinted there by permission from Dudley Fitts, ed., *Poems from the Greek Anthology* (New Directions, 1956).

## Notes to Chapter 3

1. Gertrude Stein, *The Autobiography of Alice B. Toklas*, in *Selected Writings of Gertrude Stein*, ed. Carl Van Vechten (New York: Vintage, 1972), pp. 1–237; 84–85.
2. Gertrude Stein, *Picasso* (New York: Dover Publications, 1984), p. 11.
3. Gertrude Stein, "Transatlantic Interview 1946," *A Primer for the Gradual Understanding of Gertrude Stein*, ed. Robert Bartlett Haas (Santa Barbara: Black Sparrow Press, 1976), pp. 15–35, 33.
4. Although Stein's writing was widely known in avant-garde literary circles, and even caricatured in the North American popular press from an early date, the success of the *Autobiography* and her resulting U.S. lecture tour moved her into an unprecedented position of public visibility. See James R. Mellow, *Charmed Circle: Gertrude Stein and Company* (New York: Avon, 1975), or more recently Diana Souhami, *Gertrude and Alice* (London: Pandora, 1991).
5. Although, as Jayne Walker argues, *Three Lives* was her first major assault on the conventions governing literary representation in the nineteenth century," Stein's engagement, "early and radically, with what we have come to recognize as the most crucial issue of modernist art—the problem of representation," began with her first literary attempts, the first draft of *The Making of Americans* and her first completed work, *Q.E.D.* Jayne L. Walker, *The Making of a Modernist: Gertrude Stein from "Three Lives" to "Tender Buttons"* (Amherst: The University of Massachusetts Press, 1984), p. xi.
6. Gertrude Stein, *Fernhurst, Q.E.D., and Other Early Writings* (New York: Liveright, 1971), p. 144.
7. Leon Katz has noted Stein's overwhelming interest in narrative during this early period, as reflected in the program of reading she began recording at the time of the first draft of *The Making of Americans* (late 1902 to early 1903) and continued "throughout the years of her writing of the novel":

The most striking fact about these lists is that not a single volume of criticism, philosophy, essays, poetry, or drama appears on them. There are
several hundred titles set down in all, and with occasional exceptions such
as the Spanish *Lazarillo de Tormes*, the *Arabian Nights*, George Sand
memoirs, Russian novels, or anthologies of Oriental tales, they are made
up entirely of major, minor, and very minor English novels and collec-
tions of tales; of diaries, letters, biographies, and autobiographies; and
compendious volumes of history like Clarendon's and Gibbon's. There is
an illuminating suggestion in this exclusiveness of her reading interest in
narrative. Her feeling for the long roll of events was formed by long reading habit and from her peculiar experience of English narrative tradition.

Leon Katz, "Introduction," Stein, *Fernhurst, Q.E.D., and Other Early Writings*, pp.
ix–xlii, xviii.

8. Richard Bridgman, *Gertrude Stein in Pieces* (New York: Oxford University Press,
1970), p. 46.

9. Bridgman, *Gertrude Stein in Pieces*, p. 46.

10. Gertrude Stein, *The Making of Americans being the history of a family's progress*
(London: Peter Owen, 1968), p. 176. Walker, *The Making of a Modernist*, also discusses "history" in *The Making of Americans*, pp. 43–74.

11. "Melanctha" is widely regarded as a recasting of the autobiographical material also
dealt with in *Q.E.D.* See Catharine R. Stimpson, "The Mind, the Body and
Gertrude Stein," *Critical Inquiry* 3, 3 (Spring 1977), pp. 489–505. Janice L.
Doane discusses *Q.E.D.* extensively in *Silence and Narrative: The Early Novels of
Gertrude Stein* (Westport, CT: Greenwood Press, 1986), pp. 1–32. Lisa Ruddick
argues for Stein's identification with Jeff Campbell and Melanctha Herbert in her
discussion of "Melanctha," in *Reading Gertrude Stein: Body, Text, Gnosis* (Ithaca:
Cornell University Press, 1990), pp. 12–55.

12. These connections broadly reinforce the argument increasingly being made by
critics of Stein, that questions of content were a significant impetus behind her
formal innovations. See Stimpson above, and also "The Somagrams of Gertrude
Stein," *Poetics Today* 6, 1–2, (1985), pp. 67–80; "Gertrice/Altrude," *Mothering the
Mind*, eds. Ruth Perry and Martine Watson Brownley (New York: Holmes and
Meier, 1984), pp. 122–139; and "Gertrude Stein and the Transposition of Gender," in *The Poetics of Gender*, ed. Nancy K. Miller (New York: Columbia University Press, 1986), pp. 1–18. See also Elizabeth Fifer, "Is Flesh Advisable: The
Interior Theater of Gertrude Stein," *Signs* 4, 3 (Spring 1979), pp. 472–485; Cyn-
thia Secor, "Gertrude Stein: The Complex Force of Her Femininity," in *Women,
the Arts and the 1920s in Paris and New York*, eds. Kenneth Wheeler and Virginia
Lee Lussier (New Brunswick, NJ: Transaction Books, 1982), pp. 27–35; Secor,
"Ida: A Great American Novel," *Twentieth Century Literature* 24, 1 (Spring 1978),
pp. 96–107; and Penelope J. Engelbrecht, " 'Lifting Belly is a Language': The Post-
modern Lesbian Subject," *Feminist Studies* 16, 1 (Spring 1990), pp. 85–114. Shari
Benstock discusses Stein's relation to conventional definitions of modernism in
"Beyond the Reaches of Feminist Criticism: A Letter from Paris," in *Feminist Is-
sues in Literary Scholarship*, ed. Shari Benstock (Bloomington: Indiana University
Press, 1987), pp. 7–29. The most recent book-length studies—Doane, Ruddick,

and Harriet Scott Chessman, *The Public Is Invited to Dance: Representation, the Body, and Dialogue in Gertrude Stein* (Stanford: Stanford University Press, 1989)—all begin with strikingly self-conscious declarations in favor of at least a partially autobiographical and thematic Stein criticism. They also suggest more continuity between the early work and Stein's experimental impulse, and the later return to narrative, than is usually accorded. At the conclusion of her excellent study, *A Different Language: Gertrude Stein's Experimental Writing* (Madison: The University of Wisconsin Press, 1983), Marianne DeKoven explicitly proposes continuities between the early experimentation and Stein's final narrative phase. Chessman has begun to trace patterns from the early work through the writings of the 1930s and 1940s.

13. In *The Autobiography of Alice B. Toklas* Stein claimed to have put aside and forgotten the manuscript of *Q.E.D.* until the mid-1930s. It was not published until 1950, in a limited edition, under the title *Things As They Are*, and not widely available until Leon Katz's 1971 collection, *Fernhurst, Q.E.D. and Other Early Writings*.

14. Gertrude Stein, *The Geographical History of America or the Relation of Human Nature to the Human Mind* (New York: Random House, 1936), p. 59.

15. Gertrude Stein, "Lifting Belly," in *The Yale Gertrude Stein*, ed. Richard Kostelanetz (New Haven: Yale University Press, 1980), pp. 4–54, 30. Linda Simon, *The Biography of Alice B. Toklas* (Garden City, NY: Doubleday, 1977), and Bridgman, *Gertrude Stein in Pieces*. See also, for readings of Stein's sexual language, Fifer and Chessman; and Stimpson, "Somagrams," for a discussion of other people's references to Stein as a "Roman."

16. Chessman also offers a reading of such historical references in "Lifting Belly," arguing, for example, that "Stein associates seeing in the poem with a nationalistic impluse leading to war," but concluding, "the war remains an emphatically peripheral phenomenon, marginal to the love of words and the love touched upon by the words" (*The Public Is Invited to Dance*, p. 106).

17. Gertrude Stein, "Didn't Nelly and Lilly Love You," in *As Fine As Melanctha: 1914–1930* (New Haven: Yale University Press, 1954), pp. 219–252, 230. Lillian Faderman also discusses this work in *Surpassing the Love of Men: Romantic Friendship and Love Between Women from the Renaissance to the Present* (New York: William Morrow, 1981), pp. 402–405.

18. Bridgman, *Gertrude Stein in Pieces*, p. 199.

19. Bridgman, *Gertrude Stein in Pieces*, pp. 197–198, quoting Stein, *How to Write* (Paris, 1931).

20. Gertrude Stein, *Lectures in America* (Boston: Beacon Press, 1985), p. 232.

21. Poetry becomes love: "So as I say poetry is essentially the discovery, the love, the passion for the name of anything" (Stein, *Lectures*, p. 235). See also Ulla Dydo's account of the relation between Stein's love for Toklas and her writing, in *The Language That Rises: The Voice of Gertrude Stein, 1923–1932* (Evanston, IL: Northwestern University Press).

22. Gertrude Stein, "We Came. A History," in *Reflections on the Atomic Bomb*, ed. Robert Bartlett Haas (Los Angeles: Black Sparrow Press, 1974), pp. 148–152, 148.

23. Gertrude Stein, "History or Messages from History," in *Alphabets and Birthdays* (New Haven: Yale University Press, 1957), pp. 219–238, 228.

24. Gertrude Stein, *Narration* (Chicago: The University of Chicago Press, 1935), p. 58. Also, "and really and truly it does not happen again not as it used to happen again because now we know really know so much that has happened that really we do know that what has happened does not happen again and so that for poor comfort has been taken away from the historian." She would return to this question of repetition within history, especially during *Wars I Have Seen*, where a renewed faith in repetition seems to be one response to the war.

25. This defeat would only be completed by World War II, as she observed in *Wars I Have Seen*: "There is neither unanimity nor faith in peace and progress, the nineteenth century is dead." It is a defeat Stein claimed her part in: "The nineteenth century was completely lacking in logic, it had cosmic terms and hopes, and aspirations, and discoveries, and ideals but it had no logic, and I like logic I really do, I suppose that is the reason that I so naturally had my part in killing the nineteenth century and killing it dead, quite like a gangster with a mitraillette, if that is the same as a tommy gun." *Wars I Have Seen* (London: Brilliance Books, 1984), pp. 104, 91.

26. The *Geographical History* is almost endlessly subdivided into randomly numbered "chapters," "volumes," "parts," "plays," and "autobiographies," ranging from a few lines to a few pages in length.

27. Gertrude Stein, "How Writing is Written," in *How Writing is Written: Vol. II of the Previously Uncollected Writings of Gertrude Stein*, ed. Robert Bartlett Haas (Los Angeles: Black Sparrow Press, 1974), pp. 151–160, 158.

28. John Hyde Preston, "A Conversation," in *Atlantic Monthly* LVI (August 1935), pp. 187–194, 193. Other examples of the rejection of "story" can be found, for example, in *Everybody's Autobiography*, where she declared, "I have told all about [my mother] in The Making of Americans but that is a story and after all what is the use of its being a story. If it is real enough what is the use of it being a story." *Everybody's Autobiography* (New York: Random House, 1973), p. 138.

29. Preston, "A Conversation," p. 193.

30. Bridgman, in his typically negative fashion, has commented on the shift in Stein's work from the late 1920s into the early 1930s: "Only when she turned back upon herself and began to explain her past did she revive. This pre-eminently a-historical woman rediscovered her energies in her own history." *Gertrude Stein in Pieces*, p. 204.

31. Stein, *The Autobiography of Alice B. Toklas*, p. 31: "It was an important purchase because in looking and looking at this picture Gertrude Stein wrote Three Lives. She had begun not long before as an exercise in literature to translate Flaubert's Trois Contes and then she had this Cézanne and she looked at it and under its stimulus she wrote Three Lives."

32. In *The Autobiography of Alice B. Toklas*, for example, it is used to mark the end of World War I (pp. 180–181).

33. For example, Gertrude Stein, *Paris France: Personal Recollections* (London: Peter Owen, 1971), pp. 3–4; and "Pictures," *Lectures in America*, pp. 62–64.

34. Stein, *Wars I Have Seen*, for example, pp. 7, 10, 13.

35. Stein, *Lectures in America*, p. 65.

36. Gertrude Stein, "Composition as Explanation," *Selected Writings of Gertrude Stein*, ed. Van Vechten, pp. 512–523, 513.

37. So, for example, in *Everybody's Autobiography* she explains, "But after all I was a natural believer in republics a natural believer in science a natural believer in progress and I began to write. After all I was a natural believer just as the present generation are natural believers in Soviets and proletarian literature and social laws and everything although really it does not make them be living any more than science and progress and democracies did me" (pp. 243–244).

38. Gertrude Stein, *Four in America* (New Haven: Yale University Press, 1947), p. 122.

39. DeKoven sees Stein's later "rapprochement of the experimental with the conventional" in terms of the theories of Julia Kristeva, as "precisely Kristeva's ideal alternation of the male and the female psychological-linguistic-political modes—her sense that we need a 'paternal identification' (time, reason, history), that we must not isolate ourselves within a female identity once we have retrieved it." *A Different Language*, p. 150.

40. "Pictures":

> I have always liked looking at pictures of battle scenes but as I say I always like looking at pictures and then once after the war I saw the battle field of the battle of Metz. For a moment as I looked at it, it was a grey day and we were on our way back from Alsace to Paris and we had seen so many battle fields of this war and this one was so historical, it almost it did almost look like an oil painting. As I say things do not generally look to me like an oil painting. And just then into this thing which was so historical that it almost did look like an oil painting a very old couple of people a man and a woman got out of an automobile and went to look at a grave at the way-side and the moment of its existence as an oil painting ceased, it became a historical illustration for a simple historical story. (*Lectures in America*, p. 64)

41. Stein disbelieves a level of cultural protestation against war. "Now why do you say you do not want war. Of course you do want war because this is a way of seeing when you look and we like to look oh yes we like to look. . . . And why not. Most everybody wants to be shown. And that is war." *Four*, p. 27.

42. War is even represented as an "explanation": "as everybody likes explanations everybody likes everything proved everybody likes a war so there has to be the war." *Four*, p. 26.

43. Gertrude Stein, *Paris France* (New York: Liveright, 1970), p. 38.

44. Gertrude Stein, *Brewsie and Willie* (New York: Random House, 1946), pp. 43–44.

45. As she is writing *Picasso*, World War II is beginning, a beginning she describes in terms of representation: "At present another composition is commencing, each generation has its composition, people do not change from one generation to another generation but the composition that surrounds them changes" (p. 11).

46. For example:

> I love my love with a dress and a hat
> I love my love and not with this or with that
> I love my love with a y because she is my bride
> I love her with a d because she is my love beside

From "Before the Flowers of Friendship Faded Friendship Faded," in Gertrude
Stein, *Look At Me Now and Here I Am: Writings and Lectures 1909–1945*, ed. Patricia Meyerowitz (Harmondsworth: Penguin, 1971), pp. 274–89, 286.

47. Gilbert and Gubar discuss lesbian writing as a conversation between lovers in *Sexchanges*, chapter 6, " 'She Meant What I Said': Lesbian Double Talk," as does
Chessman in *The Public Is Invited to Dance*.

48. Chessman discusses "caresses" as part of her consideration of Stein's representation
of the female body, *The Public Is Invited to Dance*, pp. 79–111.

49. Gertrude Stein, *Geography and Plays* (New York: Something Else Press, 1968), p. 16.

50. Marianne DeKoven discusses the possibility of both/and under the rubric of what
she argues is a characteristically modernist *sous-rature* in *Rich and Strange* (Princeton: Princeton University Press, 1992), pp. 3–16. Nevertheless, although she
analyses Stein's "Melanctha" and "Tender Buttons," DeKoven "would argue that
'Melanctha' is the point at which Stein's work coincides most closely with modernism—after the (almost) modernist 'Melanctha,' Stein moves beyond or outside
modernism into avant-garde experimentalism" (p. 68).

51. Stein also comments: "For which in might they be in union./ Is there not one. Is
there not two" (p. 116). This seems to be an allusion to Marianne Moore's "Marriage," which concludes with reference to Daniel Webster and his statue in New
York City's Central Park: " 'Liberty and union/ now and forever';/ the Book on the
writing-table;/ the hand in the breast-pocket" (Marianne Moore, *Collected Poems*
(New York: Macmillan, 1979), p. 78.

52. See Chessman's discussion of "*Ida* and Twins," *The Public Is Invited to Dance*, pp.
167–98.

53. Gertrude Stein, *The Mother of Us All*, in *Last Operas and Plays*, ed. Carl Van
Vechten (New York: Vintage, 1975), pp. 52–88, 54–55.

54. "I did not realise then how completely and entirely american [sic] was Gertrude
Stein. Later I often teased her, calling her a general, a civil war general of either or
both sides." Stein, *The Autobiography of Alice B. Toklas*, p. 15.

55. As Stein writes, "And so to go back to historical wars. I naturally liked history and
Shakespeare's plays and historical novels and there was always war. Of course ancient history was full of wars and the Decline and Fall of the Roman Empire was
full of war but these did not any of them interest me as wars. English wars interested me, some French wars and the American civil war. And I was right because
the American civil war was the prototype of all the wars the two big wars that I
have completely lived. Also the American civil war" (*Wars I Have Seen*, p. 8).

56. Their survival was also the result of their social and political connections, including their friendship with the Fascist sympathizer and Vichy minister for culture,
Bernard Faÿ.

57. At the beginning of *The Making of Americans*, Stein wrote about leaving America
as an unwanted "singular," to write for herself and "strangers." By *Wars I Have
Seen*, her singularity has been reconstituted benignly into the status of American
and writer with a range of readers.

58. If Wilde's imprisonment is to be seen as a paradigm for the wartime universe,
Stein's late description of her own experience of the occupation seems an image
of what she would not have called the closet:

It is impossible to make anybody realise what occupation by Germans is who has not had it, here in Culoz it was as easy as it was possible for it to be as most of the population are railroad employees and the Germans did not want to irritate them, but it was like a suffocating cloud under which you could not breathe right, we had lots of food, and no interference on the part of the Germans but there it was a weight that was always there and now everybody feels natural. (*Wars*, p. 236)

There are similar passages in Stein's "fictional" account of the war years, *Mrs Reynolds*, where Hitler is represented by the figure of "Angel Harper": "It was a long way to wait and in the meantime every day there was a dark cloud, a very dark one. An Angel Harper cloud said Mrs Reynolds and she said as long as Angel Harper lived there would be every afternoon and sometimes even in the morning and quite likely at noon a very big dark cloud in the sky even if it did not make any lightning nor any hail." *Mrs Reynolds* (Los Angeles: Sun and Moon Press, n.d.), p. 90.

59. "A Message from Gertrude Stein," *Selected Writings*, ed. Van Vechten, p. vii.

## Notes to Chapter 4

1. Djuna Barnes, *Nightwood* (New York: New Directions, 1961), p. 50.
2. Djuna Barnes, *Ladies Almanack* (New York: Harper and Row, 1972), p. 71; *The Antiphon*, in *Selected Works of Djuna Barnes* (New York: Farrar, Straus and Giroux, 1962), pp. 81–224, 207.
3. Dolly Wilde, Oscar Wilde's niece, appeared in the *Ladies Almanack* as Doll Furious, as Andrew Field notes in his discussion of the book in *Djuna: The Life and Times of Djuna Barnes* (New York: G. P. Putnam's Sons, 1983), p. 124. Barnes also satirized Radclyffe Hall and her lover, Una, Lady Troubridge, in the *Ladies Almanack*, where they appear as Tilly-Tweed-In-Blood and Lady-Buck-and-Balk (pp. 18–26). The Dreyfus affair was inevitably present in the background of her account of both of the Volkbeins, and is suggested particularly by Guido's apprehension in the presence of military men. Dreyfus was crucial to Proust's account of Jews and homosexuals. See ahead for a discussion of the Volkbeins and the relation between *Nightwood* and the work of Proust.
4. Andrew Field is only too eager to repeat what may have been Barnes's own equivocations about her sexuality in *Djuna*. Two of the earliest and most interesting discussions of Barnes as a lesbian writer were Bertha Harris, "The More Profound Nationality of Their Lesbianism: Lesbian Society in Paris in the 1920s," *Amazon Expedition: A Lesbian Feminist Anthology*, eds. Phyllis Birkby, Bertha Harris, Jill Johnston, Esther Newton, and Jane O'Wyatt (Albion, CA: Times Change Press, 1973), pp. 77–88, and Susan Sniader Lanser, "Speaking in Tongues: *Ladies Almanack* and the Language of Celebration," *Frontiers* 4, 3 (Fall 1979), pp. 39–46. For more general background information on the lesbian circles in which Barnes moved in Paris, see Gayle Rubin, "Introduction," Renée Vivien, *A Woman Appeared to Me*, trans. Jeannette H. Foster (Naiad Press, 1976), pp. iii–xxxvii, as well as Shari Benstock's *Women of the Left Bank: Paris–1040* (Austin: University of

Texas Press, 1986). Most recently, a range of the essays in *Silence and Power: Djuna Barnes—A Re-evaluation*, edited by Mary Lynn Broe (Carbondale: Southern Illinois University Press, 1990), address the question of lesbianism. This chapter initially appeared in that collection. See also *The Review of Contemporary Fiction* special issue on Djuna Barnes, 13, 3 (Fall 1993).

5. Djuna Barnes, *Ryder* (New York: St. Martin's Press, 1979), pp. 302–314.

6. For an account of the Nazi persecution of homosexuals, see Heinz Heger, *The Men With the Pink Triangle*, trans. David Fernbach (Boston: Alyson Publications, 1980), and Richard Plant, *The Pink Triangle: The Nazi War Against Homosexuals* (New York: Henry Holt, 1986).

7. J. E. Rivers, *Proust and the Art of Love* (New York: Columbia University Press, 1980).

8. Proust even alludes to the Dreyfus and Wilde cases so as to imply their parallel lessons for Jews and homosexuals. He describes homosexuals thus:

> Their honor precarious, their liberty provisional, lasting only until the discovery of their crime; their position unstable, like that of the poet one day fêted in every drawing-room and applauded in every theatre in London, and the next driven from every lodging, unable to find a pillow upon which to lay his head . . . excluded even, save on the days of general misfortune when the majority rally round the victim as the Jews rallied round Dreyfus.

Marcel Proust, *Remembrance of Things Past*, Vol. II, *Cities of the Plain*, trans. C. K. Scott Moncrieff and Terence Kilmartin (New York: Vintage Books, 1982), pp. 623–1169, 638.

9. In her introduction to the 1972 reprint of the *Ladies Almanack*, Barnes referred to that work as "neap-tide to the Proustian chronicle" (p. 3). Her library, which has been deposited at the McKeldin Library of the University of Maryland, contains copies of *A la recherche du temps perdu* in French and English. These volumes contain extensive notes made by Barnes, particularly on the first part of *Sodome et Gomorrhe*, in which Proust discusses homosexuality most explicitly. (Private conversation, Nancy Levine, October 8, 1984.) George Wickes, in *The Amazon of Letters: The Life and Loves of Natalie Barney* (New York: G. P. Putnam's Sons, 1976), says that Barnes discussed Proust's work in her correspondence with Natalie Barney, "both disapproving of Proust's treatment of lesbianism" (p. 179). The influence of Proust's account of lesbianism and male homosexuality on the work of other lesbian writers can be seen, for example, in Colette's *Ces plaisirs* (1932, reprinted as *Le pur et l'impur*, 1941).

10. It has often been argued either that the Volkbein story was added simply as a cover to distract readers' attentions from Barnes's lesbian subject, or that it constitutes the "real" focus of the book. See for example Field, *Djuna*, pp. 78, 140.

11. Field, *Djuna*, pp. 183, 165. Elizabeth Pochoda, in "Style's Hoax: A Reading of Djuna Barnes's *Nightwood*," also argues that "the theme of de-evolution or of bowing down . . . has implications for the act of writing." But she suggests, "The book moves backward. Beginning with an amusing historical flourish in its famous first sentence it eventually turns its back on history, on faith in coherent ex-

pression, and finally on words themselves. The novel bows down before its own impotence to express truth; its author wrote no successors." *Twentieth Century Literature* 22, 2 (May 1976), pp. 179–191, 180.

12. See Harris, "The More Profound Nationality of Their Lesbianism," for another discussion of Barnes, lesbian history, and the father.

13. The briefest glance at Barnes's publishing history indicates that publication was usually problematic for her. While *Ryder* was a best-seller for its day in the United States, it was also censored. The *Ladies Almanack* was only published and sold privately in Paris in the 1920s before its 1972 second printing, and was then out of print again for another twenty years. *Nightwood* was rejected by seven publishers, according to Andrew Field, *Djuna* (p. 20), before it was forced on a reluctant Faber and Faber by T.S. Eliot; all of its editions to date have been burdened by Eliot's prefatory references to "freaks."

14. Djuna Barnes, "Cassation," *Selected Works of Djuna Barnes*, pp. 12–20, 14.

## Notes to Chapter 5

1. The standard biography of Virginia Woolf remains Quentin Bell's *Virginia Woolf* (New York: Harcourt Brace Jovanovich, 1973); it was followed by more liberal and more conservative efforts, such as Phyllis Rose's *Woman of Letters: A Life of Virginia Woolf* (New York: Oxford University Press, 1979), and Lyndall Gordon's *Virginia Woolf: A Writer's Life* (New York: Norton, 1984). There have been biographies concentrating on psychiatric issues, including Roger Poole, *The Unknown Virginia Woolf* (Cambridge: Cambridge University Press, 1978) and Stephen Trombley, *"All That Summer She Was Mad": Virginia Woolf and Her Doctors* (London: Junction Books, 1981); and more recently on sexual abuse, as in Louise DeSalvo, *Virginia Woolf: The Impact of Childhood Sexual Abuse on Her Life and Work* (Boston: Beacon Press, 1989). It has been the publication of Woolf's letters and diaries over the last fifteen years that has provided the basis for discussion of her lesbianism.

2. Virginia Woolf, *Mrs. Dalloway* (Harmondsworth: Penguin, 1974), p. 35.

3. See Jane Marcus, *Virginia Woolf and the Languages of Patriarchy* (Bloomington: Indiana University Press, 1987), pp. 117–118; and Sandra M. Gilbert and Susan Gubar, *No Man's Land*, Volume 3, *Letters from the Front* (New Haven: Yale University Press, 1994), p. 21.

4. Homosexuality is also often represented as inseparable from heterosexual failure in the lesbian novels of the period, such as *The Well of Loneliness*.

5. Elizabeth Abel, *Virginia Woolf and the Fictions of Psychoanalysis* (Chicago: The University of Chicago Press, 1989), p. 37.

6. Virginia Woolf, *Three Guineas* (New York: Harcourt Brace Jovanovich, 1966), p. 142.

7. Virginia Woolf, *A Room of One's Own* (New York: Harcourt Brace and Company, 1929), pp. 35–36.

8. Virginia Woolf, *To the Lighthouse* (Harmondsworth: Penguin, 1974), p. 215.

9. Virginia Woolf, *The Years* (New York: Harcourt Brace and Company, 1937), p. 281.

10. Pamela L. Caughie, *Virginia Woolf and Postmodernism: Literature in Quest and Question of Itself* (Urbana: University of Illinois Press, 1991).

11. Jane Marcus, *Virginia Woolf and the Languages of Patriarchy*, p. 5. For a reading of Woolf as a historical novelist that predates the feminist interest in her work, see Avrom Fleishman, *The English Historical Novel: Walter Scott to Virginia Woolf* (Baltimore: Johns Hopkins University Press, 1971). For other discussions of history in Woolf's writing see Gillian Beer, "Virginia Woolf and Pre-History," in *Virginia Woolf: A Centenary Perspective*, ed. Eric Warner (London: Macmillan, 1984), pp. 99–123; Chapter 10 of Lyndall Gordon's *Virginia Woolf: A Writer's Life*; and *Virginia Woolf and War: Fiction, Reality and Myth*, ed. Mark Hussey (Syracuse, NY: Syracuse University Press, 1991).

12. Sandra Gilbert and Susan Gubar, *Letters From the Front*, p. 13.

13. See Rachel DuPlessis's discussion of *Mrs. Dalloway* in *Writing Beyond the Ending* (Bloomington: Indiana University Press, 1985); Sherron Knopp, "'If I Saw You Would You Kiss Me?': Sapphism and the Subversiveness of Virginia Woolf's *Orlando*," *PMLA*, 103, 1 (January 1988), pp. 24–34; and Suzanne Raitt, *Vita and Virginia: The Work and Friendship of V. Sackville-West and Virginia Woolf* (New York: Oxford University Press, 1993).

14. For a denial of Woolf's lesbianism see also Ellen Bayuk Rosenman, "Sexual Identity and *A Room of One's Own*: 'Secret Economies' in Virginia Woolf's Feminist Discourse," *Signs* 14, 3 (Spring 1989), pp. 505–634.

15. As Rachel Blau DuPlessis observes, "After the first two novels, heterosexual romance is displaced from a controlling and privileged position in [Woolf's] work. It will never again appear as the unique center of narrative concern." DuPlessis, *Writing Beyond the Ending* (Bloomington: Indiana University Press, 1985), pp. 47–48. Gilbert and Gubar note this shift into history also, but pose it as a rejection of the "family romance" rather than the heterosexual plot: *Letters From the Front*, p. 20.

16. For a discussion of *Jacob's Room* and *One of Ours*, see Josephine O'Brien Schaefer, "The Great War and 'This late age of world's experience' in Cather and Woolf," in Mark Hussey, ed., *Virginia Woolf and War*, pp. 134–150.

17. Alex Zwerdling observes, "As her first readers in 1922 would certainly have known, Flanders was a synonym for death in battle," and quotes John McCrae's "In Flanders Fields," "the most popular poem of the war." *Virginia Woolf and the Real World* (Berkeley: University of California Press, 1986), p. 64.

18. Virginia Woolf, *Jacob's Room* (Harmondsworth: Penguin, 1971), p. 164.

19. She proposed an alternative women's history: "a mass of information; at what age did she marry; how many children had she as a rule; what was her house like; had she a room to herself; did she do the cooking; would she be likely to have a servant? . . . why should they not add a supplement to history? calling it, of course, by some inconspicuous name so that women might figure there without impropriety?" (pp. 77–78). Such questions as "Would she be likely to have a servant?" indicate that Woolf is still primarily concerned with middle- and upper-class women, despite Marcus's analysis of her political solidarity with working-class women in *The Languages of Patriarchy*.

20. When she predicts the future of women's writing, she predicts a historically grounded fiction, in which the "men and women" women writers create "will not be observed wholly in relation to each other emotionally, but as they cohere and clash in groups and classes and races." Virginia Woolf, *Collected Essays: Volume II* (New York: Harcourt Brace Jovanovich, 1970), p. 147.

21. Virginia Woolf, *The Waves* (Harmondsworth: Penguin, 1975), p. 193.

22. Virginia Woolf, "A Sketch of the Past" (1940), *Moments of Being,* ed. Jeanne Schulkind (New York: Harcourt Brace Jovanovich, 1985), pp. 61–159, 80.

23. The homosexuality of St. John Hirst is implied in Woolf's first novel, *The Voyage Out,* by his commitment to the exclusively masculine world of his Oxbridge college, and his reading of Sappho.

24. In a device Woolf will continue to use, his sexuality is also represented through the social hostility it evokes: "Now *he's* a dark horse if you like. And there these gossips would suddenly pause. Obviously they meant to hint at his peculiar disposition—long rumoured among them" (*Jacob's Room*, p. 146).

25. This response was more complicated than Jane Marcus has suggested in *Virginia Woolf and the Languages of Patriarchy,* where she describes Woolf's necessary hostility to, "in her own generation and the one before it . . . a homosexual hegemony over British culture" (p. 76). While Woolf recorded E. M. Forster's antilesbian comment on the occasion of the Radclyffe Hall trial—"He said he thought Sapphism disgusting: partly from convention, partly because he disliked that women should be independent of men"—she also joined with Forster in writing a letter to the *Nation and Athenaeum,* on September 8, 1928, protesting the banning of *The Well. The Diary of Virginia Woolf: Volume 3, 1925–1930,* ed. Anne Olivier Bell assisted by Andrew McNellie (New York: Harcourt Brace Jovanovich, 1980), p. 193. There are also sympathetic gay male characters in Woolf's fiction, especially Nicholas in *The Years,* and William Dodge in *Between the Acts.*

26. For other readings of Clarissa's lesbianism, see Emily Jensen, "Clarissa Dalloway's Respectable Suicide," in *Virginia Woolf: A Feminist Slant,* ed. Jane Marcus (Lincoln: University of Nebraska Press, 1983), pp. 162–179; and Elizabeth Abel, "Narrative Structure(s) and Female Development: The Case of *Mrs. Dalloway,*" *The Voyage In: Fictions of Female Development,* eds. Elizabeth Abel, Marianne Hirsch, and Elizabeth Langland (Hanover: University Press of New England, 1983), pp. 161–185, 169.

27. Clarissa's father, Justin Parry, "'never liked anyone who—our friends,' said Clarissa; and could have bitten her tongue for thus reminding Peter that he had wanted to marry her" (p. 47). And Peter remembers, "old Parry disliked them [he and Sally] both equally, which was a great bond" (p. 67).

28. Jane Marcus analyzes Clarissa's decision in terms of an "erotics of chastity," which she proposes as "a screen for her lesbian imagination." Clarissa's "honor," she claims, "seems to have derived from her failure to be Richard's sexual partner." "The Niece of a Nun," *Virginia Woolf and the Languages of Patriarchy,* pp. 117–118. I am arguing against Marcus's emphasis on "chastity," but also the idea of a "lesbian imagination" (the contents of which we can assume), and its necessary "screen."

29. This passage echoes *Jacob's Room*, where Woolf represented Bonamy's feelings for Jacob in similar terms: "Bonamy would play round him like an affectionate spaniel; and . . . (as likely as not) they would end by rolling on the floor" (p. 157).

30. Woolf will later be explicit about the connections between crime and love in her characterization of Nicholas, in *The Years*, where his sexuality is introduced through the information that he "ought to be in prison." See ahead to the discussion of Nicholas. Ed Cohen discusses the effect of Oscar Wilde's trials on the public construction of male homosexuality in *Talk on the Wilde Side: Toward a Genealogy of a Discourse on Male Sexualities* (New York: Routledge, 1993).

31. Alex Zwerdling, for example, seems to think that Woolf intended shell shock to be the explanation for Septimus's state (*Virginia Woolf*, p. 29–31).

32. Rachel Blau DuPlessis sees in the pairing of Clarissa and Septimus a "structural coup, the creation of an unsexual, nonromantic central couple," reflecting Woolf's refusal of the heterosexual plot. But she fails to recognize the gay connection between them, and therefore the extent to which these two mark a rejection of the plot (*Writing Beyond the Ending*, p. 57).

33. It must also be noted that the British edition of *Mrs. Dalloway* does not credit Richard here. "Odd, incredible; she had never been so happy," Woolf writes (p. 205), and goes on to describe Clarissa not simply "having done with the triumphs of youth" but losing and then finding again an unspecified happiness.

34. It is not entirely clear in the following passage whether religion or lesbianism is the objectionable element: "'Kilman arrives just as we've done lunch,' she said. 'Elizabeth turns pink. They shut themselves up. I suppose they're praying.' Lord! He didn't like it; but these things pass over if you let them" (p. 132). Miss Kilman also evokes one of the few connections Woolf makes between lesbian emotion and the (unconscious) primeval: "and stand she did, with the power and taciturnity of some prehistoric monster armoured for primeval warfare" in Clarissa's hallway (p. 139).

35. Woolf's portrait of Miss Kilman is profoundly hostile, partly a reflection of Clarissa's jealousy, and perhaps partly as a propitiatory sacrifice to either homophobic convention or her own internalized anxieties about her portrait of Clarissa and of the love between Clarissa and Sally. Another possible victim of this anxiety in the novel is Milly Brush, Lady Bruton's secretary, "who observed men with unflinching rectitude, and was capable of everlasting devotion, to her own sex in particular, being knobbed, scraped, angular, and entirely without feminine charm" (p. 118). If it is the war that masks the connection between Clarissa and Septimus, it is Woolf's emphasis on both Clarissa's and Kilman's awareness of their class difference that serves to obscure their kinship. This pattern echoes the role of class differences between Tom Outland and Rodney Blake in Cather's *The Professor's House*.

36. Not only does Kitty's devotion to Lucy stand little chance, but even after Kitty marries into the aristocracy, she has access to their possession of the history of England, embodied in its land, only so long as her marriage lasts. Her husband (a colonial governor) dead, everything must be relinquished to his son and heir.

37. Woolf's attitude to the history that structures her text in *The Years* is fundamentally ambivalent. World War I is recorded, but through the dinner party at which Eleanor meets Nicholas, which continues through an air raid. Sara insists that

North, off to the front, is joining the "Royal Regiment of Rat-catchers" (p. 285). The ending of the war is observed from the perspective of Crosby, a pensioned-off servant, who at the moment of the Armistice is most intent on hobbling across Richmond Green to the High Street for her shopping. On their way to the novel's final family gathering in the late 1930s, Peggy observes to Eleanor that the statue honoring World War I martyr-heroine Nurse Cavell, "always reminds me of an advertisement of sanitary towels" (p. 336). Yet it is during the wartime scenes that Nicholas, who is publicly gay, is introduced not only to Eleanor but into the novel.

38. Peggy asks herself, "Did she envy [Sara] because she was happy, or was it the croak of some ancestral prudery—did she disapprove of these friendships with men who did not love women?" (*The Years*, p. 327).

39. See Paul Fussell's *The Great War and Modern Memory* (New York: Oxford University Press, 1979), for a discussion of references to St. Sebastian in late Victorian and early-twentieth-century British homoerotic poetry.

40. The manuscript version reveals that Woolf deleted lesbian references from this novel. See Grace Radin, " 'I Am Not a Hero': Virginia Woolf and the First Version of *The Years*," *Massachusetts Review* 7, 1 (Winter 1975), pp. 195–208, and " 'Two Enormous Chunks': Episodes During the Final Revision of *The Years*," *Bulletin of the New York Public Library* 80, 2 (Winter 1977), pp. 221–251.

41. Jane Marcus, in *Virginia Woolf and the Languages of Patriarchy*, also suggests that Mrs. Ramsay is in some way responsible for the deaths of her children: "Mrs. Ramsay's insistence on marriage and traditional roles results in the death of her son in battle and of her daughter in childbirth" (p. 77).

42. Compare the final scenes of *The Years* during which Peggy sits at Eleanor's knee to have her vision of "living differently."

43. Lily thinks of Mr. Carmichael's loss of Andrew:

> Yes, he looked the same, but somebody had said, she recalled, that when he had heard of Andrew Ramsay's death (he was killed in a second by a shell; he should have been a great mathematician) Mr. Carmichael had "lost all interest in life." What did it mean—that? she wondered. Had he marched through Trafalgar Square grasping a big stick? Had he turned pages over and over, without reading them, sitting in his room in St. John's Wood alone? She did not know what he had done, when he heard that Andrew was killed, but she felt it in him all the same. (*To the Lighthouse*, p. 221)

44. Virginia Woolf, *Between the Acts* (Harmondsworth: Penguin, 1972), p. 67.

45. Many critics have overlooked the fact that Miss La Trobe is identified as a lesbian. Mitchell A. Leaska, on the other hand, argues for the significant relation of Vita Sackville-West to this novel, and so implicitly for a lesbian reading, in the afterword to his edition of the drafts, *Pointz Hall: The Earlier and Later Typescripts of "Between the Acts,"* ed. Mitchell A. Leaska (New York: University Publications, 1983).

46. See my introduction for a discussion of Woolf's own description of the necessity of literary convention in her 1921 essay "Mr. Bennett and Mrs. Brown." See also

Elizabeth Ermarth, *Realism and Consensus in the English Novel* (Princeton: Princeton University Press, 1983).

47. Judith L. Johnston also copnsiders the significance of history in this novel, in "The Remediable Flaw: Revisioning Cultural History in *Between the Acts*," in *Virginia Woolf and Bloomsbury*, ed. Jane Marcus (London: Macmillan, 1987), pp. 253–277.

48. Alex Zwerdling discusses the novel in the context of the war in "*Between the Acts* and the Coming of War," *Novel* (Spring 1977), pp. 220–236.

49. Jane Marcus also points to this equation in *Virginia Woolf and the Languages of Patriarchy*, p. 95.

50. Gillian Beer notes that in this book of Mrs. Swithin's Woolf "amalgamates" H. G. Wells's "*The Outline of History* with his *Short History of the World*, and writes her own version rather than quoting Wells directly": "Virginia Woolf and Pre-History," p. 115. What does this reference to Wells mean, given her early construction of her own work in opposition to the writings of "Mr Galsworthy, Mr Bennett and Mr Wells"? Is this a sign that the world represented by the Victorian Age's policeman Budge has won?

51. Virginia Woolf, *The Voyage Out* (Harmondsworth: Penguin, 1974), p. 64.

52. Pamela Caughie argues that, in *Between the Acts*, "the artist (e.g., La Trobe) no longer represents her kind (women, lesbians, feminists)," as if this is a breakthrough. But it has never been possible to assume that the lesbian artist could or would "represent her kind," as it remains unclear what "represent[ing] her kind" might mean. *Virginia Woolf and Postmodernism*, p. 57.

53. Critical examples of the community thesis include Judy Little, "Festive Comedy in Woolf's *Between the Acts*," *Women and Literature* 5, 1 (Spring 1977), pp. 26–37; Maria DiBattista, *Virginia Woolf's Major Novels: The Fables of Anon* (New Haven: Yale University Press, 1980), pp. 191–234.

54. Elizabeth Abel opens her discussion of *Between the Acts*, in *Virginia Woolf and the Fictions of Psychoanalysis*, by stating that "(Hetero)sexuality is repeatedly insinuated as our covert truth" (p. 108). She goes on to refer to the novel's "assumption of women's innate heterosexuality" (p. 128), and concludes with a celebration of Miss La Trobe's "replac[ing] a fully discredited matricentric narrative with the heterosexual plot that originates, for women, with the father" (p. 130). Abel does not seem to notice that Miss La Trobe's presence calls into question "women's innate heterosexuality." While reading the novel's ending as "launch[ing] a new text and a new cycle of history" (p. 130), she fails to mention that it also heralds the beginning of World War II, which hardly seems like "a new text" or "a new cycle of history."

55. Beer, "Virginia Woolf and Pre-History," p. 103.

56. Note, for example, the terms of the well-known passage in *A Room* in which she argues that

> Women have served all these centuries as looking-glasses possessing the magic and delicious power of reflecting the figure of man at twice its natural size. Without that power probably the earth would still be swamp and jungle. The glories of all our wars would be unknown. We should still be scratching the outlines of deer on the remains of mutton bones and

bartering flints for sheepskins or whatever simple ornament took our un-sophisticated taste. Supermen and Fingers of Destiny would never have existed. The Czar and the Kaiser would never have worn their crowns or lost them. Whatever may be their use in civilised societies, mirrors are es-sential to all violent and heroic action. (pp. 60–61)

## Notes to Afterword

1. Dr. Richard von Krafft-Ebing, *Psychopathia Sexualis* (New York: Paperback Library [1886–1903, 12th ed.] 1965), p. 27.
2. Erving Goffman, *Stigma: Notes on the Management of Spoiled Identity* (New York: Simon and Schuster, 1963), p. 25.
3. Cindy Patton, "Tremble, Hetero Swine!" in *Fear of a Queer Planet*, ed. Michael Warner (Minneapolis: University of Minnesota Press, 1993), pp. 143–177, 174. Kevin Kopelson, in his *Love's Litany*, claims that "Homosexuality is a literary effect insofar as it is structured by readings of 'literary texts,'" although he has a more limited view of "the literary" than Goffman, arguing specifically "More 'inverted' lesbians, it is safe to say, have read, and recognized themselves in, *The Well of Lone-liness*, than have read Richard von Krafft-Ebing's *Psychopathia Sexualis*. And more gay men have read *Dancer From the Dance* than Alfred Kinsey's *Sexual Behavior in the Human Male*." *Love's Litany: The Writing of Modern Homoerotics* (Stanford: Stanford University Press, 1994), p. 10.
4. Kopelson refers to his own interest in "the literary" as "somewhat unfashionable" (*Love's Library*, p. 10).
5. Alan Sinfield, "Beyond Englit," *Cultural Politics—Queer Reading* (Philadelphia: University of Pennsylvania Press, 1994), pp. 60–82.

# Index

**Julie Abraham** is professor of Lesbian, Gay, Bisexual, and Transgender Studies at Sarah Lawrence College. She is the author of *Metropolitan Lovers: The Homosexuality of Cities* (Minnesota, 2008) and the editor of *Diana: A Strange Autobiography.* Her reviews have been published in *The Nation* and *The Women's Review of Books*.